International Country Music Journal 2021

Don Cusic, Editor

International Country Music Journal
Don Cusic, Editor
Copyright 2021

All rights reserved.
Printed in the United States of America

ISBN 978-0-9990537-6-8

Brackish Publishing
P.O. Box 120751
Nashville, TN 37212

Production Coordinator
Jim Sharp
Sharp Management

Cover and Interior Layout Design
www.PricelessDigitalMedia.com

Acknowledgments

The International Country Music Journal is an outgrowth of the International Country Music Conference, an academic conference held annually at Belmont University in Nashville the weekend after Memorial Day. The Conference is hosted by James Akenson and Don Cusic with assistance from Greg Reiss and Olivia Beaudry. In addition to presentations, the Conference also presents the annual Belmont Book Award for the Best Book on Country Music published the previous calendar year. We are indebted to Mike Curb and the Mike Curb Family Foundation for the funding of the International Country Music Journal.

Table of Contents

The Trials of Eva Thompson Jones: A Tainted Legacy
By Dave Sichak and Don Cusic 9

Reinterpreting Country Music in Japan:
The February 2019 Issue of Guitar Magaziner
and the Legacy of the "Anything but Country" Attitude
By Mari Nagatomi 45

"I'll Be Locked Here in this Cell 'Til my Body's Just a Shell":
Hank Williams on Crime and Punishment
By Tim Dodge 71

Marg Osburne: National Singing Star of Don Messer's Jubilee
By Linda J. Daniel 91

"Classifying Operations": Constructing and manufacturing
identities in Irish and American country music
By Christina Lynn 127

Jo Val and Herb Applin
By Bill Nowlin 151

"Rank Stranger"—The Stanley Brothers (1960)
By David W. Johnson 195

The Legendary Phipps Family: The Old-Time Country Music
Singing Family of Kentucky
By Kenichi Yamaguchi 205

Two Brothers, Two Sisters and Their Dreams—The Story of
Sleepy Hollow Ranch
By Dave Sichak 233

Milton Estes: A Forgotten Star
By Don Cusic 291

The Trials of Eva Thompson Jones: A Tainted Legacy

By Dave Sichak and Don Cusic

WSM's first broadcast was on October 5, 1925, and on November 2 they hired George D. Hay to manage the station. He arrived in Nashville a week later.

Hay had developed his writing and broadcast skills first in Memphis, where he created a character, "Howdy Judge," for a newspaper column. It featured dialogues between a white judge and various black defendants that featured dialect and ethnic stereotypes. Hays' newspaper columns were popular and led to him broadcasting on WMC in Memphis. He became so popular that he acquired the nickname "The Solemn Old Judge."

In 1924, Hay was hired by Sears and Roebuck for their new station, WLS in Chicago. WLS created "The National Barn Dance" when they went on the air in April, 1924 and Hay became a popular announcer on that program. That same year, a magazine, *Radio Digest*, awarded Hay a Gold Cup for being the most popular announcer in the nation. The award was determined by radio fans across the country voting.

The National Barn Dance was the first nationally popular barn dance—defined as a radio variety program for a rural audience which emphasized what later became known as "country music"—and the first to be a regular ongoing program.

It was because of Hay's popularity at WLS that WSM hired him.

Before Hay arrived, WSM's programming was directed "at the varied and rather sophisticated tastes of Nashville," wrote Charles K. Wolfe in his book, *A Good Natured Rio: The Birth of The Grand Ole Opry*. "Some traditional music was occasionally heard, but a great deal of the fare was light or semi-classical music, dance bands and ladies' string trios." Hay "knew that a much vaster audience than the Nashville urban area lay within range and demanded a reconsideration of programming." (Wolfe 9)

Hays had witnessed the popularity of The National Barn Dance and, after his arrival, "told Eva Thompson Jones that he wasn't entirely satisfied with the programming direction of the station and asked for suggestions." (Wolfe, 9) Jones was a staff musician on WSM at this time (she sang light classical music and played the piano) and suggested booking her uncle, known as Uncle Jimmy Thompson, to perform on the air. Jones invited Hay to her home "for an informal audition" on Friday night, November 27. Hay was impressed and invited Uncle Jimmy Thompson to perform with his niece the next night. (Wolfe 77).

There had been traditional or "folk" artists who had appeared during WSM's opening and Dr. Henry Bate, Uncle Dave Macon and Sid Harkreader had performed occasionally on WSM before Hay arrived. However, there was no regular program on WSM that featured this music.

On Saturday night, November 28 at 8 p.m., Uncle Jimmy Thompson and Eva were scheduled to perform for an hour. The fiddling was so popular that they stayed on for two hours because a deluge of telegrams came in, requesting tunes. This is the first performance of what came to be known as the Grand Ole Opry. At that time, Uncle Jimmy was seventy-seven and Eva had just turned 34.

Eva Thompson Jones was a graduate of Ward-Belmont College, a girl's "finishing school" that evolved to become Belmont University. She had received a Bachelor of Music Degree from the school and was a staff musician at WSM, playing piano and singing. This places Belmont University as a key factor in the creation of the Grand Old Opry and, ultimately, in Nashville becoming "Music City U.S.A."

According to Wolfe in his book, and based on articles in the *Nashville Tennessean* newspaper, on December 26 "Uncle Jimmy Thompson, the South's champion barn dance fiddler, and Eva Thompson Jones, contralto, will present a program of old-fashioned tunes" for two hours. "We get a hint that Eva Thompson Jones was doing more than playing piano backup. She is billed as a 'Contralto,' suggesting that she also sang," stated Wolfe. (Wolfe 69)

The next day the *Tennessean* newspaper announced that "old-time tunes" would be a regular Saturday night feature on WSM. Joining Uncle Jimmy Thompson was Uncle Dave Macon for those Saturday night shows. The newspaper noted that Uncle Jimmy Thompson "is usually accompanied by his niece, whom he refers to constantly as 'Sweetmeats.'" (Wolfe 70)

The article further stated that "Uncle Jimmy is old-fashioned and is proud of it. For that reason, when he had his picture taken with his niece, he insisted that she let her hair down. 'I don't like these new fangled styles women wear,' says Uncle Jimmy." (Wolfe 71)

WSM had commissioned a photographer to take pictures of their new stars and in one photo there is "a haunting pre-Raphaelite pose with Eva sitting on the arm of a chair while her uncle, fiddle in hand, gazes up at her." (Wolfe 71)

Eva Thompson Jones was born on October 19, 1892 in Smith County, Tennessee, the daughter of Robert Lee and Mary Trousdale Thompson. Uncle Jimmy was Robert Lee's's brother. The family lived about 80 miles east of Nashville, near Baxter, Tennessee, a few miles west of Cookeville or about half way between Nashville and Knoxville. Lee Thompson's family must have been somewhat affluent for his daughter to attend Ward-Belmont.

Before the Civil War, the Thompson family (Jimmy had at least two brothers) had moved to Texas. After the Civil War, they apparently moved back to Tennessee although Uncle Jimmy returned to Texas where he settled around Bonham, northeast of Dallas. (Wolfe 72-73)

In 1912, Uncle Jimmy was sixty-four, his children had grown and his wife was dying of cancer so they returned to Tennessee and bought a farm near Hendersonville in Sumner County. Shortly after he returned his wife died. Thompson had grown too old to farm so he turned to his fiddle to make a living.

In Wolfe's book, he states, "By this time Eva Thompson, Uncle Jimmy's niece was starting to teach music in rural Tennessee schools. As a young girl, Eva became quite naturally enamored of classical music and of Victorian parlor music, considered semi-classical. She liked to accompany her father into Nashville so she could watch the touring shows playing the Nashville theaters while her father did business at the stockyards. Later, she studied at Ward-

Belmont College, then as now a widely respected center of musical study, and later recalled going by horse and buggy to give music lessons. In 1915, Eva was teaching in Sumner County. (Wolfe 73)

Uncle Jimmy spent time travelling around to courthouses and "busking" to earn money. He was often accompanied by Eva Thompson Jones and/or his wife, known as Aunt Ella. (Around 1916, when he was sixty-eight, Thompson had re-married.).

During the early months of 1926, Uncle Jimmy and Eva continued to perform on Saturday nights at 8 p.m. for an hour, although occasionally the show ran for two hours. However, Uncle Jimmy was fond of his moonshine and his drinking "was probably the most immediate reason why he stopped broadcasting. 'They would have to watch him,' recalled neighbor Jim Thompson. 'In fact, they told him they didn't want him to come down there drinking. His business down there just finally played out on that account.'" (Wolfe 81)

Uncle Jimmy Thompson continued to fiddle but rarely played on the WSM "barn dance" which, by 1927, was known as the Grand Ole Opry. In November, 1926, he went to Atlanta and recorded four songs for the Columbia Phonograph Company; he was accompanied there by Eva. When he did appear on the Opry, his time allotment was cut back to 30 minutes. Shortly after his first appearance on WSM, he had suffered a stroke that left him blind in one eye and it was increasingly difficult to get around. In April, 1930, he recorded two sides in Knoxville for the Brunswick-Vocalion company.

(NOTE: It is possible to hear a recording of Uncle Jimmy and Eva on YouTube. She provides a rhythm on the piano, chording behind Uncle Jimmy's fiddling.)

Meanwhile, the Grand Ole Opry grew, adding cast members as WSM acquired more wattage that allowed them to cover the United States, but Uncle Jimmy Thompson did not grow with it. When he died in 1931, Eva Thompson Jones was the only member of the Opry to attend the funeral.

Eva Thompson had married Turner Lewis Jones and had a son, Turner Lewis Jones, Jr. After Uncle Jimmy's death, Eva Thompson opened The Eva Thompson Jones Studio at 415 ½ Church street in Nashville where she gave piano and voice lessons. Recitals by her students were given at schools or halls around the city by literally dozens of students and articles in the *Tennessean* and *Banner* newspapers listed the recitals and the students names.

During the early 1940s, she began to diversity the courses of instruction offered to students, offering guitar lessons for $40 with a pay as you learn arrangement. She hired or took on an associate, Mr. Marvin Boone, formerly of Hollywood, who was a distinguished instructor in Ballroom and Tap Dancing. That led to classes for various dances – tap, ballet acrobatic, ballroom and rhumba.

In August, 1942, the life and career of 40 year old Eva Thompson Jones changed dramatically. Jones, who lived at 400 21st Avenue North, was arrested in violation of the May Act, which was directed against prostitution near military and naval establishments. Violation of the act was punishable by a fine of not more than $1,000 and imprisonment of not more than a year.

Eva was held without bond for questioning by federal authorities and Nashville City Police charged her with disorderly and offensive conduct. Chief of Police John Griffin stated that Mrs.

Jones "was arrested with a soldier in an automobile in the alley off Church Street" (behind her studio). There were seven officers at the scene listed in the article. Both the man, who was not named and Eva gave statements to the police, which were then turned them over to the FBI.

A federal warrant charged that Jones "unlawfully did engage in prostitution and did solicit for the purpose of prostitution." A U. S. Marshal escorted her from the city jail to the U. S. Courthouse where she posted a $250 bail. The arrest apparently came after an investigation over several weeks.

During World War II Nashville was swarming with young soldiers, especially on the weekends. There were training facilities in nearby Tullahoma and Clarksville and soldiers could get a "weekend pass" to visit Nashville—and many did. The audiences at the Grand Ole Opry will filled with young servicemen enjoying the show.

In the classified ad section of the newspaper, it stated that Mrs. Jones studio was now operating under the management of Robert Morgan.

There were a series of articles in the Nashville newspapers documenting Eva Thompson Jones' legal problems. It appears that the arrest was a test case for enforcement of the May Act in the Nashville area. The attorney for Mrs. Jones argued that because of the manner in which the Man Act was invoked it did not apply legally to Davidson County or any of the 26 counties listed in the federal order. Her attorney also argued points of technicality that made the arrest invalid.

Col. Millard F. Waltz, Jr., post commander of Camp Forrest at Tullahoma, declared that Jones' studio was out of bounds for men in the armed forces and that Military Police stationed in the Nashville area were ordered to prohibit service men from entering the place.

At the hearing it was a alleged that Mrs. Jones asked the arresting officer (J. M. West) to not arrest her because it would ruin her. She said she would give him a check or go with him to get some money. Her attorney contended that the government had not proven a violation of the May Act.

There was such an interest in the case that the case had to be moved from the Commissioners' small chambers to the larger Federal Court room.

The case became more interesting when her attorney alleged that the arresting officer promised her that she could avoid all publicity in the matter if she made a full and complete confession of guilt and signed it. She did so but her attorney alleged that the confession constituted a promise on their part, nullifying her statement. Prosecutors countered that when she signed the statement of guilt, she was signing it of her own free will and without promise.

Mrs. Jones attorney claimed that the arresting officer was working with the arrested soldier as an agent for him to test Mrs. Jones. During a question and answer period it was alleged that the soldier was paid $10 by Inspector R. W. Jett (then in the army) who arranged for him to have two days additional leave if he managed to catch Mrs. Jones.

Commissioner Brock declared that the defendant was probably guilty and bound her over to the federal grand jury. He rejected the defense attorney's motions to dismiss the case. Jones posted bond of $250 and was released.

Mrs Jones was arraigned before Judge Elmer D. Davies and pled not guilty and a trial was set to be held in Federal Court in Nashville on October 7.

During the trial the judge stated that if women were in violation of the May Act, then so were soldiers who were arrested. FBI Agent Fleming stated that it was his understanding that a violation of the May Act decreed that only the woman was subject to prosecution. Under cross examination, Agent Fleming stated that he learned that the car in which Mr. Criswell (the man arrested with Mrs. Jones) and Mrs. Jones were found was furnished by the city police.

During her testimony Mrs. Jones said that the two $5 bills found in her purse had been planted. She claimed that she had never engaged in prostitution with Criswell or anyone else and that she had first met Criswell on the night of August 13 when she stood outside her studio around 10:30 pm to make sure that none of her girls left with a soldier.

Criswell had been dancing with two of Mrs. Jones' nieces and Criswell asked if he could take them home in a car. She said she consented with the provision that she accompany them in the car. Criswell asked her to go with him to get the car from a parking lot and she stated that she was in the car for only a few seconds but when she started to get out that Criswell pulled her back in and two officers arrived to make the arrest. When they took her to the police station, the officer attempted to get her to admit that she had relations with Criswell and would not let her call an attorney.

Federal Judge Elmer D. Davies declared that "some day Nashville police may learn that federal prisoners are entitled to have counsel and are entitled to call counsel. If they are to enforce the May Act, then have to abide by federal regulations."

When the trial proceedings were complete, the jury debated for about 30 minutes and Mrs. Jones was acquitted.

Although it is difficult to know the specifics, it seems that soldiers were attracted to Mrs. Posts' dance club because there were girls there and the city police and Federal agents set up a "trap" to arrest Mrs. Jones and shut down the club.

You have some other factors in play as well. First, you have a woman running a business in a patriarchal culture. Next, Tennessee was a "dry" state and Nashville was a "dry" city so young men bringing in liquor was against the law. Finally, Nashville was "the buckle of the Bible belt" where there were numerous churches and most of them declared that dancing was sinful. Mrs. Jones was an easy target for the military police as well as the local police.

Mrs. Jones decided to change her business operations for her studio/dance establishment and advertisements began appearing that listed her facility as a place where people could learn how to dance. She held a music and dance recital in May, 1954, in the school auditorium and on June 4, 1954, opened the venue as the Club Pla-More. She held another dance recital on December 9 in what was to be a series of Christmas recitals and parties in the school auditorium.

Legal issues continued to hound her. She was ordered to attend a General Sessions court hearing on a charge of contributing to the delinquency of a minor. The warrant was sworn out by the father of a 15 year old girl who claimed his daughter was frequenting the dance hall and was allowed to have dates with soldiers. The case against Mrs. Jones was going to be handled by juvenile authorities per the order of Judge John L. Drape but it was apparently never taken up with juvenile authorities.

However, that began another round of legal entanglements.

The *Tennessean* printed a front page story on July 31, 1955, stating that city police had raided her Pla-More Club and arrested 20 soldiers, charging them with being off-limits and charged civilian men with disorderly conduct. Several teen-age girls were taken to the police station but released without charge

Mrs. Jones and eight others were tried in City Court on August 1, 1955 stemming from the raid. She was charged with aiding and abetting the delinquency of a minor and operating a disorderly house. The others were charged with loitering about a disorderly house. Two of the eight were Fort. Campbell soldiers charged with disorderly and offensive conduct. Twenty-seven soldiers were not charged, but were referred to military authorities. A police inspector indicated that about 30 to 35 people escaped by running down a back fire escape. The military had declared the place off-limits the week before after they learned soldiers were frequenting the establishment.

The story was front page news in the newspapers and included pictures. The police, led by Inspector F. W. Muller, had blocked off Fourth and Fifth Avenues on Church Street during the raid and made a surprise entry where they found the dimly-lit upstairs hall filled with swaying couples, including girls aged 14 and up with numerous soldiers and bottles of liquor on the floor.

A four-piece Negro band was playing in the dance hall.

Testimony stated that Mrs. Jones was sitting on a landing when police entered. She was registering her young customers, charging admission of a dollar to soldiers and civilian men. It was reported that Mrs. Jones had set off a warning buzzer when the raid started.

The *Tennessean* had been tipped off and a reporter was inside the hall before the raid and wrote that it appeared that most of the girls were under the age of 18. By 9 p.m. the large floor was crowded with dancers so Mrs. Jones was charged with operating a disorderly house and running a dance hall without permission. During a four-hour trial, the judge imposed a fine of $50 for each case. Mrs. Jones stated that she always tried to conduct a nice, clean place for youngsters to come to but could not account for the conduct of a few who sneak in through windows.

A grand jury was empaneled to interview witnesses from the raid. Teenagers were reportedly met with stony stares as they passed Mrs. Jones to enter the attorney general's office until District Attorney Carlton Loser ordered her away from the premises so she could not intimidate witnesses.

Mrs. Jones was set to appear before Criminal Court Judge Charles Gilbert and be charged with a rarely invoked statute that charged her club was a "breeding place for fornication, lewdness and adultery."

Joe Lackey, the attorney for Mrs. Jones, attacked the validity of the Grand Jury charge of "operating a common law nuisance."

He claimed that it should be dismissed on two counts; (1) it was unlawful and (2) no such crime or misdemeanor as common law nuisances existed in Tennessee law. However, Judge Charles Gilbert denied the dismissal and set the trial for the January term of Criminal Court if she pled innocent.

She lost a bid to dismiss two prior convictions and $50 fines. The next step was for the case to be placed on the non-jury docket and a trial date was set for February 7, 1956 on the charge that she had been operating a common nuisance on December 7, 1955.

General Sessions Judge John L. Draper ordered Mrs. Jones to turn the club over to the Nashville Trust Company, which stated her lease expired December 31. Her lawyer stated that she had operated the club at the Church Street address for almost 30 years and notified the trust company that she wanted a one-year extension in August. Her attorney, Mr. Lackey, stated that the Trust company had agreed to do so.

Newspapers reported that Mrs. Eva Thompson Jones "sat erect and sphinx like" as her attorneys worked on jury selection. However the jury selection ran into problems because many of the men called said they had religious scruples against dancing and the drinking of liquor although some said they could set aside that beliefs. Jury selection was done shortly after noon and the news reported the names and addresses of the all-male jury.

At the time of the trial, liquor was illegal in Nashville; the city did not allow liquor by the drink until November, 1967.

The trial began on February 7 and was set to be a lengthy trial because George Carlisle, the criminal court officer, had issued subpoenas for about 90 witnesses.

One of the first witnesses, Leland Stallcup, caused an uproar when defense attorney Joe Lackey confronted him, stating that he had not been in the club itself but had only gone to a desk and spoken with Mrs. Jones about playing his trumpet in the club band. Leland Stallcup responded, "That's a lie" and tempers arose in the courtroom with that response.

Two teenage girls testified. The seventeen year old said that she had met a soldier at the club and he was the father of her baby girl. A fifteen year old said she had been married when she was 13 and testified she had only been drinking at the club. A witness the previous day had stated that she gave birth to a child after meeting a man at the club. The girls testified that the acts happened off the premises.

The trial was major news in Nashville and spectators packed the small courtroom. Those watching could not recall any trial that spurred so much interest.

Police officers testified they had heard wolf whistles by men from the windows in the Pla-More Club directed at women on Church Street. The defense insisted that Mrs. Jones was not aware of any wrong doing. One witness was asked about a popular dance called "The Bop" that had been labeled "obscene dancing" and stated that it was only obscene in the eye of the beholder. The dance fit well with the advent of rock and roll. You can see an example of "The Bop" on YouTube under "Dancing Through the Years, The 1950s—The Bop." If you watch, you will see that it was rather mild by today's standards. Still, all dancing was taboo in the religious community and those churches were a powerful force in Nashville during the 1950s.

Military Police Sergeant Hilyward Medlin testified that there were about 30 military personnel there and the club was off limits, but they were all in civilian clothes.

Assistant Attorney General Joe Binkley asked Mrs. Jones if she had "obtained strippers and arranged stag parties" at the club. He asked a defense witness if she knew that Mrs. Jones "booked most of the strip acts." That caused a courtroom outburst and the jury had to leave the room. One witness indicated that one of her daughters had been taught music and voice for eight years by Mrs. Jones and had gone to the club.

Mrs. Jones took the stand and stated that she felt her place was patronized by "nice boys and girls" and that she had operated a respectable, well supervised establishment. As part of her "character," the jury was informed that she was a former church choir director. Mrs. Jones testified that the persons charged with being drunk during the July 31 raid had followed the police into the club.

Prosecuting Attorney Mr. Binkley, cross examined her and it was revealed that she had lost her dancing license in 1954 or 1955 and then had turned her venue into a club. When asked why she lost the license she simply said "I don't know."

One witness claimed that he didn't see anything wrong at the club on July 31 but Leonard Montgomery testified he heard a buzzer signal from the second to third floor because Mrs. Jones had "buzzed upstairs for change." Mrs. Jones related there was a buzzer system on the third floor but it was used for dancing instructors to call students and teachers.

Attorney Joe Lackey asked her questions about her background and what she had done during the past 32 years.

Mrs. Jones replied that she was a member of Westminster Presbyterian Church, had taught music in Davidson county schools for a number of years and had been choir director at First Presbyterian Church and McKendree Methodist Church. She stated that she was a music teacher and had mastered musical instruments and had been associated with opera and opera stars such as James Melton. She stated that she had given Dinah Shore her first public appearance in Nashville and was with her Uncle Jimmy Thompson when he helped start the Opry as its first performers.

Mrs. Jones testified that some of the girls who had been in and near the courtroom during the trial were members of her club and that some of the girls who were snapping their fingers and singing, "Oh Rudy, tutti, fruitti" during the noon recess called the music "bop."

(NOTE: That phrase comes from Little Richard's hit, "Tutti Frutti." This trial was held during 1956 when Elvis and rock and roll exploded in the nation. There were concerns that rock and roll led to juvenile delinquency. It seems likely that a jury pool of men who disliked liquor and/or dancing would not be fans of Elvis or rock and roll.)

On the last day of testimony the District Attorney asserted that there was a linkage to a terrorist with a witness. He asked the young lady about her Pachuko tattoo. The witness said it was just a fad, although that mark was the mark of a terrorist group in California. The witness admitted that she had brought in a couple bottles of whisky to the club, but none larger than the pint in her pocketbook. She then showed the bottle to the jury and showed them her tattoo before she stepped back and flippantly asked, "Anyone else want to see?"

The "common nuisance" trial of Eva Thompson Jones went to the all male jury shortly after one in the afternoon. A verdict was expected before sundown but in a startling development, the all-male jury returned in just seventeen minutes with a verdict of "Guilty" of operating a "common nuisance" and fined her $1,000, an amount set by the jurors.

That should not have been a surprise in a state where "temperance" was a key issue in Tennessee politics, where dancing was considered "sinful" and condemned by the church and where the churches played a major role in state and community issues. Add those factors to a woman owning a dance club, teenage sex and the threat of rock'n'roll music and you can see that the deck was stacked against Eva Thompson Jones from the start.

Defense Attorney Joe Lackey stated that the grand jury verdict was "corrupt" with "filthy allegations" that had not been proven during the four day trial. He said the three page accusation was born out of the mind of a "sex fanatic." Her other attorney, Mr. Hardin, said they had the best lawsuit for malicious prosecution ever seen.

The arrest and trial seems to have been part of a generation shift. It was a "young people" problem that caused fear and concern from the older generation and led to accusations and trials like this. It seems like this was part of The Rock and Roll Revolution when teenagers were less inhibited than their parents and like their music with a new beat—which their parents and other older folks, who came of age during the Big Ban era, could not stand.

Eva Thompson Jones' legal problems were not over. She continued efforts to keep the lease on her club but the jury verdict hampered that effort. She also faced a decision by the Judge that could sentence her up to 11 months and 29 days in prison.

That verdict was appealed and arguments for a new trial were to be heard by Special Criminal Court Judge C. Vernon Hines on April 2. Mrs. Jones was offered the suspension of a 90-day workhouse sentence and sought a full reversal of her $1,000 fine and jail term. Judge Hines said he would be willing to suspend her sentence if she did not appeal to the State Supreme Court and, since her attorneys would not agree to that demand, Judge Hines on May 14 stated that the 90-day workhouse sentence he imposed on Mrs. Jones would stand. He also denied the appeal for a new trial.

There were hopes for clemency so she could escape her County Workhouse sentence. A reporter said a "source close" to the Davidson County District Attorney General was looking at the matter as a 'test case' to help determine the correct procedure in future "nuisance" cases. It was expected there would be some relief granted to Mrs. Jones.

Mrs. Jones hoped for a favorable decision from the State Pardons and Paroles Board, but Charles Crowe, an executive on the board, indicated the case would need further study the following week.

On August 7, 1957, a story in the *Nashville Banner* indicated that the State Pardons and Parole Board recommended executive clemency in Mrs. Jones' case regarding the Pla-More Club although the sentence was previously upheld by the State Supreme Court. Governor Frank Clement was expected to act on the case quickly. If the Governor accepted the clemency recommendation, Mrs. Jones would not have to serve the 90 days in the workhouse sentence, but would still have to pay the $1,000 fine. The Governor was on a trip to Cuba at the time and would review it upon his return.

In late September, the State Pardons and Paroles board withdrew their recommendation of a pardon for Mrs. Jones. Charles W. Crow, Board Secretary, indicated the action was taken because of additional information received from past court records, but did not elaborate.

On October 11, Circuit Court Judge Richard P. Dews set aside his order evicting Mrs. Eva Thompson Jones from her music establishment and granted her a new trial. On August 24 he had ordered Mrs. Jones to vacate the suite she occupied at 417 ½ Church Street and turn it over to the Crescent Amusement Company. She was fined $1,000.

The case was an appeal made by her attorney Joe Lackey from General Session Court Judge Dews who said he might have erred in his ruling on the case. He stated the case boils down to an interpretation of a lease agreement and related circumstances.

Mrs. Jones maintained that she had a right to extend the lease for one year to December 31, 1956 and had informed the amusement company of her intent.

It was reported that a final appeal was going to be made by friends of Mrs. Jones, not her attorneys. A new attorney was representing her along with Joe Lackey, but neither attorney would identify who those friends were. The order to start serving her sentence was postponed to allow her friends to file the 11th hour appeal.

On November 12, 1957, Mrs. Jones was ordered to begin serving her 90 day County Workhouse sentence and attorney Joe Lackey would bring her to the workhouse that afternoon. Criminal Court Judge Charles Gilbert formally accepted and made it a part of the court's record of the State Supreme Court's decision upholding Mrs. Jones conviction.

That decision came after the State Pardon and Parole Board, which had heard two pleas, ruled it would not consider Mrs. Jones' case any further. She was to be put to work in the Workhouse laundry room or sew the tattered clothes of inmates; those were the kind of jobs assigned to women. However, Mr. Crow, the Executive Secretary of the Parole Board said that as soon as she had served a day of her sentence, she had a right to appeal to Governor Clement for commutation of her sentence "to time served." Another option was to petition the Criminal Court for a suspended sentence, but only after she had served at least 30 days.

Governor Frank G. Clement, upon a recommendation from the Board of Pardons and Paroles, signed papers commuting her sentence to time served, but she still had to pay the $1,000 fine and $148 court costs. She had entered the workhouse on November 12, 1957. If she did not pay the fine and court costs, she would have to remain there and earn those amounts by working for $2 a day, excluding Sundays.

In December of 1957, the long saga of the 'common nuisance' of her Pla-More Club was over. She paid the $1,000 fine and also

$148 in court costs. Her attorney Joe Lackey paid the amount at noon and went to the workhouse to secure her release.

About five months later, in May, 1958, a heavy thunderstorm hit Davidson County in with heavy rains flooding Highway 100. Just before nine that evening, lighting struck the home of Eva Thompson Jones at 3824 West End Avenue, causing a fire in the top floor apartment and an estimated $700 worth of damage. Three Vanderbilt students had moved into the apartment that afternoon and they lost almost all of their clothing but were not in the apartment when the lightning struck.

In 1962, Eva Thompson Jones was arrested and went on trial for a petty larceny charge. She was charged with shoplifting several inexpensive items from the W. T. Grant store at 601 Church Street. Mrs. Jones claimed she had purchased the items but could not produce the receipt. She appeared before Judge Andrew J. Doyle but her lawyer, Carl Bishop, did not want her tried there. Her regular lawyer Joseph Lackey was absent.

During the trial, each time Judge Doyle asked Mrs. Jones if she wanted to be tried in City Court, her lawyer stated she wanted to be bound over to the grand jury. Judge Doyle repeated his question several times and told her that if the case was settled in his court and she was found guilty, she would only have to pay at the most $50, adding that he knew she had encountered a lot of trouble during the past few years.

She maintained that she had bought the merchandise in question, but told the judge that she'd rather settle the case in his court and be rid of it. He told her she didn't want to have her record blemished by a petty larceny conviction.

In 1965, the *Tennessean* ran a classified ad that she was not responsible for anyone's debts but her own.

Dolores Smith wrote an article about the piano in 1968 that offered some insight into Mrs. Jones approach to music. She spoke about how piano teaching had changed. She said her approach was not to make the student learn classical music but "After they learn notes, harmony and theory, if they want to play rock and roll, we teach 'em rock and roll." Another change in teaching piano was that instead of playing scales for weeks when starting out, the new approach encouraged a student to learn simple, perhaps even popular tunes while learning the fundamentals.

In 1967, Eva Thompson Jones was still teaching piano and voice. She had opened a new Eva Thompson Jones Studio on 123 5th Avenue North in Nashville.

In April of 1969, she filed suit to get her Uncle Jimmy Thompson's fiddle back or $15,000 from Roy Acuff. The suit claimed that she gave the fiddle to Acuff in 1963 to display but had no intention of giving him the rights to the fiddle.

In October of 1969, an advertisement showed that she had a new studio on 1121 Church Street.

An article on page two of the *Tennessean* on Wednesday, March 22, 1972, carried the headline, ""Both Musical, Police Circles Knew of Eva Thompson Jones." Mrs. Jones had died of a heart attack two days earlier at her home on 3825 West End Avenue.

The obituary stated that Mrs. Jones had a music and dance studio for over 50 years but "her distinction as a music teacher, however, was complicated considerably—and rather frequently—

two to three decades ago by the insistent interest of the police in her activities." (Nashville Tennessean, March 22, 1972, p. 2)

Eva Thompson Jones was guilty of being caught in the times more than by any crimes. By hosting young soldiers at her dance club, she became the victim of a heavy handed justice that tainted her name.

Eva Thompson Jones was 72 years old at the time of her death and was survived by her son, Turner Lewis Jones, Jr. and three grandchildren.

Credits & Sources

NOTE: Dave Sichak did the original research on this article and Don Cusic did additional research and wrote the final draft.

"Abetting Delinquency Hearing Set June 24," *Nashville Banner,* June 6, 1955

"Both Musical, Police Circles Knew of Eva Thompson Jones," *Nashville Tennessean,* March 22, 1972

"Brock Studies Jones Case, as Test Indicated

"Brunet, Tattoo Stir Club Trial; Pachuko Mark Just Fad, She Explains; Jurors Look, May Get Case By Noon, *Nashville Tennessean,* February 10, 1956

"Bulletin," *Nashville Banner,* August 7, 1957

"Bulletin; July 31, 1955"

"Burial Services Held For Mrs. Jones," *Nashville Tennessean,* March 23, 1972

"Classified Ad; *Nashville Tennessean,* September 11, 1965"

"Clemency Recommended For Mrs. Jones," *Nashville Banner,* August 8, 1957

"Club Operator Loses Bid To End Charge," *Nashville Tennessean,* November 29, 1955

"Constitutional Test Of May Act Scheduled," *Nashville Banner,* September 1, 1942

"Dance Hall Case Action Due Friday," *Nashville Banner,* October 6, 1955

"Dance Teacher Held To Jury; Commissioner Refuses Defense Plea That May Act Case Be Dismissed," *Nashville Tennessean,* August 23, 1942

"Dancing School Out of Bounds, " *Nashville Tennessean,* August 21, 1942

"Dancing Teacher Case Shifted To Juvenile Court," *Nashville Banner,* June 25, 1955

"Dancing Teacher Is Arrested Here," *Nashville Tennessean,* August 14, 1942

"Deadline Set For Jones Appeal," *Nashville Tennessean,* May 15, 1956

"Eva Jones 90-Day Sentence To Stand," *Nashville Banner,* May 14, 1956

"Eva Jones Faces May Act Charge," *Nashville Tennessean,* August 15, 1942

"Eva Jones Gambles On Court Reversal," *Nashville Tennessean,* April 3, 1956

"Eva Jones Loses Building Lease," *Nashville Tennessean,* January 31, 1956

"Eva Jones' Hearing Slated Next Friday," *Nashville Banner,* August 15, 1942

"Eva Thompson Jones (Ad)," *Nashville Tennessean,* October 12, 1969

"Eva Thompson Jones School Plans Recital," *Nashville Banner,* December 9, 1954

"Eva Thompson Jones Trial Delayed," *Nashville Banner,* February 6, 1956

"Ex-Dance Hall Owner Trial Set," *Nashville Banner,* May 9, 1962

"Fine, Costs Paid, Mrs. Jones Freed," *Nashville Banner,* December 12, 1957

"From Witness Stand ... Testimony About Screens," *Nashville Tennessean,* February 9, 1956

"Gilbert Denies Bid To Dismiss Counts," *Nashville Banner,* November 29, 1955

"Hearing Due In Eva Jones Case," *Nashville Banner,* April 27, 1956

"Hearing October 7 For Mrs. Eva Jones," *Nashville Tennessean,*

"Jones Music, Dance Recital Set Monday, *Nashville Banner,* May 18, 1954

"Judge Does Flip In Eva Jones Rent Hearing," *Nashville Banner,* July 12, 1956

"Judge Overrules Eva Jones Motion," *Nashville Tennessean,* December 2, 1955

"Men Not Held In May Cases; Judge Declares Both Should Be Arrested As Jones Trial Opens," *Nashville Tennessean,* October 9, 1942

"Mrs. Eva Jones Accused Of Theft," *Nashville Tennessean,* May 10, 1962

"Mrs. Eva Jones Can Go Free If She Pays $1,148," *Nashville Banner,* December 11, 1957

"Mrs. Eva Jones To Be Tried In City Court," *Nashville Banner,* August 1, 1955

"Mrs. Eva T. Jones Conviction Is Upheld," *Nashville Banner,* April 1, 1957

"Mrs. Eva T. Jones To Get New Trial," *Nashville Tennessean,* October 11, 1956

"Mrs. Jones Appeal Arguments Slated April 2 By Judge," *Nashville Banner,* March 8, 1956

"Mrs. Jones Arraignment Set Monday," *Nashville Banner,* November 23, 1955

"Mrs. Jones Clemency Plea Sent Governor," *Nashville Tennessean,* August 8, 1957

"Mrs. Jones Fined $1,000" (Page one headline), *Nashville Banner*, February 10, 1956

"Mrs. Jones Freed In 30 Minutes, *Nashville Tennessean*, October 14, 1942

"Mrs. Jones Gets Hope Of Clemency, *Nashville Banner*, July 26, 1957

"Mrs. Jones Ordered To Workhouse," *Nashville Banner*, November 12, 1957

"Mrs. Jones To Appeal City Court Convictions," *Nashville Banner*, August 2, 1955

"Mrs. Jones To Request New Hearing," *Nashville Banner*, September 11, 1956

"Mrs. Jones' Friends Plan Final Appeal," *Nashville Banner*, November 5, 1957

"Mrs. Jones' Pardon Chances Slashed," *Nashville Tennessean*, September 25, 1957

"Nice Asks For Fiddle, *Daily News-Journal*, April 10, 1969

"No Action Taken In Eva Jones Case, *Nashville Tennessean*, June 27, 1955

"Officers Watch Club Patrons...Carry Out Evidence, *Nashville Tennessean*, August 1, 1955

"Parole Board Delays Action On Jones Case," *Nashville Banner*, July 27, 1957

"Pla-More Club Defendants Face Charges Today," *Nashville Tennessean*, August 1, 1955

"Pla-More Club Presentment Called Invalid," *Nashville Banner*, November 28, 1955

"Pla-More Operator Faces Trial Today," *Nashville Tennessean*, February 7, 1956

"Pla-More Trial Set February 6," *Nashville Banner*, December 7, 1955

"Plea Of Innocent Entered In Pla-More Case," *Nashville Banner*, November 30, 1955

"Policewoman's Auto Tires Cut, *Nashville Banner*, February 10, 1956

"Prosecution Hit In Jones Trial; Policeman's Search Of Defendant's 'Hall' Is Declared Illegal," *Nashville Tennessean*, October 13, 1942

"Special Goings On – Ad," *Nashville Tennessean*, January 22, 1967

"State Witness Hurls 'Lie' At Jones Attorney," *Nashville Banner*, February 8, 1956

"Was Framed Says Mrs. Jones; Dancing Teach Denies May Act Violation; Judge Scores Police," *Nashville Tennessean*, October 10, 1942

Armour, Joan. "Only Place To Go, Club Girls Say," *Nashville Tennessean*, August 5, 1955

Classified Ad: New manager of Eva Thompson Jones Studio," *Nashville Banner*,; August 19, 1942

Havighurst, Craig. *Air Castle of the South: WSM and the Making of Music City*. Chicago: University of Illinois Press, 2007.

Keel, William, "Witnesses Get Stoney Stares," *Nashville Tennessean*, October 6, 1955

Keel, William. "Jail Possible For Mrs. Jones," *Nashville Tennessean*, February 11, 1956

Keel, William. "Police Describe Wolf Whistles," *Nashville Tennessean*, February 8, 1956

Keel, William. "Ran Nice Place, Mrs. Jones Says; Club Pla-More Operator Testifies Liquor, Drunks Were Barred," *Nashville Tennessean*, February 9, 1956

McLinden, Mickey. "Begs Fight Outside Courtroom," *Nashville Banner*, February 8, 1956

McLinden, Mickey. "Closing of Pla-More Forecast," *Nashville Banner,* February 11, 1956

McLinden, Mickey. "Judge Bars 'Stripper' Query in Jones Trial," *Nashville Banner,* February 9, 1956

McLinden, Mickey. "Jury Returns Verdict In 17 Minutes," *Nashville Banner,* February 10, 1956

McLinden, Mickey. "Mrs. Jones Unmoved By Selection Of Jury," *Nashville Banner,* February 7, 1956

Setters, Jack. "Attempted Bribery Charged At Eva T. Jones' May Act Hearing, *Nashville Tennessean,* August 22, 1942

Smith, Dolores. "Don't Sell The 'Ole Piano Short!," *Nashville Tennessean,* January 28, 1968

Wolfe, Charles K. *A Good-Natured Riot: the Birth of the Grand Ole Opry.* Nashville: Country Music Foundation and Vanderbilt University Press, 1999.

In a break from the traditional way of listing sources, I'm listing the sources chronologically so the reader may see how the cases of Mrs. Jones were pursued by the news media.

Chronological Listing of Sources

"Brock Studies Jones Case, as Test Indicated

"Hearing October 7 For Mrs. Eva Jones," *Nashville Tennessean,*

"Dancing Teacher Is Arrested Here," *Nashville Tennessean,* August 14, 1942

"Eva Jones Faces May Act Charge," *Nashville Tennessean,* August 15, 1942

"Eva Jones' Hearing Slated Next Friday," *Nashville Banner,* August 15, 1942

Classified Ad: New manager of Eva Thompson Jones Studio," *Nashville Banner,*; August 19, 1942

"Dancing School Out of Bounds, " *Nashville Tennessean,* August 21, 1942

Setters, Jack. "Attempted Bribery Charged At Eva T. Jones' May Act Hearing, *Nashville Tennessean,* August 22, 1942

"Dance Teacher Held To Jury; Commissioner Refuses Defense Plea That May Act Case Be Dismissed," *Nashville Tennessean,* August 23, 1942

"Constitutional Test Of May Act Scheduled," *Nashville Banner,* September 1, 1942

"Men Not Held In May Cases; Judge Declares Both Should Be Arrested As Jones Trial Opens," *Nashville Tennessean,* October 9, 1942

"Was Framed Says Mrs. Jones; Dancing Teach Denies May Act Violation; Judge Scores Police," *Nashville Tennessean,* October 10, 1942

"Prosecution Hit In Jones Trial; Policeman's Search Of Defendant's 'Hall' Is Declared Illegal," *Nashville Tennessean,* October 13, 1942

"Mrs. Jones Freed In 30 Minutes, *Nashville Tennessean,* October 14, 1942

"Jones Music, Dance Recital Set Monday, *Nashville Banner,* May 18, 1954

"Eva Thompson Jones School Plans Recital," *Nashville Banner,* December 9, 1954

Keel, William. "Police Describe Wolf Whistles," *Nashville Tennessean,* February 8, 1956

"Bulletin; July 31, 1955"

"Abetting Delinquency Hearing Set June 24," *Nashville Banner,* June 6, 1955

"Dancing Teacher Case Shifted To Juvenile Court," *Nashville Banner,* June 25, 1955

"No Action Taken In Eva Jones Case, *Nashville Tennessean,* June 27, 1955

"Mrs. Eva Jones To Be Tried In City Court," *Nashville Banner,* August 1, 1955

"Officers Watch Club Patrons…Carry Out Evidence, *Nashville Tennessean,* August 1, 1955

"Pla-More Club Defendants Face Charges Today," *Nashville Tennessean,* August 1, 1955

"Mrs. Jones To Appeal City Court Convictions," *Nashville Banner,* August 2, 1955

Armour, Joan. "Only Place To Go, Club Girls Say," *Nashville Tennessean,* August 5, 1955

"Dance Hall Case Action Due Friday," *Nashville Banner,* October 6, 1955

Keel, William, "Witnesses Get Stoney Stares," *Nashville Tennessean,* October 6, 1955

"Mrs. Jones Arraignment Set Monday," *Nashville Banner,* November 23, 1955

"Pla-More Club Presentment Called Invalid," *Nashville Banner,* November 28, 1955

"Club Operator Loses Bid To End Charge," *Nashville Tennessean,* November 29, 1955

"Gilbert Denies Bid To Dismiss Counts," *Nashville Banner,* November 29, 1955

"Judge Overrules Eva Jones Motion," *Nashville Tennessean,* December 2, 1955

"Pla-More Trial Set February 6," *Nashville Banner,* December 7, 1955

"Plea Of Innocent Entered In Pla-More Case," *Nashville Banner,* November 30, 1955

"Eva Jones Loses Building Lease," *Nashville Tennessean,* January 31, 1956

McLinden, Mickey. "Begs Fight Outside Courtroom," *Nashville Banner,* February 8, 1956

"Eva Thompson Jones Trial Delayed," *Nashville Banner,* February 6, 1956

"Pla-More Operator Faces Trial Today," *Nashville Tennessean,* February 7, 1956

McLinden, Mickey. "Mrs. Jones Unmoved By Selection Of Jury," *Nashville Banner,* February 7, 1956

"Mrs. Jones Appeal Arguments Slated April 2 By Judge," *Nashville Banner,* March 8, 1956

"State Witness Hurls 'Lie' At Jones Attorney," *Nashville Banner,* February 8, 1956

"From Witness Stand … Testimony About Screens," *Nashville Tennessean,* February 9, 1956

Keel, William. "Ran Nice Place, Mrs. Jones Says; Club Pla-More Operator Testifies Liquor, Drunks Were Barred," *Nashville Tennessean,* February 9, 1956

McLinden, Mickey. "Judge Bars 'Stripper' Query in Jones Trial," *Nashville Banner,* February 9, 1956

"Brunet, Tattoo Stir Club Trial; Pachuko Mark Just Fad, She Explains; Jurors Look, May Get Case By Noon, *Nashville Tennessean,* February 10, 1956

"Mrs. Jones Fined $1,000" (Page one headline), *Nashville Banner,* February 10, 1956

"Policewoman's Auto Tires Cut, *Nashville Banner,* February 10, 1956

McLinden, Mickey. "Jury Returns Verdict In 17 Minutes," *Nashville Banner,* February 10, 1956

Keel, William. "Jail Possible For Mrs. Jones," *Nashville Tennessean,* February 11, 1956

McLinden, Mickey. "Closing of Pla-More Forecast," *Nashville Banner,* February 11, 1956

"Eva Jones Gambles On Court Reversal," *Nashville Tennessean,* April 3, 1956

"Hearing Due In Eva Jones Case," *Nashville Banner,* April 27, 1956

"Eva Jones 90-Day Sentence To Stand," *Nashville Banner,* May 14, 1956

"Deadline Set For Jones Appeal," *Nashville Tennessean,* May 15, 1956

"Judge Does Flip In Eva Jones Rent Hearing," *Nashville Banner,* July 12, 1956

"Mrs. Jones To Request New Hearing," *Nashville Banner,* September 11, 1956

"Mrs. Eva T. Jones To Get New Trial," *Nashville Tennessean,* October 11, 1956

"Mrs. Eva T. Jones Conviction Is Upheld," *Nashville Banner,* April 1, 1957

"Mrs. Jones Gets Hope Of Clemency, *Nashville Banner,* July 26, 1957

"Parole Board Delays Action On Jones Case," *Nashville Banner,* July 27, 1957

"Bulletin," *Nashville Banner,* August 7, 1957

"Clemency Recommended For Mrs. Jones," *Nashville Banner,* August 8, 1957

"Mrs. Jones Clemency Plea Sent Governor," *Nashville Tennessean,* August 8, 1957

"Mrs. Jones' Pardon Chances Slashed," *Nashville Tennessean,* September 25, 1957

"Mrs. Jones' Friends Plan Final Appeal," *Nashville Banner,* November 5, 1957

"Mrs. Jones Ordered To Workhouse," *Nashville Banner,* November 12, 1957

"Mrs. Eva Jones Can Go Free If She Pays $1,148," *Nashville Banner,* December 11, 1957

"Fine, Costs Paid, Mrs. Jones Freed," *Nashville Banner,* December 12, 1957

"Mrs. Eva Jones Accused Of Theft," *Nashville Tennessean,* May 10, 1962

"Ex-Dance Hall Owner Trial Set," *Nashville Banner,* May 9, 1962

"Classified Ad; *Nashville Tennessean,* September 11, 1965"

"Special Goings On – Ad," *Nashville Tennessean,* January 22, 1967

Smith, Dolores. "Don't Sell The 'Ole Piano Short!," *Nashville Tennessean,* January 28, 1968

"Nice Asks For Fiddle, *Daily News-Journal*, April 10, 1969

"Eva Thompson Jones (Ad)," *Nashville Tennessean,* October 12, 1969

"Both Musical, Police Circles Knew of Eva Thompson Jones," *Nashville Tennessean,* March 22, 1972

"Burial Services Held For Mrs. Jones," *Nashville Tennessean,* March 23, 1972

Reinterpreting Country Music in Japan: The February 2019 Issue of *Guitar Magazine* and the Legacy of the "Anything but Country" Attitude

By Mari Nagatomi
Setsunnan University

1. Introduction

In its February 2019 issue, *Guitar Magazine,* a major Japanese music magazine that features information and techniques for guitar players, devoted what its cover described as an "unheard volume of 116 pages" to country music and its iconic guitarists. "Country is the Best" read the cover of the magazine, which featured Merle Travis on a red motorcycle, surrounded by Joe Maphis, Jimmy Bryant, Don Rich, Hank Garland, Eldon Shamblin, Grady Martin, Jimmy Wyble, Chet Atkins, Les Paul, and Jerry Reed. This magazine pleased Japanese country music fans and musicians. As one male fan, Ryoichi Ito, 1 asked on his Facebook page, "When was the last time that a mainstream magazine featured country music?" (Ito). The prolific banjo player Yoshihiro Arita was thrilled to post about the magazine issue on Facebook, writing,

"This should be kept forever in your collection!" (Arita). But others wondered why it featured mostly guitarists who had already died. The country guitarist Hiroyuki Kitaguchi wanted the magazine "to feature other players" to represent country guitar, rather than a few contemporary players within the alternative country and Americana field (Kitaguchi). Moreover, it featured few female artists and musicians in the magazine.

The February 2019 issue of *Guitar Magazine* appeared to mark a transition in how the Japanese viewed and described country music in mainstream popular music culture. In the past 50 years or so, mainstream magazines have not covered country music so extensively, and this magazine issue was not unique in reinterpreting country music in Japan. In January 2020, another mainstream music magazine, Record Collectors, released a special issue with 190 pages exclusively devoted to country music albums. These "transitions" in country music in Japan also challenge, if not add critical views to, previous studies about country music in Japan. By dealing with only country fans and musicians in Japan, they tend to give the impression that Japanese country fans have loved the genre in the same way over the years and have adopted stereotypical views on country music in the United States (Furmanovsky; Thompson; Mitsui). As a result, they fail to address various ideas constructed by both devotees and critics at various times concerning country music and its image. For example, Thompson argues that the Japanese consumed country music to indulge themselves in an "imagined" past (38). His view can help us uphold the idea that country music is inherently nostalgic and cannot be reinterpreted. However, as I address in my dissertation, the Japanese have interpreted the meaning of country music in various ways over time (Nagatomi). Second, previous studies, including my dissertation, focus only on the "golden era" *of* country music in Japan, the period from the end of World War II to the mid-1960s when the genre was popular. Studies on the reception of country music in Japan after it lost its popularity have just started being published (Nagatomi). In this paper, I deal with current major press coverage of country music, which has not involved country music communities that previous scholars have studied, and challenge previous views on country as inherently static music. In so doing, I use the February 2019 issue of *Guitar Magazine* as a case study. The reason is that this issue was the first of any major music magazine in the last several decades in Japan to treat country music favorably.

While this magazine altered the negative images surrounding country music in Japan, it also reflects the legacy of how music journalists have criticized country music since the late 1960s. For example, like its predecessors, the magazine describes country music in masculine terms, targeting its imagined male audience, despite the fact that female Japanese fans of Taylor Swift have been changing the image of country in Japan for more than a decade. Therefore, I ask how the magazine persuaded their male readers, who had what Hubbs terms an "anything but country" stance (3), to appreciate country. What socio-cultural ideas in Japan can we glean from their current description of country music? To explore these questions, this paper investigates how the writers of the February 2019 issue of *Guitar Magazine* narrated, described, and represented country guitarists. To understand how this magazine "transformed" previous ideas about country music by mainstream journalism, it also briefly traces how rock journalists from the late 1960s to the early 1970s portrayed country music.

Analyzing narratives and representations in mainstream magazines, however, does not offer us comprehensive views on the current reception of country music in Japan, because it does not examine their interactions with country music fans and musicians. However, I believe how the mainstream media, which mostly targets rock music fans, views country music as being important for understanding how people treat country music in Japan. It is because journalistic views that target rock music fans, since the late 1960s, have played a major role in shaping the mainstream Japanese popular music culture, which allowed the mainstream music fans to like any music but country as their "normal" musical taste. By this, I do not mean that rock fans and journalists destroyed country music in Japan. The internal dynamics, schisms, and hierarchies within the community of country musicians and fans in Japan are no less important to the demise of country music and should be examined further. But I believe that normative narratives and representations of country music presented by rock journalists in contemporary Japan help us to think further about what kind of ideas Japanese people constructed through the transpacific circulation of American country music and relations between the genres of rock/pop and country music.

2. The "Anything but Country" Stance in Japan

To understand how *Guitar Magazine* reinterpreted, if not manipulated, conventional views on country music in Japan, it is important to understand how rock journalists have criticized country music since the late 1960s. It was from the late 1960s to the early 1970s, the period that Nadine Hubbs claims was "the politicizing moment of country music" in the United States (63), that the critics increasingly repudiated country music in Japan in political terms. While Japanese journalists had been criticizing country music since the early 1950s, they merely denigrated the genre as "unmodern" and "unsophisticated," describing country musicians as lacking in musical technique and knowledge (Nagatomi 81–85). But the ways in which they described country in the late 1960s, particularly in rock magazines, made a huge impact in consolidating rock normalcy, if not the "anything but country" stance, in the Japanese popular music landscape. These rock journalists began portraying country musicians and fans in the United States as "conservative whites" from the Jim Crow South or the Wild West and stressing their hyper-masculinity. As a result, they stigmatized country and its fans and musicians as morally wrong. By doing so, they underlined the rebellious stance they and their readers took against society.2

One prominent example of this is the work of the influential music critic Tōyō Nakamura, who is known for openly denouncing country music. Considered a father of rock journalism in Japan with his launch of New Music Magazine in 1969, Nakamura helped sow the seeds of rock music's popularity in Japan. One of his most notable anti-country articles was "Why I Hate Western," published in his magazine in 1972. Nakamura blasted American country music, and singer Hank Snow in particular, for his support of the segregationist presidential candidate George Wallace (42). Nakamura claimed that country promoted racial violence against blacks and Native Americans and called it pseudo-folk music (43). By racializing and politicizing country music, Nakamura showed readers his "rock spirit."

But one might wonder why such an "American" context around country persuaded Nakamura and his readers. One way in which Nakamura drew his readers' attention to the U.S. context surrounding country was to link the "white men" of country music with Japanese country-and-western fans and musicians. To do so, he created contrasting male images to represent either rock or country music, so readers could choose which male figures to emulate. For instance, when reviewing the album The Band by the Band, Nakamura criticized the notion that it was a country album. He wrote that he could imagine "the perseverance of a desperate man" represented by "the rough hand of a farmer" rather than "a greasy sheriff in the restaurant in the rural South in the movie Easy Rider," which is whom he imagined when he heard country-and-western records (99). Thus, when he criticized country in the "Why I Hate Western" article, his illustration of Japanese country-and-western fans as rough and dangerous people who "might raid" the demonstrations organized by the New Left and other leftist students might have been convincing for his readers (42). Nakamura dismissed as American imperialist "colonial subjects" those Japanese who appreciated country music. In so doing, he not only "othered" American country music and the masculine images that he imagined from it, but he also defined himself and his followers as authentic Japanese, independent of U.S. hegemony and the less-than-ideal male images that he constructed from it.

For Nakamura, the ability to talk about popular music would confirm his respectable masculinity. In his edited volume *149 Strategies to Achieve Male Sound: The Beginners' Book for a Study of the Spiritually Sophisticated,* Nakamura asked his readers: "In our modern age, who would be an authentically culturally refined man?" (2). He continued, "He would be a man who understands and loves 'sound!'" (3). Furthermore, Nakamura claimed, "If you are a man who cannot talk about sound at all in front of women, you should not live in this modern age!" (3). In this book, Nakamura stressed that explaining music to women helped maintain a man's superior status as a teacher and the woman's submissive status as his student. Nakamura included a chapter on country music by the scholar Toru Mitsui. In it, Mitsui wrote a section titled "Men Can Be Consoled Without Women If They Listen to Country and Western," which implied that country fans could be homosocial or homosexual (118–120). And his assertion that "country's social criticism tends to be right-wing" implied that country fans had a hyper-masculine, violent nature (125–130). In short, this book further confirmed why country fans could not be a respectable man.

Contemporary music fans and musicians were influenced by Nakamura's interpretation of country music. The article "Why I Hate Western" was reprinted in his anthology in 2011 (Nakamura, reprinted). The artist and composer Ryūichi Sakamoto, well-known for his film scores for the movies *The Last Emperor* (1987) and *Little Buddha* (1993) and his techno-pop group Yellow Magic Orchestra, said in the 2011 interview that he would "not say bad things about music, except for country music and Hawai'ian," because he disliked those types of music (Sakamoto). The blogger Amane declared on her blog that she liked all kinds of music except country. She disliked country because "the songs always tell a sad story," "you can only line dance to the beats," and "there is only one black country singer" (referring to Darius Rucker), "it is not stylish" (featuring Billy Ray Cyrus's picture in the 1990s), and "their English accents" were unacceptable (Amane). Amane's statement echoed Nakamura's opposition to country music. She claimed country was the music of rednecks, who she claimed supported neo-Nazis and white supremacists (Amane). All in all, those contemporary dissenters of country music repeated Nakamura's criticism of country. They seemed to confirm their good taste and their respectability by portraying country as "Other" and as uncool and morally wrong.

However, after Taylor Swift fans in Japan began altering this negative image of country starting in the late 2000s, one rock music Web magazine began to redeem country music from its negative reputation. The ways in which the Web magazine *Tap the Pop* attempted to transform its readers' image of country music shows how ideas about gender, particularly male readers' masculinity, are closely related to the discourse around country music in Japan. In 2018, Mitsuhiro Nakano, a staff writer for *Tap the Pop*, introduced nine female country artists to change "conventional images toward country music" in the article "Taylor Swift Is Not the Only One: Country Singers Include Many Good-Looking Women"

(Nakano). Instead of highlighting their songwriting and singing skills, Nakano used much of the space to describe their looks and feature their pictures and videos. When introducing Julie Roberts, Nakano wrote that she had a "deep voice despite her good looks" and warned readers not to mistake her for the Hollywood actor Julia Roberts. He praised the way Rebecca Lynn Howard looked on the cover of her album Forgive and commented, "We cannot help buying this album if she gazes at us so lovingly with her perfect short hair." By recreating an image of country as a space where Japanese men could fulfill their sexual desire for a woman, Nakano attempted to impose his own definition on the country genre, which was previously imagined as hyper-masculine. But this approach did not help make country music more visible in Japanese media. It was because this article failed to provide masculinist "knowledge" about country music, by dismissing country as visually acceptable only for its female bodies and looks (the article also failed to recognize those female singers' musical talents, their techniques, and their songwriting skills). How did *Guitar Magazine* "alter" conventional images of country?

3. The Reinterpretation of Country Music in *Guitar Magazine*

Guitar Magazine is published by Rittō Music and has been one of the best-known magazines for guitar players in Japan since its launch in 1980. In the past few years, they have dedicated over 100 pages to specific themes, such as country music and city pop, to increase their readership (Mitsui 139). The current editors think it is essential to feature "stories" of certain genres or/and musicians, such as the historical backgrounds of and influences on current music scenes, because readers can easily obtain guitar technique and artist information online (Mitsui 139). The February 2019 issue of the magazine thus covered the history of country music, iconic guitar techniques and scores, current country music artists and Japanese guitarists, and key businesspeople in country music. The entire issue focused on six country guitar players—Merle Travis, Les Paul, Chet Atkins, Hank Garland, Jimmy Bryant, and Don Rich—whom it called "the avengers of country guitarists." It introduced their biographies in brief, their albums, and the musical scores of their iconic guitar playing. With those featured articles, the magazine invited readers to take a journey, which the magazine called "Electric Country Gold," to the world of country with the goal of improving their guitar technique (*Guitar Magazine* 33).

3-1. "The Avengers"

First, I would like to analyze how and why the magazine called those six guitarists "avengers." This word "avengers" (*abenjāzu*) was written in katakana syllabary, instead of using the Japanese translation for an avenger. Because katakana syllabary is often used in the transcription of foreign languages, we can read, in this case, that the term "avengers" here does not refer to those who take revenge. Instead, it connotes the heroes in Marvel comics and the Marvel film *The Avengers*, released in 2012 in Japan. Like the six heroes in *The Avengers*, who employed different abilities and techniques to combat their enemies, the magazine listed the six guitar players—Travis, Paul, Atkins, Garland, Byrant, and Rich—each with their own unique styles. And with their different styles, those guitarists can, if not help us, "rescue" the conventional guitar culture that surrounds the magazine readers, like the Avengers in the movie combat their violent enemy, Thanos.

What are the avengers fighting against in this case? What kind of conditions does the magazine want these six guitarists to rescue their readers from? In the beginning, the editors of the magazine expressed concern about the contemporary situation, in which "nobody really appreciates the beauty of country music enough, even though most guitar players are influenced by it" (33). Thus, for the writers and their targeted readership, country music, if not country guitar, was "a frontier too broad to grasp" (72) because of its "versatile history and styles" (33). Then perhaps "the enemy" was the current ignorance of readers regarding country music and country guitar. And this ignorance, according to the magazine, hindered readers from understanding fully "what influenced the Beatles, Eric Clapton, and John Mayer" (33). Finally, the magazine encouraged its readers "to defeat the condition" of knowing little about country music (33).

3-2. Pioneers/Outlaws

Calling these guitar giants "avengers," the magazine portrayed them as rebellious outlaws who also broke through the music scenes in which they performed. In the articles narrating their life histories, the writer Yasushi Kuboki made this point. Among those life stories, Kuboki's portrayal of Merle Travis clearly shows how those rock journalists placed importance on the (paternalistic) "origin" of rock music and the "rebellious" attitudes of musicians. Asserting that Travis was a guitarist "every country guitarist would admire forever" (74), Kuboki emphasized Travis as a father and originator of country guitar, whom he thought that readers should learn and remember. Needless to say, Kuboki highlighted his invention of the solid-body electric guitar with Paul Bigsby and Travis's signature picking as his achievement (75). But he reinforced his rebellious persona by calling Travis "a guitarist (*zenryoku guitāristo*) at full force" (74). In so doing, Kuboki connected Travis's life with the boy in the popular song by Japanese artist Sukima Switch, "Being a Boy at Full Force" (*Zenryoku Shōnen*), which encourages a grown-up man to be brave like the innocent and fearless boy he had been once (Sukima Switch). Featuring a picture of Travis in his double-breasted suit with his ten-gallon hat riding on a motorcycle with several guitars, Kuboki reinforced Travis's innocent and fearless persona (*Guitar Magazine*, 75). In the caption, Kuboki wrote, "he must be the one who created the iconic American image of 'a motorcycle and a guitar,'" and emphasized Travis's outlaw status (75). All in all, Kuboki concluded, Travis "embodied our admiration of electric guitar" (75).

Kuboki, seeking others with Travis's pioneer spirit and rebellious persona, constantly linked other "avengers" to rock musicians in anecdotes. In an anecdote about Les Paul making his own harmonica rack, Kuboki reminded readers that such a rack was used by Bob Dylan and John Lennon. Kuboki attempted to position Paul, in his early career as a country singer with a guitar and a harmonica, as a predecessor of prominent rock musicians

(76). Kuboki stressed that Hank Garland's hit "Sugarfoot Rag" was recorded by "rock guitarist Duane Eddy and the Ventures" (80). And he featured Garland's picture with Elvis in what he calls "one of his signature sessions" (81). Don Rich was portrayed as a pioneer who formed a perfect duo with Buck Owens; Kuboki compares them to Mick Jagger and Keith Richards (84). Kuboki emphasized that Rich's Telecaster sound influenced the Byrds' Clarence White and concluded that "what we imagined as 'country guitar' originated from the sound of Don Rich," tracing a paternal lineage from country to rock music.

3-3. Racial Tolerance/Respectability

But to be accepted by rock guitar fans, these country guitar pioneers could not give the impression that they were like the cowboys Nakamura depicted, who oppressed Native Americans and African Americans. One way that the writers pre-empted such violent and racist associations was to emphasize that these country musicians had musical interactions with African Americans or the musical forms seen as belonging to African Americans. For example, Kuboki used one-fourth of his article on Garland to discuss Garland's love for jazz music (80). Kuboki inserted an anecdote about his frequent performances in New York with Charlie Parker (81). He added that George Benson used to listen to Garland's album *Jazz Winds from a New Direction* as he was training to become a professional guitarist (81). In commemorating Chet Atkins, Kuboki claimed that "it was Chet's achievement to make possible the debut of the first black singer in country music,

Charlie Pride" (79). Kuboki does not fail to mention Arnold Shultz as a major influence on Merle Travis's guitar style (75).

Perhaps the column titled "Country Guitarists Who Played Jazz" suggested the writer Kuboki's intention to blur boundaries between "white" country and "black" jazz to attract a wider readership for this magazine issue. Kuboki introduced Jimmy Wyble, who was in Bob Wills's Texas Playboys, as he had already played "modern solos" popular among bebop musicians in the early 1950s (86). He also claimed that Junior Barnard was strongly influenced by Charlie Christian (86). This emphasis on the connections between western swing and jazz for Japanese readers reveals some conventional ideas about American popular music that the Japanese have had since the 1970s. That is, white musicians play with a white sound, and blacks play with a black sound. And somehow these journalists have assumed that the listeners could distinguish which was which. In fact, elsewhere in this issue, another writer, Keita Fukusaki, claimed that the country guitar sound was symbolically white. Following Fukusaki's idea, Kuboki found that jazz and country guitar players played jazz differently. According to him, "jazz guitarists play dramatically at the end of the solo," whereas "[Les] Paul and [George] Burns play enthusiastically from the beginning"; Kuboki speculated that those differences resulted from "their thinking patterns and tastes" (87), implying that if whites and blacks had essentially different ideas and tastes about music.

4. Accidental Country Guitarists

What kind of "sound" should Japanese musicians, who cannot be placed in a white/black racial binary, play after learning to play country guitar? "Country Talk," an article featuring a series of interviews with Japanese guitar players and key businesspeople, gives us some clues. The interviewer Keita Fukuzaki asked the guitar player Ryōsuke Nagaoka if he defined his guitar sound as black or white, because he always felt "blackness" from Nagaoka's playing, even though Nagaoka had learned country music, which, for this interviewer, "symbolizes whiteness" (61). Nagaoka told the interviewer that his guitar "does not sound white or black" and claimed instead that it sounded "weird and mediocre" (61). Perhaps he described his guitar sound this way as a form of self-deprecation. But at the same time, his answer can be read as both excitement and regret that his own sound would stand outside the black/white binaries that he imagines authenticate popular music. The interviewer added that Nagashima's guitar "sounds a bit muggy" rather than having a "crisp country guitar sound." Nagashima responded, "Maybe because I am from Japan, where the weather is warm and humid?" By essentializing musical sound according to race, Nagaoka may have imagined that he, as a Japanese, could not play country guitar. But we might also interpret him as playing down the influence of country music on his work in order to assert his creative independence. In fact, Nagaoka concluded, "I like country, but strangely, my band does not have even a whiff of country" (61).

The veteran guitar player Hirofumi Tokutake justified his preference for country music. Tokutake explained that he used to feel country was "boring music" when he was young because it was a type of music that his elders listened to (52). He also lamented that his elders did not share their knowledge about country with him (52).3 Tokutake asserted that he "did not fall in love with country," claiming that he just "wanted to learn how to play country guitar" (52). He listened to country because his heroes, "the Ventures and many rock 'n' roll bands learned guitar from" country (52). All in all, Tokutake concluded, he wished the young readers "could understand country as white blues," because "British and blues were not the only roots of rock music" (54). Tokutake reckoned that his younger followers could take advantage of country guitar to enhance their creativity because they had already studied rock music thoroughly. Tokutake defended his and his young followers' "rebellious" and "creative" energy, which defined their rock norms, by describing country as a tool to expand their own musical frontiers.

The multi-instrumentalist Ren Takada also pointed out that he understood that country was not cool music. Growing up as a son of the prestigious folk singer Wataru Takada, he claimed that he grew up with what he called "white music" (56). But this interview's tagline read, "The only weak point of country music is that we cannot buy country albums by their cover design" (57), in favor of their readers' imagined "anything but country" stance. "Everybody has had the experience," Takada presumed, "of buying soul and blues records because of their cover design to find their sound was not so good" (57). Then he declared that country would be the opposite and encouraged readers not to "be afraid of unfashionable country album covers" (57). Although Takada acknowledged his own musical heritage in country music and recommended that readers listen to country, he defended "general" rock fans' perception of country as "uncool."

The guitarist Kenta Suzuki, from the band D. W. Nichols, unapologetically shared his love for country music with the readers, hoping that more people would appreciate "the beauty of country music because of this issue" (65). However, the editor maintained that Suzuki's musical pedigree came from rock music. The interviewer started with a pull quote that read "Bob Dylan helped me broaden my musical world" (64). Thus, the interviewer did not define Suzuki as a country guitarist. Instead, he called Suzuki "the one and only guitarist who adds his excellent country taste to his pop songs" (64). All in all, the interviewer appeared to make a special point of describing country as a mere musical element to enhance readers' musical creativity.

Indeed, these Japanese musicians were not visually represented in the magazine as outlaws, as Travis was in his photo with two guitars on a motorcycle. The Japanese artists appear to retain a more respectable, approachable, and sophisticated aura than the six country guitar giants illustrated with thick lines and shadows. For example, Hiroshi Asada, the founder of the booking agency Tom's Cabin, was photographed facing the camera head-on in his striped button-down polka-dot shirt with knitted multi-colored vest. He sat in front of the white wall and flipped the pages of concert pamphlets on the desk. His round-shaped glasses with a thin golden flame added to his polished mien (68). The tagline of the interview read, "The view of country music in Japan and the U.S. from the man who saw legends over the years" (69). Asada, represented as a respectable man, gave the impression that he had been "supervising" such "wild" country music created by outlaws when importing it to Japan.

The guitarist Suzuki, who unapologetically announced his fascination for country music, was photographed on a river walk behind the unfocused green grass and trees (64). The green shades and his denim shirt and relaxed jeans evoked a laid-back atmosphere, as one could find in the countryside, but unfocused images of tall buildings were placed behind him (64). His smile while singing, and his tortoise-shell-framed glasses, emphasized that his music was embedded in city life. Nagaoka's photograph reinforced the idea that country should be accepted as part of popular music in today's Japan. Nagaoka's picture was filtered through pastel shades of color and made his face hazy. His button-down shirt looked light pink, and his thin-framed glasses and his short hair made him look like a young man in a city. The shades of color in this picture remind us of the latest Taylor Swift album Lover and produced a futuristic aura (60). As the magazine described Nagaoka as a guitarist who plays "in the edgy pop scene in Japan," Nagaoka was represented as an embodiment of how Japanese guitarists should use country guitar styles for their own music. Ren Takada was pictured leaning on a white brick wall in his gray T-shirt and black trousers with loose black suspenders, wearing a black, wide-brimmed fedora. The monotone shades of his picture, contrasting with the pastel colors in which Nagaoka was painted, suggested his music was subtle and elaborate (56). All in all, those representations reinforced the idea that Japanese guitarists should only "blend" country guitar and musical elements and not imitate or be totally absorbed by country music.

While the magazine set the stage for Japanese readers to use country guitar to broaden their musical creativity, rather than to teach them to play and compose country music, it encouraged readers to use country guitar as a weapon to surpass their rivals' guitar technique. For example, the magazine featured the scores of iconic guitar phrases by the six "avengers" with the title "The Deadly-Blow Country Guitar Phrases" (99). The writer assured readers that "if you learn their signature styles, you will see the new horizon!" (99) Concerning Hank Garland's signature techniques, the writer remarked, "His marvelous speed and technique is his most powerful weapon" (107). He called Bryant's first solo on "Flippin' the Lid" "marching dominant motion," which involves playing phrases with a chord change where a dominant chord moves up 4th above (5th below) to resolve to the next chord. The writer also encouraged his readers to "master his technique, which would knock out" their fellow guitarists (109). While the magazine urged readers to embody "outlaw" masculinities that they thought country guitarists embodied, it encouraged them to deploy the "country weapon" to outshine their fellow guitar players. As a result, the magazine defended its readers' "authority" to create their own music, which cannot be categorized as either a white or a black sound.

5. Conclusion

The special features of country music in the February 2019 issue of *Guitar Magazine* marked a turning point in Japanese interpretations of country music. Unlike the previous era, in which rock journalism urged its followers to listen to "anything but country" by negating its musical elements, the magazine re-evaluated country as a worthy musical source and inspiration for contemporary musicians. In the past, the rock journalists in *New Music Magazine* denied country's musical influence, for example, on James Burton's guitar. In the article "The Development of Rock Guitar," the writer found a strong country-and-western stylistic influence on James Burton's playing, but he negated it by claiming, "Country-and-western instrumentalists would not have a rock spirit," which he felt Burton's playing had (35). However, 2019 *Guitar Magazine* hailed Burton as a player based on "the West Coast, the mecca of country music" (147). The February 2019 issue of *Guitar Magazine*, devoting a great deal of space to country music, managed to promote it as a worthy musical form by which Japanese could enhance their musical creativity.

Yet this magazine maintained an ideological paradigm that convinced Japanese music fans to treat an "anything but country" stance as normal. Indeed, the magazine redeemed country music from music critic Toyo Nakamura's repudiation of it as racist and hyper-masculine by underlining country guitarists' interactions with African Americans and their musical forms. It rescued the genre from perceptions that it was hyper-masculine and conservative by representing and narrating country guitarists as pioneer outlaws who opened new guitar horizons for their rock successors. However, the magazine featured only a few living guitarists, including Pete Anderson and Jim Campilongo. It covered contemporary scenes in only two pages. This lack of proportion between dead guitarists and living ones can give readers the impression that country music thrived only in the past.

The ways in which the magazine represented Japanese musicians and businesspeople familiar with country music further stressed this point. As I demonstrate, they were portrayed as respectable men, not outlaws, who used musical elements from country musicians to create their own music in other genres. In other words, the magazine portrayed them not as musicians who could rewrite the history of country music, which should be open to performers anywhere in the world, but creators who used "static country music" in their own music, embedded in the Japanese popular music scene. Moreover, the magazine obscured the small but vibrant country music scene in Japan by featuring a small note that read, "Japan had an unprecedented country boom in the past" (38). As a result, the magazine failed to give equal prominence to young guitarists who have played country guitar in Japan, such as Tamasaburō Yamaguchi, Takashi Nishiumi, Shime, Hiroyuki Kitaguchi, and Kazuaki Furuhashi, as well as the female singer Keiko Walker, who worked with such guitar players and advanced country music scenes in Japan.

Finally, the magazine inherited the male-oriented views that helped Nakamura to criticize country in the early 1970s. The magazine's constant usage of militaristic and masculine words to narrate the life stories and guitar techniques of country guitarists tell us that they targeted primarily male readers. Moreover, it suggests that the magazine encouraged male readers to use the new techniques and knowledge of guitar to assert their superiority over fellow guitarists. In short, the magazine depicted country-music knowledge and technique as a weapon their readers could deploy in order to proclaim their superior masculinity. While Nakamura promoted his masculinity by denouncing country, his contemporaries promoted theirs by adopting musical elements of country. Regardless of whether they denounced or accepted country, these male journalists and their targeted male audience used country music (or perhaps other genres of music) to affirm their masculinity, based on their knowledge and technique. Furthermore, the magazine's persistent search for the "origin" of its rock heroes by tracing their paternal lineage confirms how gendered Japanese rock journalism is and how rock music should be most "authentic" music. In short, these men used country music and popular music to explore and define what the scholar of masculinity R. W. Connell calls "hegemonic masculinity" (76).

This male-oriented paradigm, if not an idea to use popular music as a battlefield of masculinity, hinders the magazine from featuring female artists and musicians. Nikki Lane and Margo Price were the only female artists featured in the magazine. This underrepresentation makes us wonder how the magazine understood the reinterpretation of country music by Taylor Swift fans in Japan. If they were inspired by her fans, they could have mentioned that those female fans played the main role in changing the "anything but country" attitude that persisted for almost half a century in Japan. To challenge such "male-oriented" discourse around country music in Japan, we must further investigate how female fans of contemporary reinterpreted country music of their own and how this has been described and narrated in the mainstream media.

Notes

1. Throughout the text, I have followed the Western convention, in which the given name precedes the family name.
2. We need to investigate further why those rock journalists racialized country as white. Their consumption of, if not identification with, rock music was linked to their support for cultural independence from the United States, their opposition to the Japanese government and the Vietnam War, and other political concerns.
3. Country fans and dissenters alike often blame the country-music community for the demise of country since the 1970s. According to them, the hierarchies and parochial culture within the country-music community in Japan did not allow younger generations to thrive in this community.

Works Cited

Amane, "Kantorī mūjikku ga kiraina itsutsu no riyū" (Five Reasons Why I Hate Country). *Amane no blog*. 28 June 2013, http://ameblo.jp/amamizu7/entry-11562406271.html. Accessed 20 Feb. 2020.

Arita, Yoshihiro. The Latest Issue of the Guitar Magazine. *Facebook*, 11 January. 2019, http://www.facebook.com/

yoshihiro.arita.9/posts/10213385077996869. Accessed 10 February 2020.

Connell, R. W. Masculinities. University of California Press, 1995, pp.76.

Fukuzaki, Keita. "Country Talk," *Guitar Magazine*, February 2019, pp.52-71.

Furmanovsky, Michael. "American Country Music in Japan: Lost Piece in the Popular Music History Puzzle." Popular Music and Society, vol. 31, no. 3, 2008, pp. 357–372.

Guitar Magazine, February 2019.

Hubbs, Nadine. *Rednecks, Queers, and Country Music*. University of California Press, 2014.

Ito, Ryoichi. Guitar Magazine. *Facebook*, 16 Jan. 2019, http://www.facebook.com/richie.itoh/posts/1493905407406057. Accessed 10 February 2020.

Kitaguchi, Hiroyuki. *Guitar Magazine*. Facebook, 16 Jan. 2019, http://www.facebook.com/kitaguchihiroyuki/posts/1975808709183297. Accessed 10 Feb. 2020.

Kuboki, Yasushi. "Rokunin no saikyō kantorī gitārisuto sono jinsei wo tadoru" (Six country guitarists and their lives). *Guitar Magazine*, February 2019, pp.72-85.

--- "Jazu wo kanadeta kantorī gitārisuto tachi (Country guitarists who played jazz). *Guitar Magazine*, February 2019, pp.86-87.

Mitsui, Haruna. "Kanbai mo zokushutu! gitā senmonshi no yakushin 100 peiji wo koeru" (Consecutive Sold-Out Issues! *Guitar Magazine* Turns to Featuring Special Issues with Over 100 Pages). *Henshū kaigi* (Editors' Meeting), 2019, pp. 139–141.

Mitsui, Tōru. "The Reception of the Music of American Southern Whites in Japan." *Transforming Tradition: Folk Music Revivals*

Examined, edited by Neil Rosenberg, University of Illinois Press, 1993, pp. 275–293.

Nagatomi, Mari. "Racializing Country Music in Japan: Toyo Nakamura and the Crisis of Japanese Masculinities from 1969 to 1971." International Association for the Study of Popular Music Conference, 27 June 2019, Australian National University, Canberra.

――― *Tokyo Rodeo: Transnational Country Music and the Crisis of Japanese Masculinities.* 2019. Doshisha U, PhD dissertation.

Nakamura, Tōyō. "Kongetsu no rekōdo: The Band" (The Records Released This Month: The Band), *New Music Magazine,* Feb. 1970, p. 99.

――― "Naze boku wa 'uesutan' ga kirai ka" (Why I Hate Western). *New Music Magazine,* Oct. 1972, pp. 41–44.

――― "Naze boku wa 'uesutan' ga kirai ka" (Why I Hate Western). *Nakamura Tōyō ansorojī,* edited by Jun Asano, *Music Magazine,* 2011, pp. 38–43.

Nakamura, Tōyō and Hisamitsu Noguchi, editors. *Otokono saundo 149 no senryaku-seishin teki oshare nyūmon* (149 Strategies to Achieve Male Sound: The Beginners' Book for a Study of the Spiritually Sophisticated). K. K. Longsellers, 1974, pp. 2–3, 118–127.

Nakano, Mitsuhiro. "Teira suifuto dakejanai! bijo zoroi no kantorii kashutachi" (Taylor Swift Is Not the Only One: Country Singers Include Many Good-Looking Women), *Tap the Pop,* 21 Nov. 2018, http://www.tapthepop.net/extra/17933. Accessed 20 Feb. 2020.

Sakamoto, Ryūichi. "No. 16 'Suki to kirai' ni tsuite iikiru" (Asserting What I Like and Dislike). *Web Magazine Openers,* 2011, http://openers.jp/article/10556. 2019.06.03. Accessed 12 Feb. 2020.

Sukima Switch. "Zenryoku shōnen." *Kūsō kurippu* (Clippings in Our Imagination), Augusta Records, 2005. *Spotify*, http://open.spotify.com/track/3Ztjw8utVpcrzms1RrsJvR?si=yqVrwpewTXmTu-m_Qdv3eQ.

Thompson, Stephen I. "American Country Music in Japan." *Popular Music and Society, vol. 16, no. 3, 1992, pp. 31–38.*

"I'll Be Locked Here in this Cell 'til my Body's Just a Shell": Hank Williams on Crime and Punishment

By Tim Dodge
Auburn University

The themes of crime and punishment, separately or together, are found throughout the history of country music recording. A few disparate examples might include "The Prisoner's Song" by Vernon Dalhart (Marion Slaughter, 1883-1948) recorded for Victor in 1924; the macabre if lively "Hangman's Boogie" by Cowboy (Lloyd) Copas (1913-1963) recorded for King in 1948; and "Ol' Red" by Blake Shelton (1976-) recorded for Warner Brothers in 2001. The original version of "Ol' Red" was actually recorded by George Jones (1931-2013) on Epic in 1990, however, Shelton's version is much more well-known. These examples just barely scratch the surface with other famous country recordings coming to mind such as Jimmie Rodgers's (1897-1933) "In the Jail House Now" (Victor, 1928) and Johnny Cash's (1932-2003) "Folsom Prison Blues" (Sun, 1955). Some country artists have actually lived the prison experience such as Lefty (William) Frizzell (1928-1975) who served a brief sentence in Texas; Merle Haggard (1937-2016) who served hard time in the infamous San Quentin Prison for several years; David Alan Coe (1939-) who spent close to 20 years in and out of correctional facilities including the Ohio State Penitentiary; and Steve Earle (1955-) who served a fairly short term in jail that has helped inform his perhaps unconventional political views and songwriting themes.

The purpose of this investigation is not so much to place Hank Williams within the genre of prison songs so much as to explore Williams's take – as evidenced in his recordings – on the connection between *crime* (what someone does) and *punishment* (prison or something else resulting from what one has done).

Unlike Haggard or Coe, Hank never had to live through the prison experience. It is true he did experience numerous brief detentions, sometimes voluntarily, in one or another sanatorium due to his serious bouts with alcoholism and he did experience at least one brief stint in jail, in Alexander City, Alabama in July 1952. No doubt some readers will have seen the sad photograph of a gaunt, shirtless, cowboy hat-wearing Hank Williams staring out blankly at the viewer from a cell in that jail. Arrested for public drunkenness and disorderly conduct, Hank was bailed out by a local friend. Reflecting on the downward spiral of Hank's life at this stage, Colin Escott notes, "Now Hank had one girlfriend, two cars, no band, no show dates and far too much time on his hands."[1],

Hank did have numerous fights with his wife, Audrey (1923-1975), some of them quite violent, which could have potentially landed him in jail (misdemeanor) if not prison (felony). The worst of these occurred around Christmas 1951 when Hank fired his gun inside the house but not directly at Audrey.[2] Not surprisingly, Hank was kicked out and Audrey firmly resolved this time to divorce him which she did several months later. While this unfortunate encounter could have ended in murder, Hank's violent behavior pales in comparison to that of another country star, Spade (Donnell Clyde) Cooley (1910-1969), who brutally beat and stomped his wife, Ella Mae Evans (1923-1961), to death in 1961 while in a jealous drunken rage.

Hank Williams's first recording to address the theme of crime and punishment was "On the Banks of the Old Ponchartrain" (M-G-M, 1947). Utilizing a fast waltz-time rhythm and prominently featuring the fiddle, what sounds like a nineteenth-century ballad presents the poignant story of the protagonist encountering a woman while sheltering under a tree during a rainstorm on the banks of Lake Ponchartrain, the very large lake located near New Orleans. This chance encounter leads to a brief romance, however, before the protagonist can settle down with the woman he loves, the long arm of the law arrests him and takes him back to the prison on "the West Texas plain" from which he had recently escaped. He never gets to say goodbye and she has no idea what has happened to him as he sits despondently in his cell hoping someday to return to "the banks of the old Ponchartrain."

As Colin Escott notes, this recording was "one of the least typical entries in his [Hank's] canon."[3] The lyrics were sent to Hank by Kathleen Ramona Vincent, a Louisiana fan, via postcard. Perhaps a little unkindly, Paul Hemphill describes the lyrics as "a bad poem scribbled on a postcard."[4] Ribowsky declares, "It was bathetic even for Hank." Supposedly, Hank later on reflected, when considering another recording he was making, that "[I'm] sure glad it ain't another damn 'Ponchartrain.'"[5] This record was one of the relatively few studio recordings made by Hank that never charted.[6] Of course, in 1947, Hank was not yet the major country star he would become once "Lovesick Blues" (M-G-M, 1948) hit the charts in early 1949.

Criticisms of the song aside, this recording presents two important themes found in most of Hank's other crime and punishment-related recordings: fatalism concerning the rightness or inevitability of punishment (for crime) and a sense of the pathos and frustration endured by the one who is being punished (the prisoner/criminal). No matter how far he has escaped from a nameless prison on the "West Texas plain," it is inevitable that the protagonist must pay for his unnamed crime when the law catches up to him. Although bitterly disappointed at his capture and rupture of his budding romance, the protagonist does not dispute his recapture and reimprisonment. There is no romanticizing of the outlaw here. Hank's soulful singing serves to emphasize the pathos of the protagonist's predicament. He is back in prison for what is likely a long time and he is unable to communicate with the woman he met at Lake Ponchartrain. He never was able even to say goodbye, so she remains in ignorance of why he has disappeared. He pictures her waiting "in vain" for his return. He hopes someday to return but, realistically, it seems unlikely the two will ever reunite.

One of the most powerful songs recorded by Hank relating to crime and punishment was "Lonesome Whistle," often listed as "I Heard that Lonesome Whistle," recorded on M-G-M in 1951. It reached the number nine position on the *Billboard* country charts that year.[7] This slow, somewhat bluesy ballad perfectly expresses both the fatalism (crime *will be* punished*)* and the pathos of punishment (the human cost of serving time in prison). Somewhat analogous to the protagonist in Johnny Cash's "Folsom Prison Blues" (Sun, 1955) who says, "but I shot a man in Reno just to watch him die," Hank's protagonist describes his crime as "Just a kid actin' smart, I went and broke my darling's heart. I guess I was too young to know." In both recordings, the crime (murder in Cash's case, unspecified in that of Williams although the resulting punishment implies it was serious, perhaps murder) seems to have been done in a casual, almost offhand manner – the act of a (very) thoughtless young man.

For the protagonist in "Lonesome Whistle," the consequences are grave and inevitable. Just as the long arm of the law found and re-imprisoned the prison escapee from West Texas hundreds of miles to the east on the banks of Lake Ponchartrain in Louisiana, the long arm of the law locates and captures the "kid actin' smart": "They took me off the Georgia Main, locked me to a ball and chain." The prison sentence is long, perhaps for life: "I'll be locked here in this cell 'til my body's just a shell and my hair turns whiter than snow."

Williams's sense of compassion or at least the pathos of such a lengthy prison sentence is quite expressive: "I'll never see that gal of mine, Lord, I'm in Georgia doin' time." However terrible the crime and however deserved the punishment, the personal cost and emotional devastation are evident to the listener. Williams's stress on the word "Georgia" is essentially a loud moan of pain; he is stuck there (apparently for life) and there is absolutely nothing he can ever do to change the situation.

A number of others have recorded "(I Heard that) Lonesome Whistle" since Hank Williams's original version including a very expressive interpretation by Johnny Cash on Sun in 1957. It appears that co-writer Jimmie Davis (1899-2000) did not record his own version until much later, in 1962, on Decca.[8] Davis's recording is given the full Nashville treatment with harmonica and piano accompaniment plus a rather prominent male vocal chorus. It is good but not nearly as expressive as Hank's version.

The most dramatic song recorded by Hank Williams in connection to crime and punishment has to be "My Main Trial Is Yet to Come" (unreleased, June 12, 1952). In this case, Hank played no part in the song's composition. "My Main Trial" was composed by Pee Wee King (Julius Kuczynski, 1914-2000) and his father-in-law, J.L. (Joseph Lee) Frank (1900-1952).[9] Pee Wee King, a fairly notable country star (and co-composer of the famous "Tennessee Waltz"), surprisingly, never recorded "My Main Trial Is Yet to Come." It was, however, recorded and released by several other artists including the Cope Brothers (King, 1947), the Blue Sky Boys (for WCYB radio in 1949 and on Rounder, 1975), Jimmie Osborne (1923-1957) on King in 1953; and the Stanley Brothers (King, 1959).[10]

Although Hank's recording is a little rough, possibly a first take accompanied only by his own guitar, he still very effectively and mournfully delivers what is, in effect, a gospel recording. The protagonist, sitting in his prison cell the night before his pending execution by electric chair, reflects on his ultimate fear or concern which is the judgment of God. He is at peace with the idea of his very imminent death – again, another expression of Hank's fatalistic attitude regarding the inevitability and rightness of punishment for a crime. He says goodbye to his mother and says "I've degraced [*sic,* disgraced] your name I know" indicating that he accepts the rightness of his conviction. Looking ahead to the next morning he declares, "The judge will give me the electric chair but that don't worry me." What does worry the protagonist is this: "It's what will the verdict be to come when I face the Judge of Eternity?" This is a chilling as well as fatalistic recording. Also, as a quasi-gospel song, this introduces the concept of crime as sin. As we know, Hank recorded a fairly large number of gospel recordings, perhaps most famously, his own composition, "I Saw the Light" (M-G-M, 1947). As a southerner brought up in the Baptist church, it seems highly likely Hank would have regarded crime as sin even if, in the conduct of his personal life, he often fell far short of the Christian ideal.

Considering the gravity of the punishments described in "(I Heard that) Lonesome Whistle" and "My Main Trial Is Yet to Come," the crimes that got the protagonist into these situations must have been of a very serious nature, most likely, murder. While Hank never elaborates on what exactly was done by the protagonist, for these two recordings and perhaps, also for "Ponchartrain,", the assumption of murder makes sense. It also fits in with the older country music tradition of Appalachian murder ballads not to mention the even earlier tradition of murder ballads of the British Isles and folksong in general. Looking at Greil Marcus's analysis of one such murder ballad, the Dock Boggs version of "Pretty Polly," can be instructive and can help situate Hank Williams in his approach to crime and punishment as well.

Dock (Moran Lee) Boggs (1898-1971) spent much of his life as a coal miner in Virginia and Kentucky. However, he developed an early expertise playing the banjo and enjoyed singing. Boggs was one of a number of southern musicians and singers who responded to recording opportunities presented by record company scouts in the 1920s to make recordings of "old-time" or "folk" music with his first recordings coming out on the Brunswick label in 1927. One of these was "Pretty Polly," a perfect example of an Appalachian murder ballad. The song is also known as "The Gosport Tragedy." Boggs's version features his very effective minor-key banjo picking and his nasal baritone voice sounds suitably grim as he relates the terrible tale.

Adopting the role of the protagonist Boggs starts off announcing "I used to be a rambler, I stayed around this town" which in itself is not too sinister. However, the story relates how this "rambler" lures Pretty Polly into walking through hills and valleys with him. The murder itself is only indirectly described as "She threw her arms around him and began for to weep and then Pretty Polly she fell asleep " – this after having announced that he had dug her grave the previous night. Boggs's banjo picking, all in a minor key, adds to the atmosphere of menace. The song ends with an ambivalent verse: after throwing dirt on Pretty Polly lying in her grave, the "rambler" departs "down to the river where the deep waters flow.' This is at least suggestive of a suicide ending. Having killed the object of his desire, if not affection, why would he want to keep on living?

Greil Marcus characterizes "Pretty Polly" as "there seems to be no will in the story, only fate or ritual."[11] Fate or fatalism seems to be characteristic in a number of Hank's songs, not just those dealing with crime and punishment. A good example is Hank's "I'll Never Get Out of this World Alive" (M-G-M, 1952), ironically, one of his last recordings. This is a humorous bluesy recitation of all of the troubles he keeps on encountering ending each verse with, "No matter how I struggle and strive. I'll never get out of this world alive." Interestingly enough, the African American vocal group, the Delta Rhythm Boys, featuring a brassy big-band musical accompaniment, recorded a version soon after, also in 1952, on the Victor label.

Marcus continues to describe Boggs's "Pretty Polly" as preordained with no surprises which also ties in with Hank's fatalism regarding crime and punishment. However, Marcus's assertion that Boggs's protagonist is "the defiant sinner" does not fit Hank's conception of the protagonist in his crime-and-punishment songs.[12] All indications are that Hank's sinner protagonists in recordings under discussion here are regretful if not repentant.

While crime or sin is not confined to any single class or type of individual, generally speaking, crime is more often connected to the lower classes thanks to factors such as lack of education, lack of financial resources, and lack of opportunity. In a 1993 article for Sociological Inquiry Edward Armstrong addresses this issue in connection to song lyrics relating to violence as found in rap and country music. While the topic of semiotics (the analysis of signs and symbols and their interpretation) is outside the scope of this article, Armstrong's contention that the rhetoric of violence is "a product of definitional efforts" is helpful when considering what Hank Williams has to say about crime and the resulting punishment.[13] The lyrics of country (and rap) are based more on social class rather than race.[14] Someone from a poor, rural southern background might well empathize with what Hank is saying in his songs, especially, as they relate to crime and punishment. "There but for the grace of God go I" might be the thoughts of many a listener.

The issue of social class might also connect with who was most susceptible to the lure of Hank's haunting "Lost Highway" (M-G-M, 1949). This song was composed by and first recorded by renowned singer and songwriter Leon Payne (1917-1969) in 1948 on Bullet. Payne's excellent original version has a somewhat jaunty, if not enthusiastic, sound. Hank's version, taken at a slightly slower tempo and featuring some wonderful bluesy steel guitar, features long, drawn-out vocals definitely exhibiting an aching, regretful sound. Perhaps this is more appropriate than the relatively happy sound of Payne's original, since the lyrics provide a warning. The song starts off announcing, "I'm a rolling stone all alone and lost. For a life of sin I have paid the cost." Once again, Hank links crime to sin. Once again the inevitability and appropriateness of punishment is made plain ("for a life of sin I have paid the cost"). Hank's version of "Lost Highway" reached number twelve on the country charts in 1949; Leon Payne's original and perhaps superior version did not chart at all[15]

Like the careless young protagonists of Johnny Cash's "Folsom Prison Blues" and Hank's "(I Heard that) Lonesome Whistle," the protagonist of "Lost Highway" is described as "I was just a lad nearly twenty-two. Neither good nor bad, just a kid like you." However, like those earlier protagonists, this one seemingly without thought makes a poor choice by giving in to the temptations of wine, gambling ("a deck of cards") and "a woman's lies." He is condemned to a life of immorality or sin if not crime, instability, and sorrow. Hank warns the listener to take his advice or else "you'll curse the day you started rollin' down that lost highway."

Although "Lost Highway" is specifically addressed to young men, Hank did not entirely leave women out of the picture. "Too Many Parties and Too Many Pals" recorded by Hank under his alter-ego, Luke the Drifter, for M-G-M in 1950, concerns the trial of "a social enemy, a lady of the evening." While prostitution is really more of a misdemeanor than a major crime such as murder, this recording fits in well with Hank's conception of crime as a sin and it certainly fits in with the wayward way of life portrayed in "Lost Highway." Hank's use of the Luke the Drifter persona was an alternative way of recording songs of a moralizing nature, most often in the form of gospel-like recitations, that Hank wanted to record but that Fred Rose (c. 1898-1954) did not. Rose was a songwriter and, together with Roy Acuff (1903-1992), the proprietor of the major Nashville music publishing venture, Acuff-Rose Music. Rose was an important figure in Hank's career, doing everything from helping to polish Hank's songwriting to promoting and marketing his career. Ribowsky describes these Luke the Drifter recordings as "songs of broken faith and fallen women."[16]

"Too Many Parties" was written by Tin Pan Alley songwriters Billy Rose (1899-1966, no relation to Fred Rose), Mort Dixon (1892-1956), and Ray Henderson (1896-1970). The first recording, a rather mellow instrumental version, dates back to 1926 by the Bar Harbor Society Orchestra on Harmony.[17] Both the melody and the moralizing lyrics sound quite old-fashioned for 1950 but, as always, Hank manages to infuse both the sung refrain and the spoken recitation with pathos and feeling. Perhaps a little unkindly, Paul Hemphill describes this recording as "one mercifully short act." However, Hemphill does note that a pre-Rock 'n' Roll Bill Haley (1925-1981) and his Four Aces of Western Swing had also recorded the song in 1948 on Cowboy.[18]

Of particular interest in Hank's version is when he provides the spoken recitation. While acknowledging that the young woman on trial is "a social enemy" and has done wrong, he emphasizes that for every fallen woman there are a hundred fallen men and that it is not unlikely that it might have been the son of a member of the jury who led the young woman down the path to prostitution. From a twenty-first century perspective, the path to ruin sounds quaint: "too many petting parties, cigarettes, and gin." The use of lipstick is mentioned as well as "the shrieks of saxophones" which connotes the jazz age and the rural listener's association of jazz with the vices of urban life. Perhaps by 1950 the "shrieks of saxophones" may have also suggested rhythm and blues, the urban African American music that was starting to prove attractive to young white listeners further suggesting possible moral depravity to some listeners of Hank's recording.

Prostitution or fallen women is an old and recurring theme in country music not to mention blues and folk music in general. Sometimes the issue is openly stated while at other times it is broadly hinted at or it can just be inferred. To use a couple of examples from Hank's own era, Kitty Wells (Muriel Deason, 1919-2012) hit number one on the *Billboard* country charts in July 1952 with "It Wasn't God Who Made Honky Tonk Angels" on Decca, a bittersweet retort to Hank (Henry) Thompson (1925-2007) and the Brazos Valley Boys' "The Wild Side of Life," which lamented the infidelity of the "honky tonk angels" who lurked in honky tonks and bars. While there is no overt reference to prostitutes, the implication is fairly obvious to the listener. Thompson's was a number one country hit a few months earlier, in March 1952 on Capitol. "The Wild Side of Life" was first recorded by Jimmy Heap (1922-1977) and the Melody Masters on Imperial in 1951 although it never charted.[19] Heap's version, with Houston "Perk" Williams (1926-1994) on vocals, and featuring some pounding piano by Arley Carter, sounds a little more rough and ready than does Thompson's version. Ironically, Wells's hit record, now regarded as something of a feminist anthem, was written by three men, J.D. Miller (1922-1996), William Warren, and Arlie A. Carter (presumably the same person as Arley Carter of Jimmy Heap's Melody Masters).[20] Both songs share the same wistful melody which, in turn, was the melody used by Roy Acuff and his Crazy Tennesseans for his wonderful country-gospel recording, "The Great Speckled Bird" (Conqueror, 1936), which, in turn, used the same melody as the Carter Family's classic "I'm Thinking Tonight of my Blue Eyes" from 1929 recorded for Victor.

Perhaps the most devastating verse in Hank's "Too Many Parties" comes at the end where, reflecting on how the young woman on trial for prostitution is not the saint her mother was, he reveals that she is his own daughter. One could hardly have a more empathetic perspective than that.

Hank's empathy if not sympathy for the convicted felon is obvious in "My Son Calls another Man Daddy" (M-G-M) which reached the number nine position on the *Billboard* country charts in early 1950.[21] Written by Acuff-Rose staff country music songwriter Jewell House (1921-1971) with modifications by Hank, "My Son Calls Another Man Daddy" is a very sentimental depiction of the frustration and despair felt by a prisoner who longs for his son but knows he'll never be able to communicate with him. Mark Ribowksy describes the recording as "backwoods bathos."[22] Escott's assessment is more scathing: "it was a contrived piece that lacked all the compelling immediacy of the songs Hank drew from his own experience."[23] While perhaps a bit "contrived," this listener finds Hank's delivery and emotional investment to be as compelling as in most of his other recordings, expressing quite convincingly the despair and frustration of the imprisoned father. The only aspect of the recording that strikes this listener as perhaps a little contrived or corny is the occasional brief interjection of a few notes on the steel guitar that, sonically, resemble weeping. Otherwise, Hank's soaring, almost piercing vocals very effectively convey the despair and sorrow felt by the protagonist. It's bad enough that his son's mother "shares a new love" with another man but what really causes Hank's protagonist pain is the loss of his son: "he'll ne'er know my name or my face." The long (life?) term in prison may be merited for the unnamed crime, but there is no denying the personal cost and emotional damage being done to the prisoner.

Hank's empathy for the despair and frustration of the imprisoned stands in contrast to the more stoic or indifferent attitude expressed in some other country songs regarding crime and punishment. One good example is "Columbus Stockade Blues." Many artists have recorded this over the decades but the first version appears to have been recorded by Darby and Tarleton in 1927 on Columbia. Tom Darby (1891-1971) and Jimmie Tarlton (1892-1979) formed a duo featuring both on vocals with Darby on guitar and Tarlton on slide guitar. They made several dozen recordings between 1927 and 1933, the best of them, such as "Columbus Stockade Blues," featuring a distinctive bluesy yet sweet sound. "Columbus Stockade "of course, refers to the prison located in Columbus, Georgia, Tom Darby's hometown. (Jimmie Tarlton came from South Carolina).

Adopting the persona of a convict from Tennessee serving time in the Columbus Stockade, they state, "Friends have turned their back on me." Regarding the separation from his woman (whether girlfriend or wife is not specified), the prisoner then says, "Go and leave me if you wish to, never let me cross your mind. In your heart you love another, believe me, darling, I don't mind." The stoicism, brave indifference, or possibly calm acceptance of a permanent rupture is encapsulated in this verse. The phrase, "Believe me, darling, I don't mind" is completely the opposite of the despair and longing expressed by Hank Williams in songs such as "On the Banks of the Old Ponchartrain," "Lonesome Whistle," or "My Son Calls Another Man Daddy." However, in another verse Darby and Tarlton seem to indicate that, perhaps, the stoical, blithely indifferent prisoner may not have been quite as sanguine about his fate as "believe me, darling I don't mind" might suggest. This verse relates, "Last night while I lay sleeping, I dreamed that I was in your arms. When I woke, I was mistaken. I was peeking through the bars." However, this moment of pathos (weakness?) is immediately followed by the refrain telling his woman to go and leave him, "Believe me, darling, I don't mind," perhaps in an attempt to convince himself as much as his ex that he really does not care.

While it is an otherwise completely unrelated song, it is interesting to note a very similar verse in the well-known "You Are my Sunshine": "The other night, dear, as I lay sleeping. I dreamed I held you in my arms. But when I woke, dear, I was mistaken. And hung my head and cried." Although Jimmie Davis (1899-2000) recorded the big hit version of "Sunshine" in 1940 on Decca, it was first recorded by the Pine Ridge Boys for Bluebird in 1939 and written by Paul Rice (1917-1988) of the Rice Brothers' Gang who also recorded it in 1939 on the Decca label.[24]

In terms of number of recordings, Hank Williams did not visit the theme of crime and punishment very often. The six recordings discussed here are dwarfed in numbers by his songs concerning love both good and bad, the honky tonk life, and gospel. Also, in contrast to most of his other recordings, Hank did not write most of these six, although, of course, he adapted or modified them to some degree to make them truly his own interpretation or statement on the subject. While it is impossible to truly know in detail what Hank actually thought about crime and punishment outside the recording studio, his choice of these songs and the way in which he sang them does reveal at least something that can be suggested. He certainly would have been conscious of what he was singing in terms of what he wanted his audience to hear. Knowing where to separate the artist from his/her art is not always clear. Be that as it may, Hank does at least in terms of these six recordings present a definite perspective on crime and punishment with several identifiable themes.

Perhaps the overarching theme or world view presented here is the rightness and the inevitability of punishment for crime. Nowhere does Hank express any opposition to his punishment whether it is a long prison term, life in prison, or death by the electric chair. There is a fatalism or sense of inevitability of punishment ranging from the surprise capture of the protagonist in "On the Banks of the Old Ponchartrain" to the capture of the protagonist on the train in "Lonesome Whistle" in both cases, with him then being directly sent to prison for his (unnamed) crime. Even the immediate prospect of execution by the electric chair the next morning does not elicit defiance or fear in "My Main Trial Is Yet to Come." In all of these examples, the protagonist has committed a crime and his punishment is both inevitable and justified.

It seems Hank's sense of the rightness or inevitability of punishment is his likely conception of crime as sin. If one has done wrong, one has gone against God and one has thus committed a sin. As a rural Southerner growing up in the 1920's and 1930's he had a church upbringing. Christian values, especially as expressed through the preaching he heard in the Baptist church, informed his sense of morality even if, as an adult, he may not have lived a particularly Christian life. This Christian perspective is evident in the numerous recordings made by Hank whether in the studio or, more often, as documented in a number of his live and radio transcription performances where he announces that it's "hymn time." Perhaps some, such as Fred Rose of Acuff-Rose

Music, may have found this moralizing less than appealing and thus partly relegated to Hank's Luke the Drifter recordings, but it likely resonated with many of Hank's listeners. Crime as sin was certainly not a foreign concept to Hank's listeners. The road to sin and ruin is effectively depicted in "Lost Highway," one of Hank's most iconic recordings.

However, Hank's unerring appeal to human emotion, feeling, or sympathy comes through in all six of these recordings too. However guilty and deserving of punishment the protagonist, only a heart of stone would not be moved by Hank's soulful delivery of the utterly hopeless predicament of the protagonist facing a lifetime of dreary imprisonment and utter, permanent separation from the woman he loves and, perhaps most affectingly, from his son: "he'll ne'er know my name or my face."

Perhaps the ultimate message delivered by Hank in these songs is as the saying goes: "don't do the crime, if you can't do the time."

Endnotes

1. Colin Escott. *Hank Williams: The Biography* (Boston: Little, Brown and Company, 1984), 211.
2. Mark Ribowsky. *The Short Life and Long Country Road of Hank Williams* (New York: Liveright Publishing Corporation, 2017), 269-270.
3. Escott, *Hank Williams*, 64.
4. Paul Hemphill. *Lovesick Blues: The Life of Hank Williams* (New York: Viking, 2005), 72-73.
5. Ribowksy, *Short Life and Long Country Road*, 128.
6. Joel Whitburn. *Joel Whitburn's Top Country Singles 1944-1988* (Menomonee Falls, Wis.: Record Research Inc., 1989), 358-359.
7. *Ibid.*, 359.
8. See *Discography of American Historical Recordings (website)*: https://adp.library.ucsb.edu/index.php/talent/detail/4955/Davis_Jimmie_vocalist . Viewed July 9, 2019.
9. Dick Spottswood. *The Blue Sky Boys* (Jackson: University Press of Mississippi, 2018), 191.
10. *Ibid.*, 191.
11. Greil Marcus. "Dock Boggs in Jefferson's Virginia," *Representation*, No. 58 (Spring 1997), 17.
12. *Ibid.*, 21.
13. Edward G. Armstrong. "The Rhetoric of Violence in Rap and Country Music," *Sociological Inquiry*, Vol. 63, No. 1 (Feb. 1993), 65.
14. *Ibid.*, 69.
15. Whitburn. *Top Country Singles 1944-1988*, 337 and 358.
16. Ribowsky, *Short Life and Long Country Road*, 203.

17. *SecondHandSongs (web site):* https://secondhandsongs.com/release/232517 . Accessed July 23, 2019.

18. Hemphill, *Lovesick Blues, 127.*

19. Whitburn. *Top Country Singles 1944-1988, 322 and 348.*

20. *SecondHandSongs (web site):* https://secondhandsongs.com/work/121568/versions Accessed July 24, 2019.

21. Whitburn, *Top Country Singles 1944-1988, 356.*

22. Ribowsky, *Short Life and Long Country Road, 168.*

23. Escott, *Hank Williams, 123.*

24. *SecondHandSongs (web site):* https://secondhandsongs.com/performance/45676/versions Accessed August 8, 2019.

Marg Osburne National Singing Star of Don Messer's Jubilee

By Linda J. Daniel

Introduction

Marg Osburne was a singer with the musical group Don Messer and His Islanders where she became known coast to coast in Canada. A female pioneer in the music business, she was one of only three women inducted into the first Canadian Country Music Hall of Fame, the other two being Myrna Lorrie and Lucille Starr. The *Official Souvenir Book, Pictures and Stories of the 25 Inaugural Inductees* states: "Of all the additions to the Islanders, none made such a wonderful difference as Marg Osburne, 'The Girl From The Singing Hills', who joined as a vocalist in 1947 and became (with Don Messer and Charlie Chamberlain), the artist most commonly identified with the group." Osburne quickly became "The Islanders' sweetheart of the airwaves" with her "naturally beautiful voice and a love for singing" (Buck 30).

Don Messer and His Islanders brought "old-time" music into Canadian homes, toured extensively across the country, and recorded over 30 LPs (Green). By the mid-20th century, largely due to its successful Canadian Broadcasting Corporation (CBC) radio and television series, the group was extremely popular in Canada

(Green and Miller). But for twenty-five years it was Marg Osburne who received the most mail from fans than any other member of the band (Jackson).

Beginnings

Verna Marguerite Osburne was born in Moncton, New Brunswick on December 29th, 1926 to a musical family. Her mother was a homemaker, father a night watchman, and she had one brother named Gerry (Bertin 201-202). In an interview with John Braddock published in the *Atlantic Advocate* in June 1967, Osburne describes her family's close connection with music and how singing was a large part of what they did on both her mother's and father's sides:

> 'My grandfather ... learned a terrific amount of folk songs, I remember. He always sang tenor in the church choir. He was a Moore – that's on my mother's side. The Osburnes on my father's side are all great singers. My brother is musical too. Almost all my relatives had either an organ or a piano at home, so we grew up with them. We all sang songs – folk songs, Stephen Foster songs, hymns, a lot of hymns – in fact my brother and I learned our harmony by ear through singing hymns.' (18)

Marg taught herself how to harmonize, "a skill that would become a mainstay." Later in her career, she was one of the first to record harmony with herself, the technique of putting a second track of her voice over the first. It was so new that listeners had no idea Marg was singing her own harmony. She once received a letter from a fan stating that she liked the harmony singer's voice more than Marg's, asking why this singer never performed on the show and received no credit (Bertin 202).

In addition to singing with extended family, Osburne began performing at school concerts and Sunday school recitals (Braddock 18). Antony Ferry reports that the singer's venture into show business happened because of a dare. At the age of 16, a cousin visiting Marg in Moncton "heard her singing at home, and bet her $5 she wouldn't phone up the local radio station, CKCW, for an audition." Osburne explains, "'I never had $5, so I went'" (19).

Initially unconcerned about her performance that day, her feelings began to change as the time drew near. She recalls:

> 'I had no idea of becoming a singer, so I went down for the fun of it. I didn't have a nerve in my body – or so I thought!'

> 'I went in. And no sooner was I inside and saw the studio and the microphones and all the people and things I got the shakes. Somehow I sang a couple of songs. I remember I was so nervous I couldn't control my voice. It kept wavering a great deal, and I thought: "Oh, this is terrible!"'

> 'Nevertheless, they must have heard something they liked because I got the job.' (Braddock 18)

The next week she was singing on a western show as a replacement for a woman who had left to get married (Ferry 19). The radio station hired her to perform on a weekly program (Bertin 202).

Joining Don Messer and His Islanders

According to Johanna Bertin, author of *Don Messer, The Man Behind the Music*, after two years of singing on CKCW Moncton, one of the announcers who believed [Osburne] had "more talent than the show required" sent a recording to Don Messer for him to consider. But it was not until three years later that Messer needed a replacement for his regular vocalist, Charlie Chamberlain, who had been injured in a car accident. "Marg filled the bill." By the time Chamberlain recuperated and came back to the show, Marg had become part of the group and would stay for the next twenty-five years until Messer's death (Bertin 202).

In the Braddock interview Marg states:

> '... I sang with them [CKCW Moncton] for a couple of years – just for the fun of it. I still never thought of making a career there. But unknown to me Don had heard the show while passing through Moncton. At that time Charlie Chamberlain had had a car accident and Don asked if I would join him while Charlie recuperated. I said: "Sure!" It was a wonderful chance.' (18)

Whether by receiving a tape of Marg singing or hearing her voice on the radio while he was driving through her hometown, the fact remains that "It was on that radio show that Don Messer first heard her and when his male vocalist had a car accident, he decided to take his chances with a female singer" ("Marg ..." 13). Albeit, as journalist John Kraglund states: "Marg Osburne had already been discovered by radio before she joined the Islanders" (15).

Don Messer was born on May 9, 1909 in Tweedside, near Fredericton, New Brunswick and began playing violin at the age of five, learning fiddle tunes from local family and friends in addition to Scottish and Irish songs from his mother. At seven years of age, he was playing at area weddings, barn dances, and other social functions (Green, Green and Miller). By 1929 he was performing on CFBO radio in Saint John, New Brunswick. He formed a band called the New Brunswick Lumberjacks that was broadcasting from CHJS, Saint John by 1934. In 1938 Messer took part of his group to Charlottetown, Prince Edward Island and formed Don Messer and the Islanders, later called Don Messer and His Islanders. Broadcast across Canada on CBC Radio from 1939 to 1958, thousands listened to the group on their radios three times a week ("Don Messer fonds").

Don Messer played a significant role in the successful singing career of Marg Osburne by hiring her as a vocalist. In 1947 Marg joined Messer's band in Charlottetown (Melhuish 47). Osburne states: "'[The Messer show] was on coast-to-coast radio those days, and I moved to Prince Edward Island for it … When Charlie got better, they couldn't get rid of me. We both became fixtures on the show, like an old couple there's no separating'" (Ferry 19).

A photograph in the Nova Scotia Archives entitled "Early Messer Group ('Don Messer and His Islanders')" is dated "1940s" and shows a young Marg Osburne seated towards the back of the group. Messer is standing front and centre. Charlie Chamberlain sits next to the piano. The picture is labelled in large white lettering: "Charlie" [Chamberlain] with a guitar, "Jackie" [Doyle] seated at the piano, "Don" [Messer] holding a fiddle, "Rae" [Simmons] with a saxophone, "Warren" [MacRae] on drums, "Harold" on trumpet, "Marg" [Osburne] as vocalist, and "Duke" [Julius 'Duke' Nielson] on trombone ("Don Messer fonds").

Messer never agreed with terms like "hillbilly" or "country and western" to describe the kind of music they did. "'It is folk music,' he stated. 'Our forefathers brought these hornpipes, jigs and reels over with them from the old country and they kept them alive.'" Yet, Kraglund ponders: "Those who have other ideas about what folk music is may find barn-dance music a more accurate description. But, then, what is barn-dancing but a folk activity?" (15).

Don Messer's Jubilee

Television came to Canada in 1952. Before that time, American shows had been "dribbling over the border" for about five years. If you had a television and lived close enough to intercept the signal coming from the United States, you could watch Lucille Ball, Sid Caesar, Arthur Godfrey, Groucho Marx or Ed Sullivan and be thoroughly captivated ("The Season …").

Bill Langstroth was working on a CBC-TV variety show in Halifax in 1954 when Don Messer and His Islanders appeared as guests on the show. He remembers the listeners' immediate response: "'it blew the switchboard right off the walls'" (Martin S8). In 1956, the group auditioned for CBC Halifax television executives, won a spot on the regional network and began appearing regularly on CHBY-TV in Halifax (Green and Miller).

Starting on August 7th, 1959, *The Don Messer Show* was broadcast nationally by CBC-TV on Friday nights at 9:30 p.m.

as a summer replacement for *Country Hoedown*. When the show returned in the fall, Messer was moved to Monday nights at 7:30 p.m. on September 28 and renamed *Don Messer's Jubilee*. From September 1959 to June 1968, the popular half-hour series retained the Monday evening time slot until its final season. From September 20, 1968 to June 20th, 1969, it was shown at 8:30 p.m. on Friday evenings. *Don Messer's Jubilee* ran an entire decade and "became one of the most beloved programs CBC television has ever produced" (*Don Messer*'s *Jubilee*).

A young energetic Bill Langstroth became the producer of *Don Messer's Jubilee* and had two main components with which he had to work: the music of the Islanders and the vocal performances of Marg Osburne and Charlie Chamberlain (Beaton and Pedersen 47). Jack McAndrew, later head of CBC-TV Variety, said Langstroth took Don Messer's main strength, – "'… he was a helluva fiddle player …,'" – and surrounded him with a supportive cast. Messer was more comfortable playing his violin than speaking so Don Tremaine was hired to host the show leaving its namesake to "speak" through his music. Marg Osburne and Charlie Chamberlain were the featured vocalists (Martin S8).

Television being a visual medium, Langstroth needed something that would help to enhance the show's attractiveness to viewers and provide a more balanced program. He decided to incorporate some dancers and contacted a well-known dance instructor working in Halifax named Gunter Buchta whose group auditioned for the show while Messer watched approvingly (Beaton and Pederson 47).

"Each Monday night when Don Tremaine announced, 'It's *Don Messer's Jubilee!*' the viewers could rest assured that for the next 30 minutes there would be no surprises or deviations from the standard script" (49). The half hour opened with Marg Osburne and Charlie Chamberlain singing "Goin' to the Barndance Tonight," followed by Messer playing a couple of fiddle tunes, solos by both Marg and Charlie, in addition to duets by the pair, regular performers like the Buchta Dancers and Johnny Forrest (a Scottish accordionist/singer), a guest performer, and, to close the show, "'Till We Meet Again," sung by Marg and Charlie as the credits rolled. Myrna Lorrie and Stompin' Tom Connors were frequent guest artists (Green and Miller). Several other talented Canadian performers were given recognition on the national show including Shirley Eikhart, Catherine McKinnon, Gene MacLellan, and Anne Murray (Martin S8).

The show's presentation was simple but effective. Sets were modest with a connection to rural life such as barns and fences. At times, props were used like Marg sitting in a rocking chair to sing "Easy Rocking Chair." Charlie liked to wear dapper hats and carry a shillelagh which he would lean on or wave in the air while he sang (Beaton and Pederson 51). The musicians provided a background for the singers, guests, and the lively Buchta Dancers. Marg Osburne and Charlie Chamberlain were the lead vocalists, "household names and minor celebrities in the early days of Canadian television" ("Don Messer fonds").

When Messer wanted to tour during the summer months which was far more lucrative, American folk singer, Pete Seeger, was suggested as a replacement. Journalist Sandra Martin writes:

"An American protest singer might seem an edgy substitute for Mr. Messer, a traditional and taciturn Maritime fiddler, but it was the era of hootenannies and glee club TV shows like *Sing Along with Mitch*." However, just before taping in June of 1961, Seeger was given a ten-year prison sentence for "refusing to testify before the House UnAmerican Activities Committee." Although his conviction was later overturned, at the time he was concerned that if he came to Canada, it might be difficult for him to return to the United States while the case was under appeal (S8).

In its place, Langstroth created *Singalong Jubilee*, showcasing a variety of musical talent and, in addition to producing, became one of its principal performers. In 1964, a schoolteacher named Anne Murray auditioned for the show but was turned down because they had too many altos. A couple of years later, encouraged by Langstroth to return, she began her assent to worldwide stardom (Grills 44-45).

While on tour in the summer of 1967, Volkmar Richter gives an account of a performance in Sarnia, Ontario on July 1st, Canada's Centennial. Marg Osburne and Charlie Chamberlain are the "stars," standing up front while Messer stays in the background. The bandleader's taste in music is heard throughout the show. He continues to play the "simple but lively" tunes he has been performing for the past fifty years, some dating back to the 17th century. Messer asserts that this kind of music has withstood the test of time and is still appealing to people, especially when played by real Maritimers (25).

By this time, many of the musicians had been with the band for years. Bass player Duke Neilson, a member for 34 years, saw

Messer more like a father than a boss, having lost his father at 10. He says Messer ran the group like a bank manager, "running the show but not the people," taking it easy and ruling by suggestion. As a result, the band was loyal: clarinetist Rae Simmons – 27 years, drummer Warren MacCrae – 25 years, fiddler Cecil McEachern – 20 years, and pianist Waldo Munro – 16 years (Ibid.). Marg Osburne had been with the group for 20 years.

Personal Life

Marg Osburne had been singing with the Islanders for about three years when she met her future husband, Austin Squarebriggs, in Charlottetown (Bertin 204). Their first child, David, was born in 1954 to little public fanfare. Throughout the pregnancy, Marg continued to perform, being filmed in such a way that the television audience would not know she was pregnant. After having the baby, she left for a few weeks and returned to the show leaving her new son with a nanny. When pregnant with her second child, the event was handled completely differently. The week before her daughter, Melody, was born, the cast of *Don Messer's Jubilee* gave Marg a baby shower on-camera. The significance of this public airing of what, in the sixties, was seen to be a private occasion shows the special place Marg held in the hearts of her fans. Gifts of booties, bonnets, and sweaters were sent to the CBC (206). Marg thinks back, "'In 1960 … I sang with the Messer show on TV until two weeks before [Melody] was born. She's the baby of the show. I got thousands of cards from the viewers …'" (Kirby n.p.).

In 1961, Marg faced a family crisis when her seven-year-old son was diagnosed with a rare malignant brain tumour behind one eye. The doctor was not hopeful but told them of an experimental treatment. His parents "jumped at the chance to save their son." When David responded to the treatment, Marg and Austin left their children with family in Sussex, New Brunswick and joined the tour out west but they soon returned home "in a panic" after learning David could not sleep for the pain in his eye. On the trip to Halifax, their son was "whimpering and crying" in the back seat when he suddenly stopped. They pulled the car over and got out, thinking the worst. As an adult David recalls: "'I just looked at them and said, "I'm hungry."'" The pain had stopped because the eye had "died" and the cancer never returned. Throughout this challenging time, Marg had the sincere backing of the band who were like an extended family. They were a close-knit group. "Whenever anything happened to one of them it was as if it were happening to all of them" (Bertin 208-209).

Osburne was residing in Sussex, New Brunswick by 1967 with her husband, nine-year-old son, and three-year-old daughter. The town held sentimental appeal since both her parents had grown up in the area. She did not find getting to work an issue because "'With modern transport,' she explains, 'you can live anywhere these days. I either fly or take a train to Halifax, but I also practise at home'" (Braddock 20).

Both David and Melody remember their mother phoning often and that she always made sure she was home for Christmas. Marg wrote letters to them and, knowing her touring schedule, they would write back. Melody recalls having many talks with her mother and, as she grew older, discussing whether she, too, would become a singer. Although encouraging, Marg always made it clear to Melody that she should "have something to fall back on because music is not an easy profession" (Bertin 214).

Musical Talent

Osburne had no formal vocal training and was unable to read music but she was still a "consummate professional," always coming to work prepared and able to learn a song within fifteen minutes (208). Marg affirms, "'I have no trouble in learning a song that I like. I know the words after going through it three times. But those I don't like I can never get!'" (Braddock 20). In the interview with Antony Ferry, Osburne addresses her lack of formal training with self-deprecating humour when she states: "'You'd hardly say I'm a trained voice … though there's many a singer learned her harmony up in a choir loft, like I did. You can learn a lot singing in church, if you've got the ear. I always sang, long as I can remember, though I never learned to read sheet music either. I still just guess at the notes as I go along'" (19).

In *Maritime Music Greats, authors* Virginia Beaton and Stephen Pedersen describe her vocal style as "middle-of-the-road" in the mezzo-soprano to soprano range saying, "... it wasn't large, but it was sweet and true." While preferring an older repertoire, Osburne also performed songs from the hit parade, country or show tunes (53). Her favourites were folk songs which she would take the opportunity to sing if interviewed by herself on radio or television. She went along with Messer's choice of songs for the show out of respect for the bandleader but would still suggest pieces she liked (Bertin 215).

It was difficult to change the mind of Don Messer on what he felt suited the show's format. Don Tremaine remembers one afternoon when he and Marg taped several tunes that they thought would be appropriate for the show. "But of 15 possible choices, Messer approved only two" (Beaton and Pederson 53). In a 1960 article covering a *Don Messer's Jubilee* show from the night before, Dennis Braithwaite marvels at Osburne's extraordinary musical talent even when singing such an abominable song as "My Tears Have Washed 'I Love You' From the Blackboard of My Heart" which would have caused any less of a singer to laugh out loud and states: "This amazing woman's natural warmth and sincerity enable her to rise above the corniest lyrics and the most dismal sentimentality. She is a wonder, that one. Her ability to communicate with the viewer emotionally is unmatched in TV today" (19).

Messer was amazed at Osburne's skill when learning a new song and confirms: "'You'll never hear Marg Osburne make a mistake.'" In later years, Bill Langstroth reflected on her outstanding vocal ability: "'She was much better than we gave her credit for at the time. She always had much more to give than you saw on the Messer show. I would be standing beside her when we would start to rehearse for a pre-recording, and she'd start to sing and be pure Rosemary Clooney, for instance. She could sing like so many people and had a terrific music ear'" (Bertin 214-215). Performances by Osburne (see "Little Arrows – Marg Osburne," "Don Messer's Jubilee," and "Don Messer's Jubilee[–]The Blue

Skirt Waltz") show a dignified entertainer who presents herself with poise and grace, a genuine singer with a pure and beautiful voice.

In addition to her musical talent, Osburne's inherent likability as a human being was expressed repeatedly. "Everyone who worked with Marg loved her." Don Tremaine states, "'She was just the finest kind of person I have ever met.'" Langstroth agrees: "'Here's a woman who travelled with six or eight men around the country, and they all treated her like a titled lady. She's royalty'" (Bertin 202).

Osburne and Chamberlain

There were times when Osburne found it difficult to work with Chamberlain. They were completely opposite in character: "She was genteel and quiet while Charlie, fond of a drink, was often boisterous and noisy." Yet, while giving "colleagues some bad moments," Chamberlain's "familiar bulky frame, sweet smile and the nods and winks he tossed at the fans made it easy for them to overlook his foibles." Often singing duets, the pair cooperated but there was frequent tension. Many viewers assumed they must be married to each other since they sang so well together (Beaton and Pederson 53).

According to Marg's son, Osburne and Chamberlain got along well: "'They had a very strong and very professional relationship … but they were good friends, too. Oh, sometimes she would be very frustrated with him and she would let him know, but she really appreciated his goodness and his talent.'" When they were living in Charlottetown, Marg would visit Charlie at his home where they would strum their guitars and sing their favourite songs (Bertin 213).

Image

The negative bias towards "old-fashioned variety" is stated clearly in *When Television Was Young, Primetime Canada 1952-1967* by Paul Rutherford:

> The male stars were neither fashionable nor debonair. ... Don Messer was also old [like Lawrence Welk], but so retiring that he rarely spoke and seemed to disappear into the background. The women were usually ordinary, not at all sexy. ... Marg Osburne of 'Don Messer's Jubilee' was a plump, cheerful woman who struck observers more as a housewife than as a television celebrity. (205)

Yet, Rutherford concludes, while the critics "were always ready to throw sticks and stones," the fact remains that these shows were popular due to "their apparent sincerity and ordinariness," compared with the flashy "unreality" of those in the "'showbiz' world" (206-207).

When in Toronto in 1961 to tape an appearance on *The Juliette Show*, one of the more glamourous Canadian "show-biz" type of variety series, Osburne is described as being "a warm-hearted rustic charmer, full of laughs and disarming candor," cognizant of the image Messer has deliberately created for his show. Compared to a family gathering for a "song-fest," this image is so convincing that she laughs heartily as she thinks about how many people believe she is married to Charlie Chamberlain (Ferry 19).

The group was able to remain who they were – genuine, sincere, real – to the delight of their viewers and never felt the need to leave the Maritimes. "In later years, when Marg Osburne, 'the Girl from the Singing Hills,' would have been recognized immediately on any street in Canada, she was simply Mrs. Squarebriggs, housewife, neighbor and church-goer in her hometown of Sussex, New Brunswick. It was as if Anne Murray was still living in Spring Hill, [Nova Scotia.]" It was a time before the "business" of music or boasting about the "industry," when the public and those dealing with the music "cheerfully allowed them to do what they like and be what they were" (Nowlan 10b).

In 1963, Marg and her daughter, Melody, were featured on the cover of the popular Canadian magazine *Chatelaine*. Yet Osburne was not affected by being a Canadian celebrity. Her warmth on the show was just as evident in her personal life. David describes his mother as being the same both on and off the stage. Her face, her clothes, the way she interacted with people, did not change. If she was answering the door or doing her grocery shopping, she was the same person whether she was in front of the camera or not (Bertin 207).

Charlie Chamberlain was 56 years of age in 1967 and had been with Messer for 34 years. He still enjoys the tours and even looks forward to the long ones. "'I love getting up there on stage, … It's not hard if you're in good shape and don't have a swelled head with a hangover.'" When asked if that has ever happened to him, he replies, "'Oh yeah. Lotta people won't admit that though … Not good for the image.'" Unlike her duet partner, Osburne is more concerned with how others might perceive her. As an example, after receiving a letter of disappointment from a fan who saw her smoking a cigarette in a restaurant, "Marg no longer does that" (Richter 25).

Tours

In his autobiography, *Ken Reynolds Presents Sixty Years in Canadian Country Music*, Don Messer's tour manager describes the tenacity of the group's only female member: "Marg was a pleasant woman with a full understanding of the rigours of long tours with all the accompanying demands on free time that radio, TV, newspaper interviews, and other engagements made on entertainers" and asserts, "She always did an excellent job singing solos and duets with Charlie [Chamberlain]" (73-74). David characterizes his mother as having a "'high tolerance for a lot of things. She was a non-judgmental person who went with the flow,'" an essential personality trait in order to get along with a group of men who were vastly different from herself (Bertin 213).

Marg took David with her on tour in 1964. They took the train from Halifax to Winnipeg where the tour bus met them. Then, zigzagging across the provinces until they reached the west coast, they turned around and did it all again in different locales on the way back. Her son has fond memories of "a strong sense of camaraderie on the bus" and the way in which the group appeared to "get along" although occasionally they could "get on each other's nerves." But he was most impressed with just how talented the musicians were: "'They were able to interpret the music, to be the music; they were never just people playing an instrument'" (209-210).

Up until David watched his mother perform in Calgary, "... he had no idea of the kind of adulation she earned. He wasn't aware that Marg had become one of the most popular members of the group, and he didn't know that the summer before, when the group was touring out west, police escorts had to protect her from the crush of fans and photographers eager to get a glimpse of Canada's most popular female performer" (210-211).

David remembers how nice the fans were to them but, even as a young boy, recognised the downside of touring and how hard the band worked. Travelling may have been exciting, but it was also extremely difficult. "'They'd travel all day to a place, set up, eat, come back to the hotel, change, and do a performance.'" Sometimes, in addition, there was a dance after the show. Then they would take down the set, return to the hotel, try to sleep, rise the next day, and repeat (210).

Osburne did not enjoy travelling to gigs. Daughter Melody, figures that was undoubtedly because "'There were too many close calls.'" Marg knew of entertainers who had died in plane crashes (Ibid.). Not wanting to fly and "not fussy about the chartered bus," her husband, Austin, would often drive her to appearances in their car (Reynolds 73-74). But there were times when "vast distances between concert locations meant the band had to travel by air." An early excursion to Newfoundland, as well as a trip through northern Canada, "fizzled" when Marg, who hated flying, did not accompany the group. Band member Rae Simmons remembers how disappointed the audiences were when the whole cast did not show up, and adds, "if he had only known how eager people were to see Marg in person, he would have rented a car and driven her from place to place rather than have her miss the entire tour" (Beaton and Pederson 55).

Many entertainers toured across the country to celebrate Canada's Centennial in 1967. Tour manager Ken Reynolds recounts:

> Don Messer's Jubilee Centennial Tour started on June 6. Beginning at Wabush, Labrador, we embarked on a monumental eighty-four-shows tour that included two appearances at the Calgary Stampede, five at Expo '67 in Montréal, and three at the Canadian National Exhibition in Toronto. The Centennial Commissioner, John Fisher, called it 'the most successful of all the Festival Canada attractions, playing the most numerous shows to more people in a three-month period.' (76)

In fact, Fisher went on to describe the group as "'the best goodwill ambassadors that Canada has ever had'" (Braddock 20). By July 1, 1967, Messer and his troupe had made seven tours across Canada since becoming known nationally on *Don Messer's Jubilee* (Richter 25). By 1969 they had completed 18 tours (Green and Miller).

The Popularity of Don Messer's Jubilee

Journalist Alden Nowlan grew up in a little village in Nova Scotia. As a child in the 1940s, he admits detesting the Messer show at a time before Osburne joined in 1947. He preferred listening to an adventure series for boys which happened to be on the radio at the same time but "My father always insisted on Don Messer." Maritimers had been listening to the group for years and felt an intimate connection due to the "roots" they shared. From a house with no electricity, the voice of Rae Simmons, who played the clarinet and doubled as emcee, would emanate from an old battery-operated Marconi saying, "'Come 'way Down East for the music of Messer and his Islanders'" (10b).

The group was broadcast three times a week on CFCY Charlottetown, Prince Edward Island, the "Friendly Voice of the Maritimes," and was heard throughout New Brunswick, Nova Scotia, Prince Edward Island, the Gaspé Peninsula and northern New England. "If you had walked through my village between 7 and 7:30 p.m. on any Monday, Wednesday or Friday, and it was summer so that the windows of the houses were open, you would never have been out of the sound of Don Messer's music." His father would come home from the sawmill after "9½ hours of catching boards as they fell one by one from the splitter saw" and, no matter how tired he must have been, "would tap his toes in time to the music." Men like his father cried when Messer died in 1973. Nolan exclaims, "How real they were, those Islanders!!" But, most remarkably, they never saw the need to leave home (Ibid.).

Reporter Wendy Lindsay recalls a time when curling up on a couch with the folks to watch *Don Messer's Jubilee* on Saturday nights was "a family ritual in many Canadian homes." People tuned in from across the country. "According to the Nielsen ratings of November, 1961, Don Messer's program of country music and dance was the favourite of both sexes and every age group. Messer and his gang even beat out *Ed Sullivan*, *Front Page Challenge*, *Bonanza* and *Hockey Night in Canada*" (C5). The critics could not believe that *Don Messer's Jubilee* had become such a hit. Sponsors, like Massey-Ferguson farm implements and Pillsbury cake mixes benefitted greatly from its success (Rutherford 206).

Osburne thinks the show was so popular because people like its "'friendly, family feeling'" and that the mail from their fans reflected this. Ferry writes: "the leading lady of Canada's most popular TV musical show said its success is simply 'the appeal of a bunch of homebodies to all the other homebodies across the country.'" She adds, "'it just plain makes your toes tap. Don's made a style all his own.'" (19). Not only did they receive an immense amount of fan mail from Canadians but also from those States within range of the CBC network like Michigan, Montana, and North Dakota. In April 1967, at the request of the trustees at the museum of Wheeling, West Virginia, Don Messer's first violin was sent because they wanted Canada to be represented (Braddock 20).

Bill Langstroth reminisces about what he thinks made *Don Messer's Jubilee* so well-liked. From a 1968 interview with the former producer, Sandra Martin reports: "[Langstroth] was philosophical about the Messer show's appeal, especially the fiddle, which he related to 'the sound of the sitar, bagpipes or the call of the muezzin from the minaret ... There is something to this business of vibrations that strikes a responsive chord'" (S8).

While this level of popularity could not be maintained, it did remain remarkably high on both the made-in-Canada and national viewing lists right up until its cancellation in 1969 (Rutherford 206). But not everyone was an enthusiast. In "Messer fans endure corn and the cold," James Bawden writes on September 8, 1970 about the 12,000 fans who attended the Canadian National Exhibition's final Grandstand Show on the windy shores of Lake Ontario, describing them as those who "will endure anything, to see and hear their hero and his pals in action." Following several dancing groups and fighting to be heard above the barking carnies and screams from the Midway, "Don and Marg and Charlie" entertained the audience of "not merely nostalgic, transplanted Maritimers but a fair sprinkling of young adults and even teen-agers (of the shorthaired variety.)" The author reveals his thinly veiled distain for the music with comments such as "Messer's brand of country corn" and describing the bandleader's personal demeanor as "dull to the point of anonymity." But it was the "fiddlin'" that they came for and that is what they got, while "Marg Osburne and Charlie Chamberlain put their considerable lung power on the line," competing with the background noise of closing night at the fair (13).

The End of an Era

By the spring of 1969, the show was no longer in the top 10. It had slipped to number 22 out of 59 national shows (Feniak C1-2). The program that had been loved by so many for over a decade ended abruptly, "creating outrage from coast to coast. Petitions were signed and questions raised in the House of Commons" (Martin S8).

Immediately following the announcement of the cancellation of *Don Messer's Jubilee* on a Monday, the CBC began receiving letters from "old people." Within a week, 500 had arrived. A sample of 13 of these letters are found in the "Entertainment" section of the *Toronto Daily Star* on April 19, 1969. From small villages to large cities, their writers are clearly upset with what they view as "a good, clean, down-to-earth presentation of Canadian talent" being taken off the air. One from Bothwell, Ontario states, "I am an old man, 74, and live alone. I am protesting that you are taking the Don Messer show off the air." Some plead that the show continue. Others ask how they can help. Sentiments such as: "I am appalled," "My heart is heavy today," and "it is striking me hard" are expressed. A London, Ontario viewer states:

> 'I am sure many, many middle-aged and senior citizens will watch TV shows like this, the same as we do, Don Messer with his own violin selections, the lively square dancers we like, and Marg Osburne and Charlie Chamberlain with their lovely songs, so familiar to us, and the special sacred hymn they always sing near the end of the program, and we hear so few of those nice hymns on TV.' ("Dear Sirs: ...")

An 81-year-old, retired railroad man from Astle, New Brunswick felt having a television was no longer worthwhile since he would not be able to watch the Messer show. A Torontonian quipped, "I am well aware of the fact that it is a pity that we old people won't just drop dead and then you could get juveniles on all your programs and be happy." But, most poignantly, a letter from Port Coquitlam, British Columbia simply inquired, "Why?" (Ibid.).

According to tour manager Ken Reynolds, the termination of *Don Messer's Jubilee* was an abrupt and cruel ending for a show that had been a Canadian favourite for years. On April 14, 1969, a telegram was sent from the Director of Programming for the CBC to the Halifax CBC television station informing them of the cancellation. It would be replaced by *Singalong Jubilee*, thought to be more appealing to a younger audience. Bill Langstroth broke the news to Messer, who was devastated. Ironically, Langstroth, who had been the producer of *Don Messer's Jubilee*, became lead singer on the replacement show. Reynolds, who had known Don since 1952, "could feel his pain and humiliation." For thirty-five years, Messer had provided excellent entertainment for the CBC and his show had become the most watched on CBC TV. Reynolds was incensed with the injustice of cancelling the long-running popular Canadian program so unceremoniously and stated: "I call it an outrageous and unforgivable decision" (81).

Journalist Peter Feniak writes that while management feared the show was "out-of-date" in an era of the "a-go-go sixties" and had to go, the effect was devastating to many:

> The howl that went up reached right to Parliament Hill. The cancellation especially gripped country people, Maritimers, and Canada's older generation. For them the fast-moving weekly set of jigs and reels, square dances, sacred ballads, and sentimental songs was a seven-day tonic. Now the people's network [CBC] was dropping the Messer show? How could they? (C1)

A trans-Canada farewell tour was organized. Reporter John Kraglund attended a show at Varsity Arena in Toronto on June 15, 1969. Although rain and poor sound quality somewhat dampen the enthusiasm of the audience, they are still happy to welcome members of the cast they have watched on television for so long. Given that the main reason for the cancellation of *Don Messer's Jubilee* was that it was too "old fashioned," for those in attendance at this show, "it was the oldest and most familiar selections, performed by the regular performers, that prompted frequent and loud bursts of applause. They even laughed loudest at the oldest jokes." And although not always in the spotlight, Messer dominated with his "familiar breakdown" (15).

The last show was broadcast by CBC on Friday, June 20, 1969, ending "one of the most successful chapters in its broadcasting history." For over 10 years *Don Messer's Jubilee* had been among the top 10 in audience ratings. Reasons for and against the cancellation were numerous, such as the culture of the Maritimes "being more than the Messer brand of folk music" and the bandleader's successful format remaining unchanged. But the Canadian favourite would not be lost completely to viewers as the independent television station CHCH-TV, Channel 11 in Hamilton, Ontario would produce the show's next season, but it would not be broadcast nationally (Ibid.).

Life After Don Messer's Jubilee

"Tapings for 1973, [Osburne's] 26th year with the show, were under way when Messer died ("Marg ... 13") in Halifax, March 26, 1973 (Jackson). With the bandleader's demise, the show on CHCH ended. The group's quiet but "almost invisible guiding force" had been lost. The musicians found it difficult to adapt to a changing music industry. They went their separate ways (Beaton and Pederson 60). It was at this time that Marg Osburne asked Ken Reynolds to become her booking agent and tour manager for personal appearances where she could feature her large repertoire (Reynolds 74).

Osburne continued to tour in addition to some television dates in Halifax. In "Marg on the one-night stands somewhere west of the Messer Show," Blaik Kirby caught up with her in a tiny village on the Quebec side of the Ottawa River near Hawkesbury in February of 1976. On a snowy winter night, she was trying to win over a sparse audience of mainly young people who had come to dance to a beat and were simply not interested in what she had to offer. Her voice was tired and she was exhausted. Looking concerned, she assures Kirby that it will be all right if she is able to rest for four days. As a foreshadowing of what was to come, the journalist astutely claims: "But there was no rest in prospect, and some day that abuse will take a permanent toll and it won't be all right." Although Osburne was familiar with "A run of exhausting one-nighters" which she had done every summer for years touring with Messer and his group, now she was trying to distance herself from "her Messer image" and re-establish herself nationally. She dreamed of a television series of her own (n.p.).

At the age of 48, everyone seems to assume that since she performed in the era of Messer and Chamberlain, now both deceased, she is older than she really is. Even with what Kirby refers to as "a ghost of worry," he compliments her "usual warm, easy-going smile, which is a great and attractive asset." She admits not knowing what they will do if she cannot continue to sing. Her husband gave up his job as a former boxer and then policeman "to go on the road with her." In three years, she has been home to Sussex, New Brunswick only five times. But she affirms not being home does not bother her and that she takes the good with the bad. She likes being with people and feels the audience is now getting to know her. "'On Mr. Messer's show, I hardly ever said a word, except maybe the title of my next song.'" While Kirby observes, "Her personality remains warm, genuine, unpretentious, natural, just plain nice. You can't help liking her," he also wonders whether that will be enough to keep her career going (Ibid.).

In fact, Osburne's dream does come true. On Friday, April 8, 1977, the CBC launched a new variety series starring Marg Osburne called "That Maritime Feeling." Reviewed by Kirby in "Maritime Feeling fails to rise above the pack," he writes that with Osburne "acting much more as hostess than as star," the show is simply "another modest, innocuous variety series." He dismisses it as "a display case for regional performers" and does not believe it "to be either expressive of its Halifax home or first-rate of any particular type." As host, "Marg Osburne is a pleasant, comfortable lady" but the journalist has difficulty finding any "distinguishing trait" to bring it "up to a standard that can make them a solid audience draw" (13).

The Sudden End

In 1977, Ken Reynolds arranged performing dates for the singer from June to October, ending at the International Ploughing Match in Kingston, Ontario. Tragically, on July 16, following a performance for the official opening of an arena in Rocklyn, Ontario and attended by an audience of three thousand, Marg Osburne died (Reynolds 74). After collapsing off-stage, she had later passed away that night from a heart attack. It was the fifth anniversary of the death of her duet partner, Charlie Chamberlain. "She was only forty-nine years old and had not yet heard that her pilot ["That Maritime Feeling"] had been accepted by CBC for a full-season show" (Bertin 216). Buried in the Pioneer cemetery in Sussex, she was survived by husband and manager, Austin Squarebriggs, son, David (22), and daughter, Melody (16) ("Marg … 13").

Tributes to Don Messer's Jubilee

January 1985, John Gray's play entitled "Don Messer's Jubilee" opened at the Neptune Theatre in Halifax. In "Tribute to a Maritime hero," Deborah Jones cites the performance as "a kind of fan letter." The only appearance its namesake makes is in the form of a large photograph which comprises part of the backdrop. The score is mainly original music by Gray with a "country flavor." Messer is portrayed only in song and through the cast of Maritimers (13).

In a scene from the play, the devastating impact of the show's cancellation is portrayed by actors, who could have been the original Buchter Dancers, performing "a macabre reel with mannikins, which they repeatedly stabbed in the back while wearing polite smiles for the audience." It was a "parody of the CBC's cancellation" – a "bitter-sweet tribute" to a show that had meant so much to so many people, and an emotional experience for those in attendance on opening night (Ibid.).

In 1989, producer Malcolm Black opened a "first-class production" of Gray's play at Theatre Plus, St. Lawrence Centre for the Arts, Toronto, in what reporter Ray Conlogue describes as a vastly different political scene from when it first played: "Gray's truculent nationalism, already frayed in 1985, seems completely on the ropes today." Clarinetist Rae Simmons, played by David Hughes, tells the story with no speaking parts given to Don Messer (who is "heard" through his violin) or any of the other musicians. To his credit, Black casts Catherine McKinnon, who sang on *Don Messer's Jubilee* when she was young, "to play her elder mentor, Marg Osburne. McKinnon performs her heart out in a tribute to Osburne. She has never sung better." David Walden plays Charlie Chamberlain. Singing duets in the Osburne/Chamberlain tradition, McKinnon and Walden have enough "chemistry together" to make the "love/hate duet, 'It's Been Going On For Years' extremely amusing" (C9).

In the early 1990s, Bill Langstroth produced and hosted a show based on old tapes of both *Don Messer's Jubilee* and *Singalong Jubilee*. Called *The Jubilee Years*, it was a 22-episode CBC series showing highlights from some of the classic shows (Martin S8). As one of its two main singers, Marg Osburne featured prominently. Feniak describes Langstroth's program as a throwback to a bygone era, a "violent cultural whiplash," but a popular one given the 650,000 to 750,000 who tuned in weekly for the "quietly successful half-hour" on CBC. Twenty-five years after leaving the airwaves, *Don Messer's Jubilee* was back (C1-2).

"Memories of a Don Messer Jubilee Christmas" first toured the Maritimes as a tribute show in 1995, coming to Ontario in 1997. Produced by Barbara Martin, it was well received, bringing back memories of "one of Canada's most revered music personalities,

Don Messer, and his famed Don Messer's Jubilee troupe." In 1999, the cast included Scott Woods as Don Messer, Anne Russo as Marg Osburne, and Tom Leadbeater as Charlie Chamberlain who played to appreciative audiences and sold-out shows ("Memories …").

In 1997, Messer's treasured instrument sparked the beginning of a musical production to commemorate Canada's iconic fiddle player and his importance. In "Fiddler on the loose," Wendy Lindsay writes that thirty years after the last television show, a play called "Don Messer's Violin" performed its world premiere in Summerside, Prince Edward Island, the place where Messer had developed his uniquely "down-home style of music" (C5).

Frank Leahy, the catalyst for the show, plays Messer in the lead role. A violin virtuoso himself and former Canadian Old Time Fiddling Champion, his hero was Don Messer. To his surprise and delight, Messer's daughter wanted Leahy to have her father's famous fiddle. He was overwhelmed. It was Leahy who decided that the story of the man and his "uniquely Canadian style of music" needed to be told. A CD of the same title was also planned (Ibid).

Conclusion

From 1956, Messer and his group continued to emerge as a prime television program in Canada, part of a "powerful musical environment defined by the tradition of Hank Snow, blues, country and Celtic music, a strange accumulation of musical styles embroidered by popular appeal and a practical approach to performing it." Well-liked in the Maritimes, it was also accepted enthusiastically in other regions of Canada (Grills 43-44). "Messer's infectious brand of toe-tapping 'down-home' music showcased the best in the musical tradition of rural North America" ("Don Messer fonds").

Gary R. Buck summarizes the Messer show's significance: "To become an institution that important to Canadians, The Islanders had to offer something special. Their specialty was zippy, simple performances of audience favourites, performed in an easy manner that brought smiles and toe-tapping fun to their faces" (31). *Don Messer's Jubilee* became a part of our family and holds a special place in Canadian television history (Braddock 20).

When asked about Osburne, Don Messer states that in addition to being smart, talented, and amiable, "Musically, she can do anything you ask her to, from pop to country and western. Marg has a personal magnetism all her own – the kind of personality that means that once you meet her you'll always remember her" (Bertin 201).

Marg Osburne became one of the most popular members of *Don Messer's Jubilee* because she exhibited a genuine quality, along with a superb singing ability, that many Canadians respected and with which they felt comfortable. Vast numbers of viewers tuned in weekly on their radios or televisions or attended her many performances on tour because they liked what they saw and heard. As a singer, Marg was unpretentious and appeared to simply enjoy singing. She connected with her audience and they loved her for it. She was a true professional right to the end.

Partial Discography

Marg Osburne*

Singles

That Easy Rockin' Chair 1957
Alberta County Soil 1972
Lonesome City 1974
Blues Comin' Round 1974
City of Tears 1974/75

Albums*

By Request (with Charlie Chamberlain) 1958	The Golden Era of Marg Osborne 1970
A Century of Folk Songs 1960	My Kind of Country 1972
Marg Osburne 1963	Country Gospel 1973
Nearer My God to Thee 1963	Old Gold & New 1974
Marg Osburne/Charlie Chamberlain 1963	Marg Osburne 1976
That Lonesome Road 1963	They Never Grow Up (with Charlie Chamberlain) n.d.
I Believe 1965	Best of (Paragon) n.d.
Sing Favorite Hymns 1966	Best of (Coral) n.d.
Songs of Faith 1966	Beyond the Sunset (with Charlie Chamberlain) n.d.
The Best of Marg Osborne 1966	Songs You Know and Love (with Ray Calder) n.d.
Marg Osburne and Charlie Chamberlain 1967	I Believe (with Ray Calder) n.d.
Sing Favorite Sacred Songs 1967	He/Songs of Reverence (with Ray Calder) n.d.

Encyclopedia of Canadian Country Music by Rick Jackson

Works Cited

Bawden, James. "Messer fans endure corn and the cold." *The Globe and Mail. 8 Sept. 1970: 13. ProQuest. Web. 16 Oct. 2016.*

Beaton, Virginia and Stephen Pedersen. *Maritime Music Greats, Fifty Years of Hits and Heartbreak. Halifax, Nova Scotia: Nimbus Publishing Limited. 1992. Print.*

Bertin, Johanna. *Don Messer: The Man Behind the Music. Fredericton, New Brunswick: Goose Lane Editions. 2009. Print.*

Braddock, John. "The Don Messer Story – Canada's Best Goodwill Ambassador." *The Atlantic Advocate June 1967: 12-20. Print.*

Braithwaite, Dennis. "Dennis Braithwaite's View, CHUM Nearly Outfoxed CBC." *Toronto Daily Star (1900-1971). 5 Sept. 1960: 19. ProQuest. Web. 16 Oct. 2016.*

Buck, Gary R. *Canadian Country Music Hall of Fame, Official Souvenir Book, Pictures and Stories of the 25 Inaugural Inductees. Kitchener, Ontario. n.d.: 30-32. Print.*

Conlogue, Ray. "Political changes put salute to Messer in different light." *The Globe and Mail. 5 Aug. 1989: C9. Web. 16 Oct. 2016.*

"Dear Sirs: Why are you dropping Don Messer?" *Toronto Daily Star (1900-1971). Apr. 1969: 97. ProQuest. Web. 16 Oct. 2016.*

"Don Messer fonds." *Nova Scotia Archives.* https://memoryns.ca/don-messer-fonds. Web. 26 Nov. 2020.

Don Messer's Jubilee. CBC Television Series 1952 to 1982. http://web.archive.org, http://www.film.queensu.ca.cbc.Doc.html. Web. 17 Apr. 2020.

"Don Messer's Jubilee." https://www.youtube.com. Web. 8 Nov. 2020.

"Don Messer's Jubilee [–] The Blue Skirt Waltz." https://www.youtube.com. Web. 8 Nov. 2020.

Feniak, Peter. "Fiddling with the past." *The Globe and Mail*. 20 Apr. 1994: C1-2. Web. 16 Oct. 2016.

Ferry, Antony. "Ours Is a Happy Show, Homebody Marg Osburne Typical of 'Jubilee.'" *Toronto Daily Star (1900-1971)*. 11 March 1961: 19. Web. 16 Oct. 2016.

Green, Richard. "Messer, Don, and the Islanders." *The Canadian Encyclopedia*. Ed. James H. Marsh. Toronto: McClelland & Stewart Inc., 1999. Print.

Green, Richard and Mark Miller. "Don Messer and His Islanders." *Encyclopedia of Music in Canada*. Ed. Helmut Kallmann, Gilles Potvin, Kenneth Winters. 2nd ed. Toronto: University of Toronto Press, 1992. Print.

Grills, Barry. *Snowbird: The Story of Anne Murray*. Kingston, Ontario: Quarry Press. 1996. Print.

Jackson, Rick. "Marg Osburne." *Encyclopedia of Canadian Country Music*. Kingston, Ontario: Quarry Press, Inc., 1996. Print.

Jones, Deborah. "Tribute to a Maritime hero." *The Globe and Mail*. 8 Jan. 1985: 13. Web. 16 Oct. 2016.

Kirby, Blaik. "Marg on the one-night stands somewhere west of the Messer Show." *The Globe and Mail. Entertainment – Travel*. 28 Feb. 1976: n.p. Web. 16 Oct. 2016.

Kirby, Blaik. "Maritime Feeling fails to rise above the pack." *The Globe and Mail*. 8 April 1977: 13. Web. 16 Oct. 2016.

Kraglund, John. "End of the Messer decade on CBC-TV. *The Globe and Mail*. 14 June 1969: 15. Web. 16 Oct. 2016.

Lindsay, Wendy. "Fiddler on the Loose." *The Globe and Mail*. 1 Nov. 1999: C5. Web. 16 Oct. 2016.

"Little Arrows – Marg Osburne." https://www.youtube.com. Web. 8 Nov. 2020.

"Marg Osburne, Singer worked with Messer." *The Globe and Mail. 18 July 1977: 13.* Web. 16 Oct. 2016.

Martin, Sandra. "A Driving Force in Canadian Country Music." *The Globe and Mail. 7 June 2013: S8.* Web. 16 Oct. 2016.

Melhuish, Mark. *Oh What a Feeling, A Vital History of Canadian Music.* Kingston, Ontario: Quarry Press, 1996. Print.

"Memories of a Don Messer Jubilee Christmas." *Country Music News. 20. 6 Sept. 1999: 7.* Print.

Nolan, Alden. "Weekend Graffiti, Silver Jubilee." Weekend Magazine. *The Globe and Mail. 24 Mar. 1979: 10b.* Web. 16 Oct. 2016.

Reynolds, Ken. *Ken Reynolds Presents Sixty Years in Canadian Country Music.* Renfrew, Ontario: General Store Publishing House. 2009. Print.

Richter, Volkmar. "After a century, Canada still has that old Don Messer soul." *Toronto Daily Star (1900-1971). 1 July 1967: 25.* Web. 16 Oct. 2016.

Rutherford, Paul. *When Television Was Young: Primetime Canada 1952-1967.* Toronto: University of Toronto Press, 1992. Print.

"The Season of '52." Weekend Magazine. *The Globe and Mail. 17 Sept. 1977: 6.* Web. 16 Oct. 2016.

"Classifying Operations": Constructing and Manufacturing Identities in Irish and American Country Music

By Christina Lynn
Dundalk Institute of Technology

A musician's image is critical to their success (Whitely, 1997, 2013; North and Hargreaves, 1999; Machin, 2010). As well as the sound of the music, it creates a connection with their audience, particularly since the advent of MTV and the music video (Banks, 1997; Frith, Goodwin and Grossberg, 2005; Lieb, 2013). Irish and American performers of country music utilise elements of social and cultural markers to create an identity for themselves. Influenced by the work of sociologist Pierre Bourdieu (1990) and its application in the study of country music (Hubbs, 2014), I will provide a comparison between American country singer Gretchen Wilson and Irish country singer Mags McCarthy.

There are many aspects of identity that are critical to understanding how the construction of an image or persona impacts on how a musician is recognised or received. Nadine Hubbs (2014) provided a comprehensive discussion on the impact of class, race and homosexuality in country music in America. She focused on Gretchen Wilson portrayal of the 'redneck' women as a contrast to the negative narrative surrounding this term.1 Hubbs suggests that Wilson utilises her identity as a 'redneck' to instil a confidence and a unity in her music and in her audience. Here I bring Hubbs concept further and critically examine two music videos to illustrate ways that both Wilson and McCarthy reflect Bourdieu's scenario of "classifying operations" (Hubbs 2014, 118). I will then demonstrate how both of these women are exemplifying a specific cultural identity. I will first detail elements of the theories put forward by Bourdieu (1990), Hubbs (2014) and musicologist Philip Austlander (2004) that have aided in the development of this paper, in which I present a new approach in analysing identity presentations and embodiments.

The performance of identity draws significantly from the social contexts from which performers emerge and with which they seek to engage. Focusing largely on education, Bourdieu (1990) engages with the concept of social classification and the choices made by culture within which individuals participate. Of particular interest is his concept of the selection of meanings:

> which objectively define a group's or a class's culture as a symbolic system is socio-logically necessary insofar as that culture owes its existence to the social conditions of which it is the product and its intelligibility to the coherence and functions of the structure of the signifying relations which constitute it' (Bourdieu 1990, p. 8).

Bourdieu goes further to detail what he means by this in his glossary. He states that the:

> Choice which constitutes a culture (choices' which no one makes) appear as arbitrary when related by the comparative method to the sum total of present and past cultures or, by imaginary variations, to the universe of possible cultures, they reveal their necessity as soon as they are related to the social conditions of their emergence and perpetuation (ibid).

The 'symbolic system[s]' that Bourdieu is discussing are the cultural symbols that exist within any given culture. These symbols are 'necessary' as markers for those within a cultural system and those outside of it. This allows for distinctions to be made between one culture and another. The choice is then instituted within that culture and is a highly charged symbolic representation of that culture. Both the symbolic system and the choice are seen as classifying operations within any given culture. While Bourdieu's concepts are taken from an examination and analysis of educational systems and their impact on the wider society, these concepts can be applied to society and culture as a whole.

Hubbs (2014) applies Bourdieu's theory to American country music. She states that 'Bourdieu's writing on class cultures illumine the cultural logic at work in so-called poverty pride songs – and indeed, in the mechanisms of working-class formation' (Hubbs 2014, p. 117). Furthermore, Hubbs highlights a deeper understanding of Bourdieu's theory when she discusses how the '"object" of sociology's classifications produces her own "classifying operations" and articulates a polemical view of the other class' (ibid, p. 118). She provides an in-depth analysis of how the aspects of cultural classification are prevalent in country music songs and identity markers, stating:

> In the context of radically separate social and cultural spheres, country music's working-class reputation and focus often inspire alienation and revulsion in middle-class audiences. But the working class has its own views and values, separate from and unrecognised by the middle-class system of values and symbolic exchange, and (as Bourdieu demonstrates) dominated by it' (Hubbs 2014, p.118).

Further to this Hubbs outlines how research by Lamont (2000) and Fox (2004) on working class values and authenticity adds to classifying operations.

Hubbs' approach is complemented by Auslander's (2004) trichotomy of performance analysis, which draws significantly on the work of musicologist Simon Frith (1998). Auslander suggests that there are three layers contained in any performance: 'the real person (the performer as a human being), the performance persona (which corresponds to Frith's (1998) star personality or image) and the characters (Frith's song personality)' (2004, p.6). Auslander's trichotomy allows researchers and audiences to analyse the embodied identities of performers through performances, both live and recorded. Auslander suggests that performances 'take place within contexts of the socio-cultural conventions of the societies in which they occur, conventions that popular music both reflects and contests' (p. 10). The idea that performances take place within the context of socio-cultural conventions also adds to the concept put forward by Hubbs and indeed Bourdieu. Auslander is specifically speaking of the performance context, yet his clear distinction of three 'personas' is useful in analysing the images presented by artists in their music videos.

The concept of the 'sincerity contract' (Rogers,1989) can be considered alongside Auslander's approach. Rogers states that there are channels of communication between a Country music artist and an audience. While Country music, like most popular music, is a medium of mass media it is also enjoyed in a private or semi-private way. This then enables the performer – the person with a message to tell according to Rogers – to create the idea of sincerity through their voice and use of language.

Rhetoric on the term 'Redneck'

In discussing the concept of the Redneck Women, Hubbs (2014) presented an analysis of Wilson's songs and image as an example of how she exemplifies the 'Redneck' women and thus cultivates an audience whom identify with the same cultural and social markers. Hubbs makes it clear that this concept of 'Redneck' is not something that she has created however, but something that can be traced back in American history that has been associated with lower-middle class or working-class people. 'Redneck' and Country music have had a long association, actually having first been associated with the 'hillbilly' music of the 1920s. American Country music is prominently and proudly associated with specific regions or places (Hubbs 2014, p. 11). Many suggest that country music comes from the south, yet there is a counter claim and research to support country music's association with California, the Southwest and the Midwest (Carney, G. O, 1977, 1979, 1980, 1994). Furthermore, Hubbs states that:

> Reception research shows that commercial country was initially a music of rural more than southern audiences; that by the 1970s its audiences were not distinctly rural or regional but preponderantly midlife, working – and lower-middle-class whites; and that in the 1980s and 1990s country made significant inroads in suburbia. Other indicators suggests that in some regions of the United States country music is less a distinct cultural object than something woven through the fabric of everyday life. (Hubbs 2014, p. 11).

Within these regions and places, the popularity of country music with audiences is most notably associated with 'objects of sociologies classification' such as working-class, predominantly white, provincial and often southern people (Hubbs 2014, Jensen 2008, A. Fox 2004, P. Fox 2009).

The relationship between country music performers/songwriters and their audience is critical. Bill C. Malone in his description of country music suggests that songwriters 'have been part of the audience for whom they write' (2010, p. 348).2 Malone further suggests that the song lyrics are 'realistic in that they concern themselves with the petty details of human existence … [and] describe life as it is, not as one might wish it to be' (ibid). The combination of descriptions put forward by Hubbs (2004) and Malone (2010) suggest that country music is music of a specific type of performer and audience. Country music's content and context are projected towards the above-mentioned subsets of societies: the music is telling a specifically relatable story to its listeners. These subsets of societies are often classed as lower or working-class, white, heterosexual and rural, and most notably associated with the term 'Redneck'.

'Redneck' like 'Hillbilly' were initially terms used by other classes as a form of exclusion. In fact, the term 'Redneck' according to the Cambridge dictionary refers to a 'poor, white person without education, especially one living in the countryside in the southern US, who is believed to have prejudiced (unfair and unreasonable) ideas and beliefs. The word is usually considered offensive' (www.cambridgeuniversitypress.com 2021). 'Redneck' according to Hubbs, is a 'pejorative term referring to white, working-class, provincial, often boorish, sometimes (but not always) southern male' (Hubbs 2014, p. 14).

Rhetoric on the term 'culchie'

Similar to the context in the use of the term 'redneck', the term 'culchie' hasn't always been used as a term of endearment or praise. Linguistic scholar Helen Kelly-Holmes (2019) suggests 'in very broad terms a culchie is an Irish person who is not from Dublin' (Kelly-Holmes, 2019, p. 353). She goes further to state that there are contrasting accounts for the use of the term culchie:

> One is that the term 'culchie' refers to a native of Kiltimagh in rural County Mayo on the west coast of Ireland on the very opposite side of the country to Dublin. An alternative theory is that the word derives from 'agriculture', and so

> it was originally used to refer to someone who works in agriculture, since this rural, farming lifestyle is seen as a key feature of a 'culchie'. Many words in Irish English come from contact with the Irish language and two other theories on the origin of 'culchie' relate to this possible etymology. Both are based on the homophonic closeness of the term to two Irish language words in particular. One is 'coillte' meaning woods, the suggestion being that this was a term for people from the woods; the other is 'cúl an tí', which means 'back of the house'. So, in other words, it was a term used to refer to servants in the big houses of landed estates of the Anglo-Irish (Kelly-Holmes, 2019, p. 353)

No matter what the origin of the term, the obvious association of the term is with people who live away from urban life in Ireland. Sociologists Anne Cassidy and Brian McGrath have suggested that

> Culchie' is usually used as a pejorative label and stereotype by Irish urban dwellers to describe rural individuals and has derogatory connotations of being backward, old fashioned and dim-witted. While the term 'culchie' is often used by outsiders in a sneering manner, in employing the word 'culchie' to describe themselves the word was positively appropriated by participants, signalling defiant pride in belonging to and membership of this community (Cassidy & McGrath, 2015, p. 26).

Only in the most recent past have Irish rural residents reclaimed this term and utilised it as a positive identity marker. The positive use of this term can also be assessed in its use by Irish expatriates in their affirmation of who they are and where they come from.3 Furthermore 'Culchie' is often associated with those in Ireland who listen to, participate in and perform country music. While there is a large percentage of rural Ireland who enjoy country music, not all residents of rural Ireland would claim to be country music fans. Furthermore, not all fans of Country music are resident in rural Ireland.4 However, those who do participate in this music have also taken the term 'culchie' and utilised it as a positive marker in the expression of identity. Many Irish country music artists have included the term in their songs as a form of inclusion, solidarity and a sense of pride.

Gretchen Wilson, An American Redneck Woman

Born in Pocahontas IL, American country music singer Gretchen Wilson (b.1973) is best known for her 2004 break through hit 'Redneck Woman. Nadine Hubbs (2014) suggests that:

> since the 1970s [redneck] has been reclaimed as a defiant antibourgeois self-designation – signalling, among other things, a rejection of the euphemistic rhetoric of the middle class (if euphemism is "the neutralization and distancing which bourgeois discourse about the social world requires and performs" it is also a frequent object of working-class perceptions of middle-class hypocrisy, duplicity, and condescension) (Hubbs 2014, p.14)

It is reinterpretation and new understanding of the term 'Redneck' that Hubbs discusses in her analysis of Wilson. She sees Wilson as using 'Redneck' in her song titles as a sense of pride and self-identification 'to create a statement of cross-gender working-class consciousness and solidarity' (ibid). In essence Hubbs suggests that Wilson is calling to arms her fellow 'rednecks' in pride songs. This specific song details a pride about who they [Rednecks] are and how they live. Wilson does this by invoking cultural markers that identify her as a 'redneck'. The cultural knowledge Wilson has of what a 'redneck' is and does, is evident in her portrayal of a 'redneck' in this music video. This specific cultural capital allows Wilson to be seen as authentic. Rogers' concept of 'the sincerity contract' is evident here, whereby 'The "sincerity contract" in country music [is] the expectation of rapport between a credible, straightforward artist and her or his audience' (1989, p. 17). Rogers' first chapter provides pivotal background reading into the creation of commercial country music, while also detailing the pitfalls for those who 'have a dream of making it big but fail' (1989, p 6). He details the 'sincerity contract' through his theory on how artists communicate with the audience through their songs and use of language (Rogers 1989). Rogers suggests that this sincerity between an artist and the audience is a vital pillar of a country music star. This allows them to create a fan base that trust in the 'message' the singer is spreading (Rogers 1989, p. 5). Richard A. Peterson (2002) has also discussed this idea of authenticity where he discusses the idea of fabricating authenticity in country music. Peterson and Rogers are discussing authenticity in different ways; Rogers discusses the concept of the' straightforward' artist, whereas Peterson is concerned with the construct of an identity that is not necessarily the same as the lived experience of the artist but relates to their artform or cultural narrative. Hubbs suggests that since emerging on the country music scene in 2004, Wilson has 'cultivated an image as a real redneck woman along the lines sketched in her songs' (Hubbs 2014, p. 119). It is this idea of the real that enables Wilson to display Rogers concept of the sincerity contract. It also illuminates Peterson's theory of authenticity in the country music artist.

Reflective of a particular identity within American society, Wilson was brought up in a trailer park and left school at the age of 14 (Wilson, 2006). She worked as a cook and a bartender until 1996 when she left her hometown to pursue a career as a country music artist in Nashville. In the music video 'Redneck Woman', Wilson is seen 'muddin' on an ATV and in a truck. This is a complete contrast to the majority of music videos in 2004 from female artists. In her autobiography Wilson details watching the 'singer-supermodels' of country music 'Shania Twain, Faith Hill and Martina McBride' while writing 'Redneck woman'. She states that she remembers exactly what she was wearing at the time: 'a wife-beater tank top, a pair of sweatpants, and flip-flops. I had no makeup on, and I had a cigarette in one hand and a bottle of beer in another' (Wilson 2006, p. 140). Wilson turned to her writing partner at the time and said 'there just no way that I can do that. No way in hell' (ibid). He was stunned and asked, 'do what' (ibid). Wilson pointed at the music videos and said she would never be able to record a music video like that: 'That. I can't do that. That's not who I am'. (ibid). Wilson is placing herself in the context of a rural, country potentially farming female who is accustomed to using an ATV and driving a truck on this terrain on a regular basis. It also alludes to the entertainment activities that these rural dwellers participate in. Wilson appears comfortable in her presentations on both the ATV and driving the Truck. She is not afraid of 'getting dirty' or appearing in a 'non-glamours way'. Wilson is portraying herself as the down to earth, home grown, real 'Redneck'. In her autobiography, also entitled Redneck Woman, she states:

> "Redneck" in "Redneck Woman" is a lifestyle, an attitude toward the world. It's about people who work hard, often in blue-collar jobs, and play hard. And they don't take no crap from anyone about who they are and where they come from (Wilson 2006, p. 141).

Re-enforcing the concept of the lifestyle of a 'redneck woman', Wilson returns 'home' in her now dirty truck to a trailer park. As evident from her biography, the audience are already aware of her own personal experience having grown up in a trailer park therefore this imagery allows the viewer once again to visualise the 'sincerity contract' in action. Wilson transfers this authenticity and sincerity to the stage when she is seen in her performance imagery. She is singing and playing guitar in a honky-tonk or a dimly lit bar. This alludes to a local, hometown performance in this context. The venue is not showcased as being a large venue with an audience base of thousands. Instead, we are drawn to a more intimate setting where the audience are in close proximity to the stage. As the music video focuses on Wilson in this performance her fashion presentation does evolve into a glamours music star. Wilson is not wearing clothing to make her stand out from the crowd. The 'difference' between her and her audience is their positioning, Wilson is on stage while the audience are on the ground.5 These images along with the words in her song enable Wilson to be identified as a 'redneck woman' by her fellow 'redneck audience'.

Engaging Auslander's theory here, he has suggested there are three personas at play in any given performance. In this instance Wilson is portraying the real person, the performance persona and the character. Yet, to the audience she is only displaying the real person. The performer is displaying what she thinks the audience wants to see. Wilson has modelled herself on the 'Redneck' persona, therefore her audience will only see the 'Redneck' as the person. The audience does not see Wilson's performance as a performance but as a portrayal of the 'straightforward' artist (Rogers 1989).

> I was discovering something much more important [during the song writing process]—what really makes a singer-songwriter connect to his or her fans and build a career

on a solid foundation and not just on hype, musical fads, or the right image for the moment. That's at the heart of country music—connecting with your audience on some level of real-life experience. The more of yourself you put in the music—warts and all—the greater the chance that the audience will take that music into their own hearts (Wilson 2006, p. 141)

Yet, the performance can be analysed from all three perspectives. The performance persona and the character are also evident here. Wilson is engaging a forceful embodiment of the 'redneck' here. Every aspect of the video and the song allows the audience to see Wilson perform the 'redneck' identity.6 This is also evident in the character of the song. The character is the 'redneck woman' whom Wilson is singing about. While this may not be entirely the lifestyle that Wilson has lived, the character is highlighting these aspects to engage with a wider audience demographic. Therefore, the character, the persona and the real person all merge into the one embodied positive identity that Wilson has displayed. The use of the sincerity contract as Rogers has suggested combined with Austlander's analysis model is what has enabled Wilson to produce this image and audience based. Wilson has used 'classifying object' to create a unique artistic identity for herself.

Mags McCarthy, An Irish Country Girl

From a farming background in Ireland, Mags McCarthy provides a contrasting Irish country music artist. McCarthy was born and raised in County Cork, Ireland and completed a university degree in music before deciding to pursue a career as a performer both in Ireland and abroad. Initially engaged primarily in Irish traditional music, song and dance, McCarthy has been part of many touring Irish dance troupes including 'Rhythm of the Dance'. She moved to Nashville in 2017 to focus primarily on her country music career. Since moving to America, McCarthy has invited to perform on a number of renowned country music stages in Nashville and has received critical acclaim for a number of her singles released in America.7 McCarthy has carved out a unique space for herself in the Nashville scene as both a singer and as a musician.

Moving back to Ireland during the Covid-19 Pandemic has provided McCarthy with the opportunity to promote herself and her music more readily to the Irish audiences through social media and television interviews.

It is through social media research that McCarthy's music video first came to my attention. The music video for McCarthy's cover of Dolly Parton's song 'Light of a Clear Blue Morning' is what will be contrasted here. In this music video, McCarthy utilised her Irish identity markers to showcase her Irishness to the audience. In a recent interview with McCarthy she suggests that she sought to evoke Ireland and an Irish sound at the start using uilleann pipes over images of Ireland. She states this:

> shows my identity and my brand and my image and who I am. I don't ever forget who I am, even when I'm in an interview in America I'll always think about how I was brought up, who I met, who had helped me, where I'm from,

most of my interviews people are probably thinking where is this dripsy place, but I love home, I love friends, I love where I come from and I love the Irish people (McCarthy 2021, Interview)

These sentiments put forward by McCarthy in her own words are illustrating her 'straightforward' and 'credible' nature that was incited by Rogers in his concept of the 'sincerity contract' (Rogers 1989) but also reflect her awareness of how instrumentation and the use of particular images can help construct and communicate an identity. McCarthy is highlighting her Irish identity through the use of music and Irish coastline imagery before she sings a single note. The first time McCarthy appears on scene to the viewer she is walking to the fields of green where the cattle are grazing, which is swiftly followed by her herding the cattle towards the farmyard.

As the music video moves through to the second verse McCarthy's image changes. In her own words, McCarthy suggested that the second half of the video highlights her passion and love for her music career: 'It shows me finishing my chores and then going out to play music for the night' (McCarthy 2021, interview). McCarthy first is seen dressed in white dancing and singing along the coastline of Cork. McCarthy is wearing a white dress that hints at a purity and innocence, yet set against the rugged coastline contrasts this meaning with a wildness: a wildness in a young Irish female.

The image changes again in the closing of the video where McCarthy is standing in the middle of a carnival or funfair setting, with carnival cars driving around her. The spotlight focuses on McCarthy and she has again changed her outfit. This is McCarthy the performer at night, in contrast to the farming working girl during the day. This image also poses another meaning. It alludes to the heritage of Irish country music performers, such as Big Tom, Declan Nerney, Philomena Begley and Susan McCann who were themselves farmworkers who also performed at Carnivals and Marquees before the eventual take-over of the dancehall and function rooms.8

McCarthy suggested that the concept for this part of the music video was to show the viewer who she really is. To show what it is like: 'a day in the life of Mags' (McCarthy 2021, interview). McCarthy is helping out on the farm, doing her chores before we see her change her clothing and appear on a beach and even later in a carnival stage. McCarthy is a rural Irish girl but, in contrast with older representations of rural Ireland, she is also mobile, educated and confident and lives in the modern world. Writing about the 'Irishness' of Irish music, John O'Flynn has pointed out, 'dominant representation of 'authentic' Irish culture attempt to reinstate aspects of essential Irishness – whether real, imaginary or a combination of both - into more recently formulated projections of a cosmopolitan and progressive Ireland' (2016, p. 197). In the opening of this video, McCarthy is utilising her 'classifying operations' to reinstate 'essential' identity markers of Irishness but relates this to her experience of living in contemporary Ireland. McCarthy is engaging in a trope of the rural Irish farming female to engage her 'sincerity contract' so that she may be seen as an authentic, straightforward, credible artist who lives what she sings. She uses the rural farming trope as a form of representation of all Irish females even though this trope is only representative of a small fraction of the population in Ireland.9

McCarthy's use of costume change and cultural display show a vast knowledge of the world that she inhabits. Similar to Wilson, she employs the sincerity contract, showcasing who she is as a person and revealing her autobiography through her music and accompanying videos. McCarthy has utilised her specific 'classifying operations' as a way of representing a specific type of Irishness that does not focus on cosmopolitanism and progressive images. Instead, McCarthy utilises rugged imagery of Irish coastlines, alongside the use of her own family farm to highlight an embodied portray of her own identity.

While based in Ireland from 2020, McCarthy has brought her American audience on her journey with her. She has utilised identity markers to show her American audience of her own roots as a rural individual. She is identifying the elements of her own unique identity while also identifying with the audience to who she sings both in Ireland and in America. McCarthy is clearly very keenly aware of her own classifying operations. McCarthy is from rural Ireland where farming is a way of life. She makes this the most prominent element of her video. McCarthy is proud of her rural Irish upbringing and its prominence shows her affinity to her heritage. Unlike Wilson however, McCarthy also incorporates her more mature and contemporary femininity into her video, thus allowing for a wider audience engagement.

As with Wilson, Auslander's trichotomy is evident here. The real person and the performance persona are one and the same here. McCarthy is trying to portray the real person, yet that person is also a character in this song. The character is evident in the video in fleeting glimpses. The reason for this is that the character of the song lyrics do not physically relate to the music video; however, McCarthy bring elements of the lyrics into her portrayal. All three merge into one as the video comes to an end thus leaving the viewer wondering which version of these images is the real Mags McCarthy.

Closing remarks

The use of cultural rhetoric – classifying operations - has enabled both Wilson and McCarthy to portray their own identities. Wilson from Pocahontas, Illinois has captured the essence of the 'redneck' women in both her lyrics and her image portrayal. Her cultural knowledge of the 'redneck' lifestyle has allowed her to portray this identity in her music. She has spoken of her aspiration to stay 'true to herself' and not 'selling out' to the 'singer-supermodel' persona's already on display in the American country music circuit. McCarthy has also taken her life experience and portrayed an altered presentation of her own identity. McCarthy has presented a particular aspect of the rural Irish experience. The essence of her identity is showcased in her display of her day-to-day life in Ireland. Furthermore, by engaging with the concept of the 'sincerity contract' by displaying their 'private lives' both women are viewed as 'straightforward' and 'credible'. They have taken cultural rhetoric, often used in a negative way, and portrayed positive images. By taking this rhetoric and engaging with the 'sincerity contract', both women have utilised 'classifying operations' in a positive way to create and display a specific personally relevant identity.

Bibliography

Articles

Banks, J., 1997. "Video in the Machine: The Incorporation of Music Video into the Recording Industry." Popular Music, 16(3), pp. 293–309.

Auslander, P. 2004. Performance Analysis and Popular Music: A Manifesto, Contemporary Theatre Review, 14(1), 1-13.

Carney, G.O., 1977. From down home to uptown: the diffusion of country-music radio stations in the United States. Journal of Geography, 76(3), pp.104-110.

Carney, G.O., 1979. T for Texas, T for Tennessee: The origins of American country music notables. Journal of Geography, 78(6), pp.218-225.

Carney, G.O., 1980. Country music and the South: A cultural geography perspective. Journal of Cultural Geography, 1(1), pp.16-33.

Carney, G.O., 1994. Branson: the new Mecca of country music. Journal of Cultural Geography, 14(2), pp.17-32.

North, A. C., & David J. Hargreaves, 1999. Music and Adolescent Identity, Music Education Research, 1(1), 75-92.

Books

Bourdieu, P., and Jean-Claude Passeron 1990. Reproduction in Education, Society and Culture. London and New Delhi: Sage Publications.

Fox, Aaron A., 2004. Real Country: Music and Language in Working-Class Culture. Durham, NC: Duke University Press.

Fox, P., 2009. Natural acts. Ann Arbor: University of Michigan Press.

Frith, S., Goodwin, A. and Grossberg, L., 2005. Sound and vision. London: Routledge.

Giddens, A., 1990. Modernity and the Self. Cambridge UK: Blackwell Publishing Ltd.

Hubbs, N., 2014. Rednecks, Queers and Country Music. Los Angeles and London: University of California Press. Berkeley.

Jensen, J., 1998. The Nashville sound. Nashville: Vanderbilt University Press.

Lamont, M., 2000. The Dignity of Working Men: Morality and the Boundaries of Race, Class, and Immigration. New York: Russell Sage Foundation.

Lieb, K., 2013. Gender, branding, and the modern music industry. New York: Routledge

Machin, D., 2010. Analysing popular music. London: SAGE Publications Ltd.

Malone, B.C., 2010. Country Music USA. University of Texas Press: Austin Texas, USA.

Martin, K., 2018. A Happy Type of Sadness. Cork: Mercier Press.

O'Flynn, J., 2016. The Irishness of Irish music. London and New York: Routledge.

Peterson, R.A., 1997. Creating Country Music: Fabricating Authenticity. University of Chicago Press: Chicago USA.

Rogers, J. N., 1989. The Country Music Message, Revisited. Fayetteville: University of Arkansas Press: Fayetteville.

Skeggs, B., 2004. Class, Self, Culture. New York: Routledge.

Whiteley, S., 2000. Women and popular music. Hoboken: Taylor and Francis.

Whiteley, S., 2013. Sexing the Groove. Hoboken: Taylor and Francis.

Wilson, G. 2006. Redneck Woman: Stories from my life. New York: Warner Books Hachette Book Group.

Music Video

McCarthy, M. (2021). Mags: Mags McCarthy Official Artist Stie. [online] Available: Http://www.Magsmccarthy.com. [Accessed 19 December 2020)

Gretchen Wilson (2004) Redneck Woman. [online] Available: https://youtu.be/82dDnv9zeLs. [Accessed: 19 December 2020].

Thesis

Millar, J., 2012. (In)Authentic Country: Country Music in Dublin: University College Dublin.

Websites

Cso.ie. 2016. Home - CSO - Central Statistics Office. [online] Available at: <https://www.cso.ie/en/index.html> [Accessed 03 January 2021].

Dictionary.cambridge.org., (2020). Redneck. [online] Available at: <https://dictionary.cambridge.org/dictionary/english/redneck> [Accessed 30 November 2020].

Netflix.com., (2019). Dolly Parton: Here I am. [online] Available at: <https://www.netflix.com/watch/81204624?trackId=14277281&tctx=-97%2C-97%2C%2C%2C%2C> [Accessed 04 October 2020].

McCarthy, M. (2021). Mags: Mags McCarthy Official Artist Stie. [online] Available: Http://www.Magsmccarthy.com. [Accessed 19 December 2020]

Oermann, R., 2018. *DISClaimer*: Dierks Bentley, Brothers Osborne, Mags Top New Releases [online] MusicRow.com. Available at: <https://musicrow.com/2018/06/disclaimer-dierks-bentley-brothers-osborne-mags-top-new-releases/> [Accessed: 19 December 2020].

Joe Val and Herb Applin

By Joe Val

Joe Val was the front man for the duo of Val and Applin. He had the lead tenor vocals, more of the stage personality, and in time fronted his own band, Joe Val and the New England Bluegrass Boys.

Joe was 10 years older than Herb Applin. He was born on June 26, 1926 as Joseph Paul Valiante in the city of Everett, Massachusetts, tucked up against Boston.

Joe's parents had similar surnames. His father was Joseph G. Valiante, listed in both the 1930 and 1940 United State censuses as a "laborer" – in 1930 as a laborer working in local coke ovens and living in Framingham, and in 1940 as "laborer WPA" and living in Somerville. He was born on October 31, 1899 in Framingham, Massachusetts of two Italian immigrant parents.

Joe Val's mother was born in Mondolfo, Pesaro, Italy on March 10, 1906. Mondolfo is on the Adriatic coast between Rimini and Ancona. When she arrived in New York on the *Ancona*, on June 9, 1913, she was recorded with the name Irma Valentini. She was known as Emma, perhaps her correct first name.

Joseph G. and Emma married on September 6, 1925 in Framingham. The 1940 census shows them with six children.[1]

Joseph G. is found working at several jobs in the Somerville City Directory, including as a gardener in 1933 and as a cement finisher in 1940. The cement work may have been done in construction of one of the tunnels under Boston Harbor. Joe's daughter Marie Westerman said of her grandfather, "He did underwater construction…in like a wet suit. He SCUBA dove. He helped build the Callahan Tunnel. I thought that was kind of cool. I also heard that at one time he was a professional boxer. He also worked as a gardener. Whatever he could do to make money, and put food on the table."[2]

Joe's sister Connie said that after the construction work, their father worked at "a big bakery place in Boston," adding, "My mother worked in a little bakery on Broadway in Somerville. She waited on people, at the counter. She came over here when she was 7."[3]

It's not surprising that Joe Val – the singer and musician – became known as Joe Val, rather than Joe Valiante. The story is that it was fiddle player Tex Logan who shortened Joe's name and it caught on. One unlikely story is that Logan found it difficult to pronounce Joe's last name. Given that Logan had a master's degree from M.I.T. and a doctorate in electrical engineering from Columbia University, the more probable explanation is that Tex simply suggested it as a stage name.

Joe was primarily raised in the urban environment of Somerville, and the family was apparently tight-knit. In a piece for the *Boston Globe*, writer Jeff McLaughlin said that Joe credited "a strong family, baseball, and music with keeping me on the right path as a youngster."[4]

Joe Val himself married and had two children. Joe married Thelma Ann Benoit (b. May 6, 1928 in Somerville) in the year 1951. She was one of the five children of Alfred R. Benoit and Nellie Day

Benoit. Alfred was listed in the 1930 census as a "chauffeur, milk company" – a milkman.

Thelma and Joe had two children, Joseph R. Valiante and Marie A. Westerman. Thelma lost Joe on June 11, 1985; she herself died on September 10, 2014 at the Newton Healthcare Center.

Joe's work was as a typewriter repairman, a job at which he worked for at least 25 years, employed by the Peter Paul Office Equipment Co., in Waltham. Joe knew how to drive, says Herb Applin, but he did not have a car of his own and relied on public transportation to visit companies whose typewriters he might be sent to repair. He carried a toolkit with him. The company was generous in allowing Joe time to travel and thus Joe and the New England Bluegrass Boys were able to make four tours of Europe, appearing in seven countries and on television for the BBC.[5]

There's another story, perhaps semi-apocryphal, that at one point he "was sent to fix folk impresario Manny Greenhill's machine. Greenhill discovered the repairman was also a musician and offered to manage his group."[6] Greenhill was based in Greater Boston and actively booked shows from the late 1950s onward, at one point serving as the longtime manager of both Joan Baez and Doc Watson. Manny's son Mitch says, "Yes, it's true that Joe was Manny's typewriter repairman. I first met Joe in Manny's office on Federal Street, where he was making a house call. Manny loved the connection, kind of like Elizabeth Cotten babysitting Mike and Peggy Seeger."[7]

Joe's interest in music started at around the age of 14 when his grandmother gave him a guitar.[8] His sister Connie remembered that and said, "He used to practice in our hallway in Somerville.

235 Pearl Street. I don't know if it's even there anymore. It had a big, high, high ceiling and he liked the acoustics in there. He would have his friends come over and they would sing with him. Once in a while, I would play the piano and sing with them.

"He was very quiet at home, but he could be very funny. Those were really, really nice times. It was all country music, yeah. And he just fell in love with it."[9]

It was local radio that first gave Joe the opportunity to hear country music in the Boston area. Radio station WCOP (1150 AM) broadcast from Boston, and then from a more powerful transmitter in Lexington, and the station came to feature a substantial amount of country music, both recorded and live from their studio.

By the early 1950s, Joe had become a performer himself, playing guitar and some banjo with a group called The Radio Rangers. Joe had gone electric more than a decade before Bob Dylan. Jim Rooney can testify to that: see his mention of Joe playing electric guitar on the WCOP *Hayloft Jamboree* in his June 1963 liner notes to the first Keith & Rooney album.[10]

The Radio Rangers were led by Larry "Lefty" Sullivan, who had started the group in his home state of Maine after returning from service in World War II.[11] Disabled with a spine injury in the war, Sullivan had first put together the Radio Rangers in Maine, toured Canada for a month with them, and then moved to Cambridge, Massachusetts and worked for the IRS. He'd put together another incarnation of the Radio Rangers with Danny Gillis (guitar and vocals), Andy Bator (fiddle), and Claude Michaud (mandolin.) Lefty played guitar as well.

One night at Boston's Hillbilly Ranch, Joe Val introduced himself and the band expanded to five pieces. Lefty recalls, "When we came off the stage after doing our 45 minutes at the Hillbilly Ranch, Joe was sitting there about 15 feet from the stage and he's all alone. He said something, so I sat down and started talking with him and he said, 'Geez, I love what you guys are doing, I play a little guitar, but I'm just learning.' I said, 'Did you ever do anything?' [playing on stage] and he said no, but he asked, 'Is there any possibility that I could get up there with you guys and sing a song?'

"I said, 'No trouble at all,' so when we went up, he went on the stage for the first time. He had his guitar and the people loved him. He ended up doing the last three sets with us.

"I took the guys home and he was in Somerville, so it was the last stop. He said, 'Can I ask you something?' and I said, 'Yeah.' He says, 'You know how nervous I was.' And I said, 'Well, that happens to all of us.' He said, 'Was there any possibility I could join you guys?' I liked him right off, and Danny Gillis and Andy Bator and Claude, they all liked him. I said, 'Well, I liked you. The other guys liked you. Let me give you a call.' I talked to the guys the next day and then I called him and said, 'Well, you're now a member of the Radio Rangers.' He joined us right then."[12]

The Radio Rangers were well-known in Boston-area country music circles but, Sullivan says, only once played the *Hayloft Jamboree*. They did play the *New England Barn Dance Jamboree*, however. "We were probably the most talked-about band around the area. We were on three radio stations at the same time, same day. We had WJDA in Quincy, and then we went over to Brookline.

WVOM. Early in the morning we went to Medford and we did a show over there. We played all the ranches around the State of Maine and New Hampshire and thereabout." One night at the Hillbilly Ranch, a man approached them about playing for a broader audience, maybe cutting a record and having their own national radio show on Saturday nights. To do that, though, they were told they'd have to change their name.

They were asked to drive to Western Massachusetts to make a demo tape. On the way there, a friend of Sullivan's named Doug Terry saw a sign along the roadside which read, "Welcome to the Berkshire Mountains." That's how they picked up the name and became the Berkshire Mountain Boys. All told, they played under one name or the other for about three years. "We were doing very, very well. Not making a lot of money, because nobody did in those days. Joe went over very big, and people liked him."

Herb Applin

While Joe Val was getting his start in music as a sideline, Herb Applin had grown up in the area, not that many miles away. He was born in Watertown, Massachusetts in 1938. He bore the same name as his father, Henry Herbert Applin, an insurance claims adjuster. His mother was the former Hilda Forster, who worked for a while as a public school teacher, but then devoted her life to raising Herb, his brother John, and sister Carol. Herb had been interested in playing drums, but what really got him going was the violin. There was a woman who played one in a field outside his family's house and that captured his attention. Like many kids of the day, his lessons were in classical violin, "ordinary run-of-the-mill classical music type things."[13]

But something else caught Herb's ear. "The thing that really got me was at the beginning of the 1950s, there was a radio station in Boston – WCOP. They were sort of like a little version of the Grand Ole Opry in Nashville. They had a regular lineup all the time of shows. They had some of the people who were the big names at that time in the country music business. They would come and go on stage and play, just like we think of as a festival today.

"It was called the *WCOP Hayloft Jamboree*, and a fellow - a friend of mine - kind of called my attention to that. He used to come home from school and we'd go down in his basement home workshop. They had all kinds of music every day on the radio. My pal there, he kind of called my attention to it. Every day after school, he'd go down in his workshop and he'd be building model airplanes and all that sort of thing. I started listening to it and I started really being attracted by one of the groups. It was a group that would usually open up one of the concerts. I went to one in Symphony Hall. The band was The Lilly Brothers and Don Stover."[14]

Herb continued, "I was also a part of the school orchestra, both in junior high school and high school, with a woman who was the director. Watertown High. I played more in junior high school."

You weren't playing old-time country music in junior high, though, were you? he was asked. "No. They would have thrown me out!"

The Lilly Brothers made a real impression. Herb continued, "They were from West Virginia. They had a fiddle player that was pretty well known, by the name of Tex Logan. He was in Boston and he earned graduate degrees in just about every school he could find. He was in engineering, but he was also a pretty doggone good fiddle player. He was pretty popular. They all knew each other real well. Tex Logan was around for a number of years and then he moved away to work for a company [Bell Labs, in Murray Hill, NJ]. He would play some on the WCOP *Jamboree*. But playing fiddle wasn't his day job.

"I became really inspired by turning on the radio and hearing Everett and Bea Lilly. Tex Logan wasn't always with them. It just fascinated me, the way the music was played and all that."

And then the *Jamboree* went off the air. It was after Herb had started college, at the University of Maine. "The WCOP didn't go on forever. Eventually, it...after a while, there was no more music like that to put on the radio after school, or in the afternoon, at night. When the *Jamboree* started to go off, at that point, for all I knew, the Lillys were gone. There was no more of that music. I took that pretty hard. It broke my heart. I was really...really in a bad way. I had really become hooked, you might say, on that music. All of a sudden, *Hayloft Jamboree* was gone. It was all gone. I had my fiddle and that was about it."

But the Lilly Brothers had not gone, and Herb learned that by happenstance one time when he was back home over the school holidays. "I happened to be in Boston – in downtown Boston – and all of a sudden I became aware of the Lillys. They were playing in one of the gin mills in Boston." It wasn't the Hillbilly Ranch, but another bar that was just about a block off the Boston Common.

"The *Hayloft Jamboree* had folded up, but they [the Lillys] still had to make a living somehow. They didn't just pack up and run back to West Virginia. They stayed in this area. There were a whole bunch of those really sleazy bars. One of these times I was back home, I just happened to be over that way and I looked and I noticed that the Lillys were playing there. I thought, 'Oh, my gosh.' I had no idea. I thought they had left Boston forever. I'd thought, 'I'll never see them again.' And here they are. Working for pennies, probably, in one of the sleaziest bars in the area.

"I went into this place where I had found out they were playing. I started to get to know them a little bit. Don Stover was not there. He had been recruited by Bill Monroe and gone to the Grand Ole Opry to be part of Bill's band. There was a fellow there in the bar with Everett and Bea Lilly, who sang. He played the banjo first, I think, before he took up the mandolin. This was Joe Val. That's where I met him.

"Joe had gotten acquainted with them and it didn't take me too long to do the same thing.

"Joe was playing the banjo and filling in for Don. Don wasn't gone all that long. He came back. The Lillys worked at different restaurants and bars, right around the immediate area. They finally – after going through maybe a dozen places – they ended up at the Hillbilly Ranch at Park Square. Don was back with them. I was getting acquainted with Joe. We got together and Joe and I kind of began to do a lot of the tunes ourselves."

Fortuitously, when Herb moved back to the Greater Boston area, he was living in Waltham "and Joe lived just a couple of blocks over, down the street." The two of them would get together and play and sing. They loved the old duet singing.

Herb worked at Itek Corporation in Lexington at the time, in the Plant Facilities Department. Itek was a defense contractor which started off specializing in cameras for satellites and other forms of visual reconnaissance and espionage. The head of the department was up from New Jersey and was renting a room in the attic of the Applin home in Watertown, owned by Herb's grandmother. His brother John worked there as well. Herb had graduated from the University of Maine and later earned a master's degree from Babson Institute in Wellesley. His field was accounting.

After a couple of years at Itek, Herb took a position with Raytheon, also in Lexington. "I started off in accounting, doing budgets and financial planning. I stayed in that for a long time. I retired about 2002, 2003, somewhere in there." It was a 40-hour-a-week position, which – as with Joe's work repairing typewriters – made it difficult for the band to ever travel any considerable distance from Boston. That said, in time, Joe's boss (in John Cooke's words) "recognized that Joe [was] his most valuable employee. When the idea for taking the CRVB to California came up, Joe's boss agreed to let him go."[15] Such was not the case with Herb's employers.

Parenthetically, it's interesting that Herb and his wife Bonnie first met at the Hillbilly Ranch in 1963. Her father had been president of Castleton State College in Vermont and Farmington State Teachers' College in Maine. He had received an honorary degree at the University of Maine in the year when Herb graduated. Bonnie marvels, "Herb passed two feet in front of his future father-in-law." Somewhat later, she and two friends were visiting downtown Boston and had been at an event in Boston's Theater District at what later became known as the Wang Center. "I can't remember why we stopped at the Hillbilly. I didn't drink." She noticed Herb in the background, playing the fiddle and he caught her eye. They got to talking, and Herb invited her to have coffee at the Trailways bus station next door to the Ranch but by the time the show was over, the bus station was closed. "Well, he's harmless," she thought to herself and invited him back to her apartment where she had an electric coffeemaker.[16]

Bonnie's mother taught home economics after graduating from Framingham Normal School before staying home to raise her daughters, Bonnie and Robin Scott.

Herb and Bonnie had been married for 52 years at the time of our 2017 interviews. They have three daughters (who played piano, flute, and tenor sax, one of them also playing guitar at one point.)

Joe & Herb and the Sixties Folk Revival

It was through association with Jim Rooney that Joe and Herb came to be welcomed into the folk music circles of the 1960s. Jim himself had started visiting some of the country music bars in Boston in the early 1950s. "I started hanging out with the Lilly Brothers back in 1952 or 1953 when they were playing those bars like the Mohawk Ranch. There were about four or five of those bars around Boston at the time. There was a group called Ray Bradley and the Tennessee Champs. As soon as Sun Records happened, he was the other half of the nightly presentation. They did rockabilly. That would have been the 50's. When I was on the *Jamboree* in '54, Ray Bradley was on the show at that time. The first place I saw them was a place called the Plaza Bar, which was right on the Common, on Tremont Street. Later, they graduated to the Hillbilly Ranch."[17]

As to Joe Val, Jim said, "I'm sure I saw him on the *Hayloft Jamboree*, when he was part of the Radio Rangers. It was kind of an electric country band. I think I might also have seen him at Bridgewater or at one id those outdoor country parks. I was aware of him as somebody who was around the Hillbilly Ranch."[18]

Jim had started playing music around Cambridge and Boston with banjoist Bill Keith and washtub bass player Fritz Richmond. They had begun playing once a week at the Club 47 on Mt. Auburn Street in Cambridge. "We had just started playing at the Club after it had reopened, after it had been closed for spurious reasons, by the police. It had reopened in January of '62. Bill and Fritz and I had started playing there, once a week. That's what we were doing. Occasionally, Manny [Greenhill] would get us a job."

One night, Rooney said, the three of them played a "little concert for the Community Church" in Boston's Copley Square. "There weren't too many people there, but there was a familiar face in the back row. It was Joe Val. Joe had been on the original *Hayloft Jamboree* as one of the Radio Rangers and had worked on and off with the Lilly Brothers at the Hillbilly Ranch. Joe had definitely paid some dues."[19]

Joe and Herb came up and introduced themselves. We started chatting and said, "Well, we get together every week over at our apartment on Dana Street. You'd be welcome to come by and join us." They picked us up on that suggestion. Herb could play fiddle. He wasn't a great fiddle player, but he could play…that gave us the full band. And Herb had a pretty good high tenor. Both of them could sing way up there. We just started working up trios and some gospel things. Joe's virtuosity immediately shone through and we were doing the 'Mule Skinner Blues' and 'I Hear a Sweet Voice Calling' and things like that. It jelled."[20] The two of them were invited to join Keith & Rooney, which thus became a five-piece band. "We were already billed at the Club as Keith & Rooney," Rooney added. "That didn't change."[21]

With Keith and Rooney now a five-piece band and working up numbers that featured Joe and Herb on vocals, Jim Rooney said, "It was incredible. We could hardly wait to get down to the Club. It was a weeknight, and it was sort of slow. I remember someone saying that we were crazy to expand. We'd never make any money that way. They were right, of course, but we could [not] have cared less, because we suddenly had what we dreamed of – a full bluegrass band – and Joe Val to boot. It was great to watch people's face when he hit those high notes. That was one of the happiest nights of my life."[22]

Keith and Rooney recorded the *Livin' on the Mountain* album for Prestige/Folklore, apparently later in 1962. The album featured both Joe and Herb with Bill, Jim, and Fritz, with fiddler Herb Hooven. Not that long afterwards, Bill Keith left the group. "Bill got a job with Red Allen and Frank Wakefield. After we did our record, Tom Morgan called Bill up and [said they needed] a banjo player. At the time, they were on the *Wheeling Jamboree* and it was a big opportunity to play with a real bluegrass band. So when he went off, it was 'Applin, Val, and Rooney' or something like that on the calendars. We kind of held onto that once-a-week spot without Bill. And then I went to Greece [pursuing academic studies on a

Fulbright scholarship]. At that time, Joe went to the Charles River Valley Boys. I don't know what Herb did."[23]

Joe himself had indeed paid his dues. For the original 1979 publication of the book *Baby, Let Me Follow You Down*, Joe said, "I've played some terrible places in my time. The Hillbilly Ranch was the best of them, and we used to call it 'The Zoo.' But at least they kept it under control. Places like the Novelty Bar were the worst. We'd alternate with a rock and roll band. On a Saturday, we'd start at two o'clock in the afternoon and go until midnight every half hour. On Sunday you'd start at one o'clock in the afternoon and go until one in the morning on the half hour. We got eight bucks apiece. There were fights and knives and bottles. We wouldn't even stay in there on our half hour off." Joe added, "The Mohawk Ranch on the corner of Dartmouth Street and Columbus Avenue was the first place to have hillbilly music – even before the Hillbilly Ranch existed. It was the only place in the word where I had a guy stick a gun in my ribs." Joe detailed what happened. No one was hurt. "I used to go home at night," he wound up, "and my wife would say, 'How'd it go?' and I'd say, 'Oh, things were pretty quiet.'"[24]

Playing at the Club 47 was a "whole different thing" for Joe – a respectful and welcoming audience; people were there to hear the music. "Even though that first time we played to only a few people and only got paid a couple of dollars, it was a joy to play there. It definitely was a turning point for me. I'd put in thirteen or fourteen years in those other places."[25]

When Jim Rooney went to Greece to study the classics, Joe and Herb formed Val and Applin at the Club 47. Joe also joined the Charles River Valley Boys. Their mandolin player, Ethan Signer, left the band to go to "the other Cambridge," the city in England. For much of the rest of the middle to late 1960s, it was CRVB with whom Joe Val played.

Joe got a parting gift from Keith and Rooney, though. "Joe had really captured our hearts. He had what he called his little 'tater bug, an A-model mandolin. He wasn't making money. We all chipped in and for Christmas we got him either an F-4 or F-5 mandolin. I can't remember if it was a 4 or a 5. He played that for quite a while. He just captured all of our hearts. He was such a wonderful person to be around, Funny, and very kind. Never a hard word about anybody. And he had a hard home life."[26]

The Charles River Valley Boys

For a few years, Joe joined the Charles River Valley Boys, one of the mainstays of the Cambridge folk scene. Bob Siggins, the banjo player of the group, says it was Jim Rooney who recommended they hire Joe. The River Boys had changing personnel. Fritz Richmond played the washtub with many musicians in town, but he departed to play with Jim Kweskin and the Jug Band. Taking his place was Everett Alan Lilly, the son of Everett Lilly of the Lilly Brothers. Everett Alan had been raised by his grandparents in West Virginia. He graduated high school in 1963 and came to Boston to work for a year before he figured out how and where he could go to college. Everett Alan ultimately earned a Ph.D. in Social Work at Brandeis University's Florence Heller School, getting his doctorate within blocks of Joe Val's Waltham home.

"I met Herb first," Everett Alan recalls. "Somewhere along the way, that first year, I met Herb Applin. Dad and Bea had already mentioned him – that he was a fine singer. He also worked there occasionally, taking somebody's place. It was soon that I met him, and I met him there. Neither Herb nor I were interested in the place. We were interested in the music and the Lilly Brothers. And Don. I was turning 19. I drank Cokes. I never even thought about having a drink [of alcohol]. It didn't even cross my mind. And I stayed out of everything else there, too. It was totally about the music.

Anyway, I met Herb and, besides being a really nice guy – you could see that he was a friend of my dad and Bea and Don. He was in that little circle. The three of them, they valued his singing. He thought the world of them and just loved their music and what they did. It was very much mutual. And I noticed that he had this clear, high voice that made him more unusual. He stood out. Lot of people came in there, to come up and play a set, but Herb was one of the standouts. He was no ordinary singer.

"I started with the River Boys [the Charles River Valley Boys] in probably September of 1964, a year after I arrived. I think it might have been Joe who called me and asked if I could play bass one night there at Cholmondeley's at Brandeis. I hadn't really met the others – Bob [Siggins] and John [Cooke]. I know Joe had said something to them. I had met Joe before that, probably at the Hillbilly Ranch. He was another one in Bea's and Dad's and Don's circle and somebody they respected. I knew he had a history with them, of playing some with them on the radio. They told me that Joe had been a country musician, playing electric guitar when he met them. Joe told me the very same thing, that he had later become a bluegrass musician. They always saw Joe as another fine musician, and somebody they liked.

"Joe was a real versatile musician. He had that background on the guitar. He was flat out a good musician. Joe was gregarious. He was charming. Everybody liked him. I never met one person who didn't. Never. The women liked Joe. They made that clear. It was his charming way. He never was out of line or anything – and that would have never been my business – but it was very clear that a lot of women liked him. I said to myself, 'Hey, I wish I had some of that charm.'"[27]

Everett Alan very much appreciated the reverence for the music that both Joe and Herb had. "Like Dad, Joe had such high regard for the music. He saw it as precious. Something to keep playing and singing, whether it was fashionable or not. It was the song itself and the tradition behind it. That always showed, even when he and the New England Bluegrass Boys were warming up. It was so heartfelt when Joe and whoever he was singing with did those songs. I felt that with him and Herb. So many times. And I saw that with Dave Dillon. It was the feeling that was in those songs, when they were just warming up. That was the real deal. I don't care where they were from. These guys are the real deal."[28]

The Charles River Valley Boys were very popular in the Greater Cambridge area during the heyday of the folk boom, playing at the Club 47 once a week, usually on Tuesdays or Thursdays. More and more musicians were coming in from afar, with bluesmen such as Son House and Mississippi John Hurt, and white musicians from the south like Clarence Ashley and Hobart Smith. The growing strength of the scene, and similar scenes such as Izzy Young's

Folklore Center and the Friends of Old Time Music in New York, made touring a real possibility both for musicians coming to the Boston area, and for musicians in Boston to be able to travel.

Holding down full-time jobs, Joe (and, though he wasn't with CRVB, Herb) was never as free to travel any significant distance except on some weekends.

A Word from Peter Rowan

The Club 47 was a magnet that drew in people, even those from the area originally, like Peter Rowan who hailed from the Boston suburb of Wayland. When he was 15, his mother would drive him to the subway so he could head into the city and see music at the coffeehouses. When he went off to college at Colgate, he missed the vibrant energy of the scene. Peter wrote some words in appreciation of Joe:

"I first met Joe Val at the old Club 47 on Mount Auburn St. in Harvard Square when Joe was playing with Bob Siggins, John Cooke, and Fritz Richmond as the Charles River Valley Boys. Joe had been singing and playing mandolin with singer-guitarist Jim Rooney and banjo innovator Bill Keith until Rooney took a hiatus to finish his classics studies in Greece. Herb Applin and Joe played as a duet in the New England country music scene and Joe was touring with the Charles River Boys, bringing his wonderful high tenor to the vocal trio with Bob and John.

"Joe and I became friends and my mom would generously drive me to his house in Waltham so that we could sing together, after Joe was home from work at his day-job as a typewriter repair man. When I got my own driving license, I would pick Joe up and bring him out to Wayland and we would sing out by the old barn down by the meadow on warm summer nights. My best friend, Bob Emery (How Banks Fail, Northern Lights) would join us and we would sing trios of Osborne Brothers songs!

"Joe Val was my first Bluegrass music mentor. He saw it as a kind of a sacred duty to teach me the correct melodies and harmony parts to the songs of the Louvin Brothers, Blue Sky Boys, and Monroe Brothers.

Joe devoted so much time to me that that his dear wife Thelma would protest. Joe was tickled when I would sweet-talk dear Thelma into letting Joe out to sing with me and Bob. Joe had a young family and their time together was precious. He was hugely generous with me.

"The subtle intricacies of the old time, Southern brother-duet-singing styles are the roots of bluegrass vocals. Without Joe Val's generous tutoring and friendship I would not have been prepared to join Bill Monroe and the Blue Grass Boys a few years later. I really owe a great deal to Joe who was always a man generous with a musical knowledge that was unique in New England. Joe Val was Boston bluegrass music's first flower!"[29]

Joe and Peter even did some gigs as a duet. "We played at the opening of a drugstore in Chelsea, among other things." It was through Joe, he said that he really started to meet others. "Before, I had really been in awe and hanging on."[30] Peter Rowan went on to forge a life and career for himself in music.

To Newport, Big Sur, and Beyond

In 1965, the Charles River Valley Boys played the Newport Folk Festival. Everett Alan enthused about the experience. It was, he said, "an incredible event...I was tireless. I didn't want to miss anything. Whenever we weren't playing, I was out in the field going to hear Maybelle Carter or Doc Watson or Bill Monroe and Bob Dylan or Joan Baez. As young as I was, I was impressed by the range of music and styles and also by the quality of the music. And then there were the parties in those mansions! Where else could you go and walk among so many truly great musicians!"[31]

That was the summer that Dylan "went electric," at Newport. It's a story that's been told widely (and sometimes a little wildly), but most thoroughly and thoughtfully in Elijah Wald's book with the apt title: *Dylan Goes Electric.*[32] The book's subtitle adds a further dimension which sees it as a dividing line in the evolution of what, to then, had been called "folk music": *Newport, Seeger, Dylan, and the Night That Split the Sixties.* Blues fans had already seen the Paul Butterfield Band "go electric" earlier in the year with their first album, fronting a full Chicago-style blues band with Elvin Bishop and Mike Bloomfield. And Muddy Waters and Howlin' Wolf had already played the Club 47.

The British Invasion was well underway. The Beatles had appeared on *The Ed Sullivan Show* in February 1964. The Rolling Stones did their first American tour in June. New groups formed in America, groups like the Lovin' Spoonful. The Byrds released their first single, "Mr. Tambourine Man," in April 1965. "Folk rock" was beginning to flower. Musical exploration and exhilaration knew no bounds. Looking back, it should perhaps not have been such a surprise that in 1966 the Charles River Valley Boys released *Beatle Country*, their full album of bluegrass renditions of Beatles songs. But it was, for many, a surprise at the time.

Jim Field had taken John Cooke's place in CRVB; John (the son of BBC's American correspondent Alistair Cooke) had gone on the first of a couple of extended trips to California. Two years later, Cooke was helping film Janis Joplin at Monterey, becoming her manager – the same Janis Joplin who had some bluegrass in her past.[33] John recalled the lure that took him west. He had "been playing with the Charles River Valley Boys for almost six years, but the invasion of the British rockers that began in 1964 had changed everything, bringing electric music to the forefront. By '67, even for a well-established bluegrass band, folk music gigs are fewer and farther between."[34]

Beatle Country turned out to be the band's last recording. Bob Siggins invited Jim Fields to take over for John Cooke on guitar and vocals. In a February 1966 show at Winterfest at Boston's War Memorial Auditorium, the band played the Beatles song "I've Just Seen Her Face" and it went over well. Joe himself remembered the reaction: "We were on right before Muddy Waters. We did our show, and the people liked it, but when we hit that song, they went crazy. Paul Rothschild [of Elektra Records] was there and told us to learn some more of those. About a week later, I saw Muddy Waters at the 47, and he said, 'You guys stole the show.'

They recorded the *Beatle Country* album in Nashville in September 1966 and released it late that year. The album did reasonably well, despite being ham-handedly promoted by Elektra as "our first country and western effort."[35]

"I didn't hear too much about it [from purists]," Bob Siggins recalled. "The only flak we got was from Joe Val initially. He was kind of edgy about it. I think he was worried about what some of his friends might say, some of his hardcore bluegrass fans. Our approach was to do it as hardcore bluegrass as we could. And I think that kind of settled his mind on it a bit."[36]

Joe Val was quoted: "Being an old traditionalist, I wasn't too keen on doing a whole record of Beatles songs, but the more they talked to me, the more interested I got. So we learned some more [songs] and made a demo tape in some basement. The next thing we knew, Paul [Rothschild] called and said that Jac Holzman liked the Beatles stuff, but that we'd have to get a whole album's worth. He didn't want to mix it with straight bluegrass. We really put our noses to the grindstone then. Fields really worked on the arrangements. 'Norwegian Wood' is the only song I recorded that my wife liked. The only one."[37]

There were, nonetheless, still opportunities and the Charles River Valley Boys played the Big Sur Folk Festival on a brief California tour in the summer of 1967.[38] There was a lot of nudity at Big Sur, and there were drugs, and Cooke characterizes Joe Val in the midst of this: "Joe likes to play the straight man. The unfettered lunacy of the scene is beyond his wildest imaginings, up to now, but he's got a sense of humor. He takes it all in with a twinkle in his eye, as he tries to stay upwind of the smoke."[39]

One wonders what Joe's wife Thelma would have thought. There was a distance between her and Joe. Eric Levenson, bass player with Joe Val and the New England Bluegrass Boys, even said that Joe "made up stories, like that women didn't go to bluegrass festivals."[40]

There were fewer gigs. The bluegrass festival phenomenon had not yet become established. That the band dissolved in 1968 and the various members each went their own ways is not surprising, given the changing times in music and the broader culture, and the fact that the band members had different career paths to pursue. None ever fully left the music, though, and all love it to this day.

Joe and Herb reunite

While Joe was off with the CRVB, Herb was concentrating on providing for his family – his wife and three daughters – and his career with Itek and then Raytheon. For his musical outlet, he had his own band, the Berkshire Mountain Boys (borrowing the name of his earlier group.) They enjoyed playing music together and performing occasionally, when the opportunity presented itself.

Joe and Herb got back together again for a while, Everett Alan Lilly recalls. "For a little while, Herb and Joe and I had a group, just the three of us. The Old Time Bluegrass Singers. It was Joe's first band, I think, post-Charles River Valley Boys, when we weren't playing regularly. Joe was just beginning to look around and try and get something together that he could lead, because he wasn't about to give up music....

"They lasted for some time, still as the Old Time Bluegrass Singers. I was with them just the first few months, before they decided to move on to other musical things."[41]

Fred Bartenstein is credited for the group changing its name from The Old Time Bluegrass Singers to the superior New England Bluegrass Boys.

Joe Val's Family

Joe had a family, too, of course—Thelma and their two children, Joe and Marie. He was comfortable playing to the Cambridge crowds, often joking, "I went through Harvard, too…and I came out with three overcoats." But there was always a tension between his family life and the music that had taken such hold of him. We note that he said the only recording he ever made that his wife Thelma liked was "Norwegian Wood." Music was in his blood. It took him out of the home, but may also have been his salvation. Everett Alan Lilly recalls, "The first time I heard Joe mention his wife – this is really comical – we were playing someplace right there in Waltham. In a gymnasium, which tells me it was probably a high school gymnasium. One of the early shows I did with them. He walks up to the microphone early in the show – it's going to be one that features him in a solo – and he said something about the 'wahden' – like the warden let him out that time. I laughed to myself. It was really funny, and it was appropriate for the audience. He made it funny. He was never cruel or anything like that. It was a funny joke."[42]

Dave Dillon, in the New England Bluegrass Boys from 1973, recalled, not meaning to be unkind, "I remember him once saying, 'at such-and-such a time period, I was never home.' He was probably as much away from home as anybody could get away with. I had the impression for many years that the two of them really just did not get along."[43]

Thelma may have resented Joe being away from home so often. No one really knows what goes on in a marriage. Joe never "misbehaved" outside the home in any way, and was a good and reliable provider to his family. There were clear indications of unhappiness, and the occasional flareups – such as the time Joe was so angered that he hit a closet door and broke his right hand. Joe's son Joe (they had different middle names) was home at the time. Asked if he thought the music was taking his father out of the house, or did he think his father was getting a break from spending time with his wife, he frankly replied, "I think a little bit of both." He added, "They didn't get along, to be honest."[44] It was kind of difficult, he said. He wished his father had been around more, but knew how much he loved the music and knew that he had a very strong work ethic.

"Joe Junior" – Joseph R. Valiante – never played any instruments, but said, "I'm really into music a lot." What kinds of music? "Beatles. David Bowie, Roxy Music. Neil Young. I could name a whole bunch…." He had been born in 1953. It was the music that his contemporaries liked. Bluegrass? "That's an acquired taste." And yet when Everett Alan Lilly's name came up in the conversation, he enthused, "He was the bass player in the Charles River Valley Boys, but he also played acoustic guitar and he was unbelievable." Did Joe Jr. ever sing? "Oh God, no! I have a horrible voice."[45]

Joe Junior got a job with Hewlett-Packard working with medical equipment as among other things a technician and assembler. He then took a position at a special education school for 10 years, as a job coach, counseling people ranging from teenagers to adults and showing them how to work. Married, with a wife who works in the electronics industry, for the last stretch he has been helping take care of an Alzheimer's patient, helping him to get dressed, to eat, and to go out for walks.

Marie Westerman was Joe and Thelma's daughter. She was born in 1954. She's retired now, but worked from her late teens on, in factories originally but then doing secretarial office work. Everett Alan Lilly remembered her as someone who had some talent on guitar. "My father gave me my first guitar when I was 11," she remembers. "He taught me some chords and I practiced them. I learned things myself, and he taught me things." What kind of music did she play? "Mostly bluegrass. Some pop music." Did she ever sit at home with Joe and sing and play? "Mostly played together. I tried to sing. But I was a smoker and my voice just got weaker."[46] She gave up singing and just kept up playing, but says it's been about 20 years since she picked up a guitar and played.

Marie, like her brother, wishes her father had been around more. "I used to love to play," she said. "I don't know if I had any talent or not." Of her father, she said, "He was gone a lot. It became par for the course."

Her mother liked other kinds of music, but "she wasn't really into music. They were total opposites." Her mother's interests? "Well, she was busy being a mom. She had a lot of health problems. She got sick fairly often." And yet Joe died in 1985, while Thelma lived to age 85, dying in 2014.

Joe's mother outlived Joe, too. Eric Levenson recalls that in Joe's final months, he and Lucille Magliozzi used to help Joe get to his chemo, to his medical appointments in Boston. The took turns driving him. Eric had met Joe's mother. "We went and had dinner with her a couple of different times. I remember when we told her stories about first going to Europe and we stayed in Holland at a thatched-roof house, but the thatch hadn't been properly maintained so it was really cold. It was January and the wind was whistling through. It was no longer a working farm but there was a small stable off the kitchen, under the roof of the house. Until you've slept in the same abode with goats, you don't really know what smell is. She just said, 'Back in the old country, when it was that cold, my parents would send us down to tuck in with the sheep, to stay warm.' She was definitely hale and hearty. I don't remember that she had a strong accent. She made really great lentil soup."

Unfortunately, Joe's two children both died in early 2019. Marie suffered from COPD and died on January 10, 2019. Just five weeks later, her brother Joe died of an apparent heart attack on February 15.

Other Friends

Lucille Magliozzi remembered happier times, "When we first met Joe, Stanley [Zdonik] took us to Passim. He said, 'You've got to hear this guy.' So we went and we heard his band and we were blown away. It was in the early 1970s. That was when Bobby Tidwell was in the band. Bobby sold Tommy [Tom Magliozzi] his bass in my brother's bluegrass band.

"We were great friends. The Magliozzis always used to have this Meals for Millions on Friday nights. Joe and Herbie would come over and just pick tunes with my brothers, who had their own little band. They were always at Raymond's house. A whole lot of people would come and we'd have dinner. Pot luck or whatever. And then the guys would play tunes. That was when my brothers were just starting to get a group together. Everybody would just come and Joe and Herbie would sing some of the most beautiful duets. Joe was just like part of the Magliozzi family."[47]

Tom and Ray became best known as "Click and Clack, the Tappet Brothers," and had their own long-running radio show, *Car Talk*. They also had their own bluegrass band, and occasionally flew to Washington to play at NPR events.

Lucille said that she and Tom shared a love of country music that went way back to days when they went, with some frequency, into Boston to see the *Hayloft Jamboree*.

Joe liked going out to hear music, too, Lucille said. "We used to go to concerts together, to go hear Sonny Terry and Brownie McGhee. I would pick up Joe. He also loved Norman Blake and Nancy. He had a life away from his house. He didn't drive. We were always picking him up. But we didn't pick him up at his house. He would always walk down to these two stone pillars and we would meet him there and leave him off there. His wife was not really all that fond of the whole bluegrass scene and his touring and all, because it took Joe away from home. I always felt like the music was like a wedge between them. She never encouraged him in any way. But thank God he did it anyway!"[48]

Ray Magliozzi said, "It's too bad that Thelma never really embraced his music. It brought him so much joy. And he brought so much joy to others with his music." Ray was living in Vermont in the early 1970s, and recalls that it was in 1972 that Tom had taken Ray to see Joe Val and the New England Bluegrass Boys at Passim. "I didn't even know what bluegrass was. I'd heard 'Foggy Mountain Breakdown' from the *Bonnie and Clyde* movie, but, boy, when I saw Joe that first time, it was like love at first sight. I loved the way they were on stage. I loved their sound."[49]

Ray had two anecdotes to tell about Joe. "Joe and Dave [Dillon], and I don't know who else was in the band at that time – probably Eric – they were playing in New Hampshire at The Stone Church. They were playing there on a weekend, both a Friday and a Saturday night. They had played Friday night and they were on the bill for Saturday night. Joe was standing in line with all the patrons waiting to get in – just as Joe would do. He wasn't about to push himself to the front of the line. He's standing there, kind of listening to the folks in front of him chatting away, and one guy says to his companion, 'Gee, who's playing tonight?' 'I don't know.' And he says, 'I hope it isn't that Joe Val. He sucks.' Joe told us that story and he couldn't stop laughing.

"Joe's voice was unique. Either you loved his voice or it grated on you. There was another time, we had gone to the Escoheag Festival and we had brought along my brother's dog. She was a fabulous dog and she was just lying there, enjoying the attention she was getting and listening to the music. Joe's band came on stage and they started playing 'Freight Train Blues.' When Joe hit those high notes, breaking into his falsetto, the dog started to howl!

And she wouldn't stop. We were trying to grab her muzzle to quiet her down. And every time he hit "freight train blue-hooooooos" – every time he hit that high note – she would howl. Finally we just gave up and everyone just enjoyed it."

Could Joe hear it from the stage? "Oh, he heard it. No disrespect was meant by the dog. It was the kind of thing that Joe would just laugh about."

Joe Val and the New England Bluegrass Boys

In 1969, Joe and Herb combined their talents to reform the Old Time Bluegrass Singers, with Bob French on banjo and Bob Tidwell on bass. Fred Bartenstein, a bluegrass magazine editor and concert promoter attending Harvard at the time, suggested they change their name to Joe Val and the New England Bluegrass Boys.

In October 1971, the first album was released on Rounder: *One Morning in May* (Rounder 0003.) It was, as the number might suggest, the third album in the company's history, and Rounder's first bluegrass record.

Five other Joe Val albums followed:

Joe Val and the New England Bluegrass Boys (Rounder 0025, released August 1975). The album featured Joe, Bob French, and Bob Tidwell, with Dave Dillon on guitar and vocals (Herb, who left the band during the album's production, was on three numbers). Bill Hall played banjo on two tracks. Herb Hooven played fiddle.

*Not A Word from Home (*Rounder 0082, released June 1977). Joe was joined by Dave Dillon, Paul Silvius on banjo, and Eric Levenson on bass.

Bound to Ride (Rounder 0109, released July 1979). The band was the same as *Not A Word from Home*.

Sparkling Brown Eyes (Rounder 0152, released June 1982). Dave Haney took over from Dave Dillon on all but one track. Paul Silvius was on banjo and Eric Levenson was on bass. Sonny Miller played fiddle.

Cold Wind (Rounder 0182, released August 1983). Dave Haney and Eric backed Joe, joined by Karl Lauber on banjo.

Dave Haney, guitar player and co-vocalist on the last two albums, said of Joe and the group, "He didn't 'run' the band – it was always 'us guys' not 'my band' – but Joe Val somehow created a vocal style, a rhythm, and a sense of dynamics that became unmistakably his."[50]

The band was featured in a cover story in *Bluegrass Unlimited* in July 1977. Increasingly, people outside the New England states had the opportunity to hear Joe and his music.

The Hillbilly Ranch closed in 1979.[51]

Joe was, in Eric Levenson's words, "very caring. I think that was why he didn't jam with people; he just didn't like the competitive OK Corral kind of atmosphere, where some other mandolin player would come in and try to out-gun him. That wasn't Joe's style at all." Ray Magliozzi said, "The thing I loved about Joe the most was that he did not have a pretentious bone in his body."[52]

Joe Val, RIP

In the first half of 1984, Joe started feeling bad. The last show he did was in December at Jekyll's Island, Georgia. He talked to friend Bill Dillon before the show, who recalled, "It was obvious he was in great pain. Yet he was a showman all the way so he went out there and tore the house down with that high tenor. They gave him a standing ovation. There never was a man that loved the music business as Joe Val did. He loved the people who loved bluegrass music. From there he went home and to the hospital, where he never arose to pick again."[53]

It was something he'd put off dealing with, perhaps out of stoicism and perhaps for economic reasons. Band member Dave Dillon says, "He just didn't seek medical attention soon enough, and the first doctors he had, from what I heard through the grapevine, weren't the most topnotch ones you could find."[54]

Joe was seriously ill, and exploratory surgery was ordered. Everett Alan Lilly was there. "The doctor told him right after the surgery, 'No cancer, Joe.' But then a little later in that same visit, Joe said, 'I really don't know. I don't know about this.' I knew he was trying to tell me something. I said, 'Joe, you're going to get better.' He said, 'Everett, I'm really not so sure.'"[55]

The initial diagnosis was wrong. Joe had non-Hodgkins lymphoma. Chemotherapy was prescribed. Joe put the best face on everything. He was optimistic to the end. But the illness was taking a toll.

Eric remembered those days. "Lucille and I, toward the end, drove Joe to a number of hospital tests and that sort of thing. Sometimes together.

"One time Lulu and I drove him to one of the downtown hospitals and I remember standing by the reception desk and as Joe was walking down the hall for his test, the look of sympathy that the nurse of the reception station gave us spoke more to where we were at with our friend. We certainly had never talked about that. It might have been very fleeting but it was clear."[56]

Lulu thought back to those days. "We all were great friends, and when Joe got sick, it was horrific. Eric [Levenson] and I did take turns, because Joe's wife didn't drive and his son was working and not available so Eric and I shared taking Joe to all his chemo. I remember when he was really, really sick at the very end. We had run the benefit for him, and I met Joe's doctor and all. The doctor said, "If love could save this man, he would be saved.""[57]

Joe's battle for his life may have helped heal his relationship with Thelma. Eric suggested, "I think Joe and Thelma got along better in the last 4-6 months than they ever had." Lucille agreed. So did Joe's son. They became closer, reconciled in some regards, and had more of an appreciation for each other again. Dave Dillon added, "When Joe passed away, though, you could tell – it took Joe's death, to make it evident – that underneath it all, she did love him. After all, when somebody takes ill, particularly seriously like that, that kind of softens things up. But there has to be an underlying relationship that makes that possible, and that was there and that was good."[58]

As Joe's illness took a turn for the worse, the bluegrass, folk, and country community came together and two benefits were held. The first was on April 18, 1985. Kevin Lynch of Traver Hollow helped organize it and they kicked off the evening, followed by Bob and Dan Paisley and the Southern Grass, Del MCoury, and the Johnson Mountain Boys.[59]

On June 9 a benefit was held at Waltham's Kennedy School. Billed as the Joe Val Benefit and Appreciation Day, as many as 20 groups performed. Herb Applin played with Bea Lilly. John Lincoln Wright, Guy Van Duser and Billy Novick, Peter Wolf, Tom Rush, Tony Rice, Tony Trischka, and Jimmy Gaudreau were among those who appeared. Dutch promoter Rienk Janssen had reportedly raised a couple of thousand dollars in the Netherlands and flown over to the benefit.[60] Some 2,000 people were said to attend, with over $11,000 raised to help with medical bills and to assist Joe's family. Lucille sat at his bedside at University Hospital in Boston and read him the *Boston Globe*'s coverage of the benefit. Joe died two days later, on June 11, 1985. He was 58 years old.[61]

Later in 1985, Joe Val was posthumously inducted into the Massachusetts Country Music Awards Association Hall of Fame. Joe is prominently featured in a display entitled "Legends of Waltham Country Music," which is housed at the Waltham Museum.

The enduring memorial to Joe Val is embodied in the annual Joe Val Bluegrass Festival, presented by the Boston Bluegrass Union each February for 32 years (through 2017) and counting. The event grew out of the Joe Val Appreciation Day benefit. For the first six years, it was a free, one-day festival held on Waltham Common and organized by Joe's friend Dr. Rod O'Neill. Bob Weiser and others presented the festival, moving it to Bentley College in Waltham in 1993. In 1994, the BBU took over the presentation and held it at Leary Field, Waltham that year and in 1995. Leary Field is next to the Kennedy Middle School.

The nonprofit BBU has presented the Joe Val Festival for every year since 1994. Beginning in 1996 and for the next two years, it was a one-day event for which admission was charged at Newton North High School. In 1999, the festival became a weekend-long event, in February. From 1999 through 2002, it was staged at the Dedham Holiday Inn. From 2003 to the present, it has been presented at the Sheraton Framingham on Presidents Day Weekend.

About 1,000 people attend the festival each day. BBU takes over the entire hotel for the run of the festival. Available rooms, divided by floor into picking and quiet camping floors, literally sell out in two minutes once the announcement is made. There are overflow hotels in the area. The festival website is the place to go for the schedule and details on hotels. See http://www.bbu.org/events/joe-val-festival/

The festival has become the premier bluegrass music event in Massachusetts and the country's largest wintertime roots music festival. The weekend typically features around 40 top national and regional bands on two stages, with more than 60 master classes and education workshops, a Joe Val Academy for Kids, and much more.

The Boston Bluegrass Union is a 501(c)3 non-profit, all volunteer organization, dedicated to preserving and promoting this original American music genre. The year 2017 marked the BBU's 40th season and the BBU is the primary source for events, education, and information on bluegrass music in the Northeast. In 2016, the BBU received the prestigious Distinguished Achievement Award from the International Bluegrass Music Association in recognition of their education mission and bluegrass performance events.

Joe Val and the Bluegrass Music Hall of Fame

In September 2018, when told that her brother Joe was being inducted into the Bluegrass Music Hall of Fame, Connie Rando was taken aback and truly pleased: "Get out of here! Oh, really? Oh, my god! Oh, my gosh!"

Joe Val was formally inducted into the Bluegrass Music Hall of Fame in ceremonies at Owensboro, Kentucky on October 18, 2018. The inductees who entered on the same date as Joe were Jake Tullock, Vassar Clements, Mike Seeger, Allen Shelton, and Terry Woodward. The event was part of the Grand Opening Celebration of the Bluegrass Music Hall of Fame and Museum.

Wrapping up

Herb Applin is still with us, of course, and he and his wife Bonnie welcomed me to their home during the course of preparing these notes.

Joe left us more than 30 years ago. For some reason, my single most enduring memory of Joe was the way he ended every phone call we ever had. When it was time to say goodbye, he simply said, "Peace."

--BN

Thanks

Thanks to the following, who shared memories regarding Joe and Herb:

Bonnie Applin
Herb Applin
Fred Bartenstein
Gordy Brown
Dave Dillon
Jim Fields
Mitch Greenhill
Dave Haney
Gerry Katz
Eric Levenson
Everett Alan Lilly
Lucille Magliozzi
Ray Magliozzi
Mike Melford
Millie Rahn
Connie Rando
Jim Rooney
John Rossbach
Peter Rowan
Betsy Siggins
Bob Siggins
Lefty Sullivan
Joe Val "Jr"
Marie Westerman
Stan Zdonik

Endnotes

1. The six children were Eleanor (b.1922 in Dorchester), Joseph (Joe Val, b. 1926 in Everett), Robert (b. 1927 in Framingham), Constance (b. 1932 in Somerville), Nancy (b. 1935 in Somerville), and Paul (b. 1937, also in Somerville.) All places are cities in eastern Massachusetts. In June 1941, Emma Valiante petitioned for naturalization as an American citizen.

2. Interview with Marie Westerman on September 25, 2017. The nearly one-mile long Callahan Tunnel was completed in 1961. It was constructed adjacent to the Sumner Tunnel (completed, 1934), allowing traffic in each tunnel to flow in just one direction. Some 14,500 tons of steel were used in the construction of the Callahan Tunnel. See https://www.bostonglobe.com/specials/insiders/2012/11/07/building-callahan-tunnel/wxqGAgXEeNV2GXTwmRcz3K/story.html

3. Interview with Connie Rando on September 22, 2018.

4. Jeff McLaughlin, "Joe Val: N.E.' Bluegrass Singer, Mandolinist and Bandleaders, at 58," *Boston Globe, June 13, 1985: 92.*

5. There was another Joe Val (no relation), the longtime sports and horse racing editor for the *New York World Telegram*, who was later in charge of establishing the Hall of Fame at Madison Square Garden. He died in 1971 at age 68.

6. Bruce Sylvester, "Joe Val plays it like it is," *Boston Globe,* May 24, 1973: 22.

7. Email from Mitch Greenhill on September 22, 2017.

8. Liner notes, Joe Val and the New England Bluegrass Boys, *One Morning in May* (Rounder 0003). See also interview with Everett Alan Lilly on September 21, 2017.

9. Interview with Connie Rando on September 22, 2018. The 235 Pearl Street home is no longer there; it was torn down and replaced by a duplex.

10 Liner notes by Jim Rooney and Linda Solomon, Bill Keith and Jim Rooney, *Bluegrass: Livin' on the Mountain* (Prestige Folklore 14002). The notes are dated June 1963.

11 Sullivan had a harrowing experience during the war. "I went overboard on this ship during a typhoon. The crew had gone below decks and tied themselves in. The ship was doing somersaults. The waves were 100 feet high and the winds were 150 miles an hour. Everybody had gone below but I was in a motor wheelboat that was hanging on the davits, outside and midships. It would go up and slam against the side. A guy yelled at me to get in and told me to try to get in. He threw me a line and I tried to secure it over the davits but the line broke and I went into the water. I just missed being sucked into the propellers. I was in the water and going up and down and taking an awful beating. The waves would go up 100 feet high and the winds would blow across the top of the waves and slam into me. I was in the water for 3 ½ hours, all alone, scared to death, laying on two jackets. I didn't dare to put them on. I was just laying on them, thinking, "What's it going to be like to die?" I was in the water for 3 ½ hours. There were two destroyers like mine that ran out of fuel and were cut in half by waves. They estimated that about 1,150 sailors – all kids like me – had drowned or been eaten by sharks." Interview with Lefty Sullivan on September 26, 2017.

12 Interview with Lefty Sullivan on September 26, 2017.

13 Interview with Herb Applin on September 15, 2017.

14 Interview with Herb Applin on September 15, 2017.

15 John Byrne Cooke, *On the Road With Janis Joplin* (New York: Berkley, 2014), 43.

16 Interview with Bonnie Applin, September 21, 2017.

17 Interview with Jim Rooney, October 17, 2017.

18 Interview with Jim Rooney, October 17, 2017.
19 Eric Von Schmidt and Jim Rooney, *Baby, Let Me Follow You Down* (Amherst: University of Massachusetts Press, 1994), 139.
20 Interview with Jim Rooney, October 17, 2017.
21 Interview with Jim Rooney, October 17, 2017.
22 *Baby, Let Me Follow You Down*, 140.
23 Interview with Jim Rooney, October 17, 2017.
24 *Baby, Let Me Follow You Down*, 139, 140.
25 *Baby, Let Me Follow You Down*, 140.
26 Interview with Jim Rooney, October 17, 2017.
27 Interview with Everett Alan Lilly, September 21, 2017. In the interview, Everett Alan told of a time the group played the Philadelphia Folk Festival. Joe had to fly down because he had work that day. "I'd driven, so I met him at the airport in Philadelphia. We came back to the motel. Joe was tired. He'd worked all day. Been on an airplane. Things just didn't seem totally right. He really looked as though he was tired. I knew that. Being like my dad and Bea a little bit, I found that comical. And I saw a machine on the bed that if I put a quarter in it, or maybe two, that it would vibrate the bed.

Joe just needed to lay down and rest for a while. That's how I knew he was really dog tired. He was on the bed and I slipped two quarters in, as a joke. And that bed started shaking, like freight trains going through an earthquake. Noisy, too! Joe yelled, 'Mother of Christ! What the hell is this?'

"I'm keeping a straight face, somehow. 'Gosh, Joe. I don't know. How're you going to sleep? This is terrible.'

"'I won't put up with this! I'm going to go down and talk to them.' At which point, I pointed to the machine and said, 'Joe, I pulled your leg.' He settled down, rested a while, and all was well."

28 Interview with Everett Alan Lilly, September 21, 2017.
29 Email from Peter Rowan, October 17, 2017.
30 *Baby, Let Me Follow You Down*, 210.
31 *Baby, Let Me Follow You Down*, 249-250.
32 Elijah Wald, *Dylan Goes Electric* (New York: Dey Street, 2016).
33 Indeed, the biographical information submitted by Janis to Big Brother manager Albert Grossman, and printed in the press release to announce Columbia's signing of the group included the phrase "Sang country music and blues with an Austin, Texas bluegrass band." The press release is reprinted on page 121 of *On the Road With Janis Joplin*.
34 *On the Road With Janis Joplin*, 17.
35 From Elektra co-producer Peter K. Siegel's liner notes to the Rounder Records 1995 reissue of *Beatle Country*, Rounder SS-41.
36 http://www.richieunterberger.com/charles.html
37 *Baby, Let Me Follow You Down*, 274.
38 They also played the Berkeley Folk Festival, the Jabberwock in Berkeley, and the Ash Grove in Los Angeles. At the Berkeley Folk Festival, the CRVB followed Country Joe and the Fish and preceded Doc Watson in the festival's grand finale.
39 *On the Road With Janis Joplin*, 48. Joe expressed worry he might get "arrested for being in company with a bunch of potheads" and chose to "keep himself at a safe remove from the goofy hippies his bluegrass cohorts have become." See page 51, 52.

40 Interview with Eric Levenson, September 17, 2017.
41 Interview with Everett Alan Lilly, September 21, 2017.
42 Interview with Everett Alan Lilly, September 21, 2017.
43 Interview with Dave Dillon, September 18, 2017.
44 Interview with Joe Valiante, October 2, 2017.
45 Interview with Joe Valiante, October 2, 2017.
46 Interview with Marie Westerman, September 25, 2017.
47 Interview with Lucille Magliozzi on October 5, 2017.
48 Interview with Lucille Magliozzi on October 5, 2017.
49 Interview with Ray Magliozzi on October 6, 2017.
50 Dave Haney, "Joe Val," *Bluegrass Unlimited,* July 1985: 7.
51 See Ernie Santosuosso, "Hillbilly Ranch Losing Homestead," *Boston Globe,* February 11, 1977: 37, and Steve Morse, "Hillbilly to Bite Dust," *Boston Globe,* February 9, 1979: 27.
52 Interview with Ray Magliozzi on October 6, 2017.
53 Bill Dillon, "Joe Val Remembered," *Bluegrass Unlimited,* October 1985: 41. Bill Dillon and Dave Dillon were not related.
54 Interview with Dave Dillon, September 18, 2017.
55 Interview with Everett Alan Lilly, September 21, 2017.
56 Interview with Eric Levenson, September 17, 2017.
57 Interview with Lucille Magliozzi on October 5, 2017.
58 Interview with Dave Dillon, September 18, 2017.
59 Dave Haney, "A Beautiful Gesture – The Joe Val Benefit Concert," *Bluegrass Unlimited,* June 1985: 75.
60 He had helped bring the New England Bluegrass Boys to Europe four times, and released a live album on his Strictly Country label. Dan Paisley played guitar and shared vocals on the live LP.

61 "Local Music Community to Salute Joe Val," *Boston Herald,* June 6, 1985: 17, and "J. P. 'Joe Val' Valiante, Bluegrass Band Leader," *Boston Herald,* June 13, 1985.

"Rank Stranger"
—The Stanley Brothers (1960)

By David W. Johnson

Every so often a song connects with deep emotions that keep the song alive in our musical consciousness for decades. Much of the power stems from the song itself, but a memorable cover version can make a difference. The Stanley Brother's cover version of the Albert E. Brumley composition "Rank Strangers to Me" had this effect on the original song, increasing its cultural significance by connecting it to new audiences.

Sentimental Song

"Rank Strangers to Me" was one of songwriter Albert Brumley's "sentimental" songs. It touched on powerful emotions, but was not explicitly religious. Brumley made his name as a writer of Southern gospel songs – called "Southern" to distinguish this branch of gospel music from the works of Black gospel songwriters such as Thomas A. Dorsey, who wrote "Peace in the Valley." He went on to become "the most popular Southern gospel writer of all time,"[1] but when he wrote "Rank Strangers to Me," he was a staff songwriter at Eugene M. Bartlett's Hartford Music Company in Hartford, Arkansas, earning $12.50 a month.[2]

By the time Brumley wrote "Rank Strangers to Me," he had composed the gospel classics "I'll Fly Away," "I'll Meet You in the Morning," and "Turn Your Radio On." The Stamps-Baxter Music and Printing Company first published "Rank Strangers to Me" in its 1942 songbook Super Specials No. 5. Publishers of Southern gospel music sponsored singing schools at Christian churches in order to increase the demand for songbooks. Gospel singers flocked to schools, camps, and "conventions" – public gatherings organized by church-going people who shared a love of singing.

Gospel Connection

In his autobiography, *Man of Constant Sorrow,* Ralph Stanley recalled the first time he and his older brother Carter listened to Brumley's song. "We were driving to a show, listening to the radio, when we heard the Willow Branch Quartet doing a song called 'Rank Stranger.' There was something there that grabbed Carter and me. We'd never heard that term 'Rank Stranger' before. . ."[3]

Ralph approved of the Willow Branch Quartet's version of the song, but "wanted to make it different. Carter and me worked out a whole new arrangement . . ." He added, "I never heard a thing about the Willow Branch Quartet since we heard them sing that Sunday morning. . ." Changing an arrangement was a way musicians could claim a song as their own. In the competitive world of old-time country and bluegrass, professionals were reluctant to acknowledge the influence of other musicians, but it was unavoidable.

The Willow Branch Quartet appears to have influenced the Stanley Brothers. Both groups made music in the same city during the same years. Both performed on radio. Carter and Ralph appeared on the "Farm and Fun Time" program on Bristol station WCYB. The Quartet had sung in churches and on radio since 1952, and released 78 rpm records between 1954 and 1956 and 45's in 1956-1957. These are now collector's items. The Quartet took its name from the Willow Branch Baptist Church in Bristol and was well-known in the region, recording "Rank Strangers" (with an "s") in 1955.[4] Also suggesting influence is the vocal arrangement on the Stanley Brothers' 1959 recording of the gospel standard "Cold Jordan," which is identical to the Quartet's arrangement recorded in 1956-1957.

When Ralph and Carter heard "Rank Strangers" on the car radio, they were listening to one of the hour-long religious programs broadcast Sunday afternoons by station WFHG in Bristol, or to a Saturday gospel sing broadcast from a school auditorium. The Willow Branch Quartet were frequent guests on the Sunday programs and participated in gospel sings. "Rank Strangers" was one of the Quartet's most requested songs. "They had a good version on it," recalled former neighbor Marvin Harlow. "I saw them sing it many, many times. It was a hit for them, too. That's where Carter and Ralph got it."[5]

The Quartet's original members were Wilda Dillon Combs, soprano and lead singer; Wilda's mother, Ettie Dillon, alto; J. C. Leonard, tenor; and Harold Shaffer, bass. Mother and daughter singing together gave the group the distinctive sound of family voices harmonizing. They sang in the old Baptist style. Wilda (sometimes Ettie) would sing a line that was repeated by two or more vocalists before the group went on to the next line.

What made the group exceptional was its lead singer's voice. "Wilda Dillon sang different than anybody I ever heard," Marvin Harlow recalled. "The closest to her was Dolly Parton." Two records by the Quartet appear to have influenced the Stanley Brothers' version of "Rank Stranger." One was the Quartet's recording of the song, and the other was their arrangement of the gospel song "Rest at the End of the Road." On "End of the Road," Wilda sang the first line of the chorus in a loud, piercing voice that sounded like Ralph singing the first line of the chorus on "Rank Stranger." The first lines have the same syllable count and both versions drop the second verse of Brumley's original.

Life in Florida

The year 1960 was a balancing act for the Stanley Brothers. The brothers and their sidemen, the Clinch Mountain Boys, recorded for two record labels that year. Carter and Ralph had a contract with Starday Records in Nashville, but in September 1958, Carter approached King Records in Cincinnati for a deal. Starday agreed to release the brothers if they recorded twenty-four more sides for the label – enough material for two albums.[6]

As performers, Carter and Ralph were making the best money of their careers. Two years before, they had struggled to make a living performing in baseball fields, drive-in theaters, and outdoor music parks. To improve their prospects, they needed to leave their native Virginia. Ralph Stanley summed up: "We had to move somewhere because we felt like we was wore out around Bristol."[7]

Offered a spot on the *Suwannee River Jamboree* radio program broadcast on Saturday night from Live Oak, Florida, the brothers took the opportunity. They moved to Live Oak in 1958, Their time on the *Jamboree* was short, but led to finding a sponsor.

The Jim Walter Corporation built shell homes that it sold to first-time buyers who planned to finish them. The Stanley Brothers and Clinch Mountain Boys promoted Jim Walter homes by hosting a radio show, performing on television, and playing at Sunday open houses. On their own time, they performed all over the state.

Live Oak is in northern Florida, halfway between Jacksonville and Tallahassee. For two brothers raised in southwestern Virginia, forsaking the mountains of Appalachia for the flatlands of Florida made them feel like outsiders. They joined a church and tried to fit in. Ralph's wife began to work at the local diner. Their sideman George Shuffler took a room in Live Oak for several years, renting a house so he could bring his wife and children to Florida. "They didn't like it and went back to the mountains," George recalled.[8] He took up fishing. When the musicians had days off, they hung out at the gas station across from the post office.

Life in Florida was not Carter and Ralph's first experience with alienation. In 1953, as the demand for personal appearances dried up, they followed a path many Appalachian men took, heading north to Michigan to work for the Ford Motor Company. Not knowing anyone else in the Detroit area, the brothers were frequent visitors to the apartment of a family from Dickenson County who moved to Michigan the previous year.[9] According to Ralph, the time in Michigan "was just for a while, to get some regular paychecks to tide us over. It may have been only for a few months, but it felt like a life sentence to me."[10]

At a performance in Live Oak, two young entrepreneurs, Tom Markham and Tom Rose, approached Carter and Ralph about recording at their new studio in Jacksonville.[11] The timing was right. The brothers needed to make good on their agreement with Starday. They had been with Columbia and Mercury, but when record sales did not meet expectations, neither company renewed their contract. Recording for major labels, the brothers worked with experienced producers and engineers in well-equipped facilities. Magnum Studios in Jacksonville was a twenty-by-twenty space in a wooden garage with a concrete slab floor.

At the end of May or in early June 1960, the Stanley Brothers spent three nights in the studio with sidemen Curley Lambert on guitar and mandolin, and Ralph Mayo on fiddle and guitar. Mayo also played with the Webster Brothers in Alabama and brought in bassist Audie Webster for the session.[12] Recording at Magnum, the brothers made do, moving microphones around until they got the sound they wanted. They recorded fifteen or twenty songs, choosing twelve to send to Starday. One of the songs was "Rank Stranger."

The Definitive Recording

The Stanley Brothers dropped the middle verse of Albert Brumley's composition to shorten "Rank Stranger" to a standard length for a 45 rpm record – about three minutes. Format and length were tailored to jukebox play and radio broadcasts. Carter and Ralph were not the first bluegrass musicians to record the song. In November 1959, mandolin player Jimmy Williams and his partner Marvin "Red" Ellis on guitar recorded "Rank Strangers to Me" and three other songs at Red's studio in Ypsilanti, Michigan. Their version was about three minutes, with a mandolin introduction and an instrumental break between verses. The Stanley Brothers' arrangement is similar.

On the definitive version, Curley Lambert's ascending mandolin riff kicks off the song. Carter sings the first verse in a wistful voice as the group hums in the background. Ralph sings the first line of the chorus at the volume of a shout. *Everybody I met/ seemed to be a rank stranger. . .* Here the word *rank* means total or complete – perhaps a meaning from Albert Brumley's roots in Oklahoma or Arkansas. Ralph's voice sounds pained, almost angry. It turns the song away from the nostalgic thoughts of a wanderer to an expression of alienation.

Carter sings the remaining three lines of the chorus with an edge. As the group repeats each line, Ralph's voice rises above the others. After Ralph Mayo's crisp guitar break on the turnaround to the second verse, Carter returns to his wistful voice as group members hum behind him. Ralph enters just as loud on the second chorus, adding emphasis to his emotion by holding the last note. Several mandolin flourishes accent the verses.

Every element in this version of "Rank Stranger" is familiar to folks who know the music of the Stanley Brothers, except the one that makes the song unique among the brothers' recordings – the deliberate contrast between Carter's gentle singing of the verses and Ralph's piercing wail on the chorus. Ralph recalled what he and Carter had in mind. "We wanted it to be like somebody surprising you from behind. Like somebody waking you up and everything seems different and you don't know if you're awake or still dreaming.[13]

"Rank Stranger" was a good fit for the Stanley Brothers. Early in their careers, Carter wrote songs that evoked similar feelings of melancholy and loss, notably "The White Dove" and "The Fields Have Turned Brown." In both, the singer's parents passed away. In "The Fields Have Turned Brown," a prodigal son returns home to find the homeplace abandoned. *But now they're both gone/ this letter just told me/ For years they've been dead,/ the fields have turned brown.*

When recorded in 1960, the Stanley Brothers' version of "Rank Stranger" did not seem as special as it does today. The recording was made without a professional engineer or producer. The recordings from the session sounded thin, and recording levels varied. The genius of the brothers was in keeping the arrangement simple – three voices, two guitars, a bass, and mandolin. The instrumentation supported Carter and Ralph's vocals without intruding.

Released as a 45 rpm single and on the album *Sacred Songs of the Hills,* the Stanley Brothers' recording of "Rank Stranger" introduced a song from the Southern gospel tradition into the repertoire of country music and bluegrass. Country royalty covered the song. Carl Story, known as "The Father of Bluegrass Gospel Music," recorded "Rank Stranger" in 1963. Kitty Wells, "Queen of Country Music," covered it in her straightforward style. Nashville traditionalist Ricky Skaggs included "Rank Stranger" on his 1997 tribute to old-time country and bluegrass, *Bluegrass Rules.* In the early 1970s, Ricky sang with the Clinch Mountain Boys alongside Ralph Stanley.

Ralph wrote in his autobiography, "I reckon it became the most popular song the Stanley Brothers ever sung. They holler for it everywhere I've ever played . . . I don't care where we've been in the world, if I mention 'Rank Stranger' on the stage, you're going to hear from the crowd. . . . It's one of those songs you know will always be sung somewhere, by somebody."[14] Other versions keep the song alive, but most listeners are drawn to the definitive recording.

David W. Johnson is the author of *Lonesome Melodies: The Lives and Music of the Stanley Brothers*. He is grateful for the assistance of Pastor Gary Combs, the son of Wilda Dillon Combs; Gary B. Reid, author of *The Music of the Stanley Brothers*; and Marvin Harlow, who knew the Stanley Brothers and Willow Branch Quartet.

Endnotes

1. Don Cusic, *The Sound of Light: A History of Gospel and Christian Music*, Hal Leonard Corporation, 2002, p. 158.
2. *I'll Fly Away: The Life Story of Albert E. Brumley*, Kay Hively and Albert E. Brumley, Jr., Mountaineer Books, 1990, p. 41.
3. Dr. Ralph Stanley with Eddie Dean, *Man of Constant Sorrow: My Life and Times*, Gotham Books, 2009, p. 384.
4. Gary Combs, e-mails to the author, August 28-September 18, 2020.
5. Interview with Marvin Harlow, August 20, 2020.
6. Personal communication from Gary B. Reid, author of *The Music of the Stanley Brothers*, University of Illinois Press, 2015.
7. Gary B. Reid, "The Stanley Brothers in Florida," *Florida Bluegrass News*, March-April 1985, Vol. 1, No. 2.
8. Interview with George Shuffler, July 6, 2007.
9. David W. Johnson, Lonesome Melodies: *The Lives and Music of the Stanley Brothers*, University Press of Mississippi, 2013, p. 114.
10. Ralph Stanley with Eddie Dean, *Man of Constant Sorrow*, p. 174.
11. Gary B. Reid, notes to *The Stanley Brothers: The Early Starday and King Years*, p. 12.
12. Personal communication with Gary B. Reid.
13. Dr. Ralph Stanley with Eddie Dean, *Man of Constant Sorrow*, p. 384.
14. Ralph Stanley with Eddie Dean, *Man of Constant Sorrow*, p. 384.

International Country Music Journal 2021

The Legendary Phipps Family -The Old-Time Country Music Singing Family of Kentucky

Kenichi Yamaguchi
Japanese Scholar

1. Greatness of the Carter Family

Before I refer to the Phipps Family, I will address the greatness of the Carter Family first, because the Phipps Family was greatly influenced by the Carters. Needless to say, the Carter Family played great roles in the popular music fields in the US. I review their greatness through these aspects; their nicknames or titles, complete collections of their works, the movie and play of the family story and so on.

1.1 The Great "Titles" of the Carter Family

For the Carter Family's great achievements, a society and several scholars gave titles to the family as follows.
"The First Family of Country Music"
 "Country Music Hall of Fame" in 1971
"The Patron Saints of Traditional Country Music"
John Adkins / "Stars of Country Music",
Edited by Bill C. Malone and Judith McCulloh, p95
"The Royal Family of Country Music"
 Fred Sokolow / "The Carter Family Collection"
"The First Superstar Group of Country Music"
  Frank M. Young & David Lasky / "The Carter Family, Don't Forget This Song"
"Their Recordings Are as Elemental as the Wind or Water"
 Charles Wolfe / "In the Shadow of Clinch Mountain," Bear Family

1.2 Great Collections of the Carter Family

There were two great collections of LPs and CDs of the Carter Family. In past years, it was not uncommon that complete albums featured one artist or a group were released. What a surprise! This 10-LP collection was released by RCA Victor Japan, far from the homeland of country music, in 1974 (Fig. 1). It was the first complete collection of the Carter Family in the world.

Twenty-six years later, a 12-CD set of theirs was released by Bear Family in Germany. I thought these two achievements showed that The Carters did really great work.

1.3 Musical and Movie of the Cater Family

The musical play, "Keep on the Sunny Side", the songs and story of the original Carter family, was first performed at the Barter Theatre in Abingdon, Virginia in 2002. It was written by Dr. Douglas Pote, a local physician, to pay homage to country music's first family. The play beautifully portrayed their life and struggles through the use of their music. It was often performed at the Theatre until around in 2010. It also entertained over 100,000 people by touring to 23 states in 2004-05. The Carter Family Fold in Hiltons, Virginia, and Barter Theatre presented six performances of the play at the Carter Family Fold during the last week in May and the first week in June, 2015.

One of the friends of the International Country Music Conference (ICMC , Ms. Beth Harrington, filmed a great movie "The Winding Stream" (Fig. 2). This was a 90-minute music history documentary that tells the story of the American roots music dynasty, the Carters and the Cashes. This saga was performed by celebrated roots music practitioners like Johnny and June Carter Cash, George Jones, Rosanne Cash, Sheryl Crow, Kris Kristofferson and others. It was shown at various cities in the United States and Canada in 2014 and 2015.

1.4 Effects on Folk Music Revival Movement

The music of the Carter Family influenced the folk music revival movement in the late 50's to early 60's. Woody Guthrie and Bob Dylan wrote songs using the old Carter Family's songs. In the case of Guthrie, he used the the Carter Family song melodies "When the World's On Fire," "Wildwood Flower," "John Hardy" and "This World Is Not My Home" for his songs "This Land Is Your Land," "Ruben James," "Tom Joad" and "I Ain't Got No Home" respectively. Bob Dylan also wrote "Palms of Victory" with the melody of "Wayworn Traveler."

Joan Baez sang a lot of the Carter's songs like "Wildwood Flower," "Little Moses," "Engine 143," "Little Darling, Pal of Mine," and "Gospel Ship" in her early albums. The Carter Family strongly influenced such great folk music heroes; therefore folk music fans all over the world recognized the greatness of the Carters.

1.5 Tributes and Followers

I now introduce the tribute records and followers to the Carter Family.

As seen in Fig 3, lots of singers and groups have released tribute LPs and CDs since the 1950s. These include Flatt & Scruggs,

Bill Clifton, Red Clay Ramblers, Antique Persuasion and other and there are several followers of the Carter Family. For example, the Phipps Family, who is the subject of this paper, the DeBusk-Weaver Family and the Romaniuk Family. Their musical style is like the original Carter Family and their repertoires contain lots of the Carter Family songs.

The first, the DeBusk-Weaver Family, consists of father, mother, son-in-Law and daughter. Their roots go back to southeast Virginia. They moved to Pennsylvania in 1960. Their Folkways release, "Meeting in the Air" was recorded at Bristol exactly 50 years later to the day of the first recording of the Carter Family.

The next follower is the Romaniuk Family. This family consists of Ed Romaniuk and his sisters. They grew up in Edson, Alberta in Canada. They had often visited A. P. Carter since 1957. They released a couple of the Carter Family style LPs (Fig. 4). So they're known as "the Canadian Carter Family".

There are followers of the Carters even in Japan. These are the bands of "We love the Carter Family" that I know.

Lassie, since 1971, Kyoto

Green Mountain. Boys, since 1971, Hyogo

Yagi-Tako, since 2009, Tokyo

640 Family Band, since 1979, Nagano

They will be promoting the Carter Family music in Japan from now on.

Next I would like to introduce the achievements of the Phipps Family which have been buried in the past for a long time.

2. Music Background of the Phipps Family

2.1 Hometown - Barbourville, Kentucky

Before introducing the Phipps Family, I will discuss their hometown Barbourville, Kentucky, their singing family tradition and their relationship with the Carter Family.

Their hometown Barbourville is in Knox County, near the southeastern corner of Kentucky. The county is one of the few coal-producing counties in Kentucky. Barbourville is the seat of the county. It lies on the Cumberland River, in the Cumberland Mountains, and is a gateway to Daniel Boone National Forest. The town was explored by Daniel Boone in 1775 and was founded in 1800 and named for James Barbour, who donated land for the town site. It turned into a battlefield during the Civil War in 1861. The current population is about 3,200. Fig. 5 is a view of the downtown taken by me in 2011. And Fig. 6 is Lovell Baptist Church which the family was the members of. Their house was near this church.

2.2 Singing Family Tradition

A.L., Arthur Leroy, Phipps, was born in 1916. His father was a singing school master and a preacher of a Baptist Church. The family organized the Phipps Family Quartet and sang at Churches, Conventions and Other Public Gatherings.

Kathleen Helton was born in 1924. She helped her parents on their farm. She joined in mother's old style family singing in her spare time, playing the guitar.

One day, A. L. attended a musical party at the Heltons. This was the first meeting for A.L. and Kathleen. They got married in 1937. Music became a large part of their lives. They decided to perform as a family singing group, together with Arthur's niece, Hester Anderson. Their debut took place at a high school in Highsplint in Kentucky, in 1942 and they started doing local performances at schools and churches. Gradually they began to appear on regular radio programs as WCPM in Middlesboro, WCTT in Corbin and WYWY in Barbourville. They were aired on the Mid-Day Merry-Go-Round at WNOX in Knoxville, Tennessee too. At times, the family was guests on more stations such as WWVA.

They received so many requests for Carter Family songs, they increasingly adopted the Carter Family style singing.

2.3 Relationship with the Carters

When the Phipps Family sang the Carter's songs at various places, A.P. Carter came back to the music stage with Sara, Janette and Joe again. They released a few records from ACME Records.

The Phippses first visited the Carters in Maces Spring, VA, in 1953. It is 100 miles between their homes. Since then the Phipps family often played at A. P. Carter Music Park. A couple of pictures of two families like Fig. 7 can be often seen in the books about the Carter Family. And A.P. Carter recommended A.L. Phipps to record songs for ACME.

A.P. wanted to do music activities more often, but he couldn't because Sara had to return to California and Janette had to look after her little babies. So A.P. asked A.L. to play together. They often booked and advertised several show dates together.

They once tape-recorded a show at Manchester Kentucky in 1954. This was released later as an LP from Mountain Eagle Label (Fig. 8). This is really precious because some A.P. Carter's solo singings and his stories of his career are included on this record.

3. Singing Family Activities

The radio programs of the Phipps family had been gradually spreading widely in the States. Then the music activities of the family had become more active. They recorded and released records on Acme, Starday, Folkways and so on.

The Phipps Family played at many historical music events like the Newport Folk Festival, Chicago Folk Music Festival, Festivals in Washington DC and others.

3.1 Recordings of the Phipps Family

1) ACME

The first record was from Janet, affiliated with ACME. As mentioned above, A.P. Carter advised A.L. Phipps to record for ACME. The owner of ACME was Reverend Clifford Spurlock and the A.P. Carter Family made their last waxing there in 1956.

A.L. asked A. P. what songs to record. As a result, the Phipps Family recorded 4 songs on 2 45s. These two disks were released around 1960.

Janet-210 Just Enough for Me / Daddy Is Mama Coming Home

Janet-211 Little Poplar Log House / We Shall Meet Beyond the River

A.L. sent these records to some 50,000 watts radio stations.

2) Starday

With radio programs and sending promotion records, the Phipps Family was beginning to become popular in the States. Some major record companies in Nashville asked A.L. Phipps to record on their labels and he finally signed on Starday Records. Since the Phipps Family was recognized to be the closest interpreter of the music of the Carter Family, two LPs of the three were all composed of the Carter's songs.

SLP 139 / Most Requested Songs of the Carter Family (1961-07)

SLP 248 / Echoes of the Carter Family (1963-11)

And the third featured their Appalachian folk songs.

SLP 195 / Old Time Mountain Pickin' & Singin' (1962)

3) Folkways

The next record was from Folkways. This was supported by Ralph Rinzler. Before this recording they performed at the Newport Folk Festival in 1964 and came to New York to record for Folkways on their way back from Newport. This record included ballads, traditional hymns, the Carter Family's songs and two originals which were Kathleen's "Forsaken Lover" and A. L.'s "The Red Jacket Mine Explosion". The songs in the LP were selected carefully, consulting with Ralph. It was released in 1965.

Folkways FA 2375 / The Phipps Family

4) Oscar Brand's Radio Program "The World of Folk Music"

While they were in New York to record for Folkways, Oscar Brand interviewed A.L. for Oscar's radio program, the World of Folk Music. This radio program was a series of 15 minute shows, sponsor by the U.S. Department of Health, Education and Welfare. A series of 15min recordings of lots of artists were featured in the series. Some of these were the Clancy Brothers, Bob Dylan, Phil Ochs, Jean Ritchie, Hedy West, the Stanley Brothers and so on.

The program of the Phipps Family was broadcast on November 2 in 1964. They sang "I Will Never Marry" and "Way Over in the Promised Land".

5) Pine Mountain

The three albums, released by Starday Records between 1961 and 1963 sold well initially, the sales eventually declined. Starday deleted their three albums from its catalogue. A.L. tried to sell them again, so he started his own label "Pine Mountain" in 1966. The name of the label was from a ridge of the Appalachians near their home place. The three LPs of Starday recordings were re-pressed by Pine Mountain Records.

PMR-139 / Most Requested Sacred Songs of the Carter Family
PMR-195 / Old Time Mountain Pickin' and Singin'
PMR-248 / Echoes of the Carter Family

During the next decade, the Family recorded eight original albums. They were composed of thematic albums of Christmas and Easter season numbers, a cappella mountain hymns, and so on (Fig.

9). A.L., Kathleen, and Truleen Helen, sons Leeman and Bowlin along with daughters Louella and Donna appeared on them.

PMR-125 / Greatest Old Time Gospel Hymns, Featuring the Phipps Family

PMR-126 / Sings about the Suffering, Crucifixion, and Resurrection of Christ

PMR-127 / Only through Grace - Early American Singing

PMR-128 / Christmas with the Phipps Family

PMR-129 / Give Me the Roses While I Live

PMR-130 / In the Sweet Bye and Bye

PMR-131 / Sings 'Em Mountain Style

PMR-134 / Just a Few More Days

Two of old ACME recordings of the Carter Family also were re-released by the Pine Mountain label.

PMR-206 / A. P. Carter's Clinch Mountain Ballads

PMR-207 / Their Last Recording

6) Mountain Eagle

A.L. started another label, Mountain Eagle and, as far as I know, released three special albums from this label. The first was recorded exactly 50 years later since the Carters' first recording. They recorded it in Bristol as the original Carter Family did.

MER-135 / the Phipps Family, Records in Bristol

This included the same 6 songs as the famous Bristol Sessions by the Carter Family in 1927.

The second was with Helen Carter, recorded at the house of Johnny Cash in Nashville.

MER-136 / Hills of Home, the Phipps Family with Helen Carter

The final was with A.P. Carter. It was based on the tape-recorded material in 1954, as shown at 2.3.

MER-137 / A. P. Carter and the Phipps Family

It was unknown why A. L. had two different labels, Pine Mountain and Mountain Eagle.

3.2 Historical Music Events of the Phipps Family

The family not only released a lot of records, but also appeared in various music events across the United States.

1) Newport Folk Festival, 1964

The first festival where they performed was the Newport Folk Festival in 1964. Around this time, old American folk songs were appreciated by the younger generation in the city, and it was a time of a folk music revival. Ralph Rinzler invited the Phipps Family. He visited their home in Kentucky in the winter of 1963 and signed them for the Newport Festival.

The program of the Festival is shown in Fig. 10. They performed four times on the stage by the beautiful harbor in Rhode Island, from Thursday through Sunday. "Helen" Truleen Phipps was 16 years old then. She was featured by a local newspaper (Fig. 11).

Vanguard Records released 2 albums including their performances. They were "Traditional Music 1964, Part 2" and "Evening Concerts Vol. 2" (Fig. 12). These 2 albums made them famous in the world.

2) Chicago Folk Music Festival and Urban Folk Festivals

Following the Newport Folk Festival, the Phipps Family was invited to the University of Chicago Folk Festival. The festival was held during February 3-5 in 1965 (Fig. 13).

Through the efforts of Ralph Rinzler and Mike Seeger, the Family was invited to a lot of events during the urban Folksong revival movement. Some were University of Pennsylvania and Delaware, Henry Ford Museum in Michigan, Local Festivals at Barbourville's Union College, Brandywine Mountain Music Convention and so on.

3) Festivals in Washington DC

The Family was often invited to the national events of American folk-life in Washington DC. The first was the Smithsonian Folklife Festival in 1973. Some of their performances there were archived through the great efforts of Berea College. They performed:

Sinless Summerland / He Is With Me All the Way

Blessed Jesus Loves You Too / Wonderful Jesus

Can the Circle Be Unbroken?

The other event was the Festival of American Folklife. They were invited twice, in 1976 and 1984 (Fig. 14). One of the local newspaper companies in Kentucky proudly reported their activity at the capital city of the United States (Fig. 15).

4) Cumberland Valley Folk Festival - Barbourville, Kentucky

A. L. Phipps started and hosted his own folk music festival at the Family's hometown in Barbourville. He must have absorbed a lot of know-how by attending many music events in the States. He named it "Cumberland Valley Folk Festival" and held it three times, in 1978, 1979 and 1980. He invited famous guests including the Bailey Brothers, Clint Howard, Roscoe Holcomb, Roy Harper, Wade Mainer and Charlie Bailey, Gloria Belle and others.

He released a compilation album recorded at the festival in 1978 (Fig. 16). Berea College archived some of their performances too.

Little Black Train, 1979
Old Cottage Home, 1979
We Will March through the Streets of the City, 1979
God Leads Us Along, 1979

5) Celebration of Traditional Music and Symposium at Berea College

Berea College did a great job for preservation of traditional music. They organized symposiums annually. In two of them, the Celebration of Traditional Music (CTM), and the Symposium on Rural Hymnody, the Phipps Family played and the College recorded and archived lots of their performances. Some of them can be seen on video

a) CTM began in 1974 by Berea College Appalachian Center. The Phipps Family played and was recorded on November 8, 1974.

Church in the Wildwood / Cyclone of Rye Cove
When the Sunset Turns the Ocean Blue to Gold
Bury Me under the Weeping Willow

b) The Symposium on Rural Hymnody at Berea College. They played and were recorded on 4-28-'79.

Church in the Wildwood / Glory to the Lamb

Longing for Home / On the Sea of Galilee
In the Sweet bye and bye / Anchored in Love
On Jordan's Stormy Bank I Stand / Room in Heaven for Me
A. L. Phipps talked about the family's musical history.

4. End of Music Activities and Conclusion

4.1 Finishing Music Activities

A.L., Kathleen and their family had been doing great music activities through the US for long periods but in 1991, doctors diagnosed Kathleen Phipps with cancer and she subsequently spent the remainder of her life in a hospital bed and the Family had to end their music career. Kathleen passed away on November 4, 1994. A local newspaper told her death (Fig. 17).

The family met with misfortune again when A.L. was murdered by one of his tenants during a home invasion at his house in August, 1995. It was a tragic day for all. The Kentucky Governor offered the condolences on A. L. Phipps's death.

Fig. 18 is the old house of the Family which was sold after his death, and Fig. 19 are graves of A.L. and Kathleen. I took both photos when I visited Barbourville in 2011. I have to add the current situation of other Phipps Family members.

A.L.'s niece Hester Anderson is struggling with illness. It was sad Leeman passed away in 1994. Truleen Helen is now in Lexington. She has been supportive of me for this paper. Other members are fine (Fig. 20). Bowlin lives in Georgia, Louella in Florida, and Donna in Corbin.

4.2 Conclusion

The Phipps Family were been active in the country and the folk music field for 50 years. They released about 20 albums. Their music was aired on many radio stations in the United States. They spread the Carter Family music too. The Family performed at many famous folk music festivals in the United States. Through their music activities, the Family visited around 32 States in the US. We can enjoy their historical live music on Berea College Digital Home. Some of the scholars and a governor expressed and evaluated the Family's achievements shortly like these.

"The Carter Family's Staunchest Admires"
by Malone and McCulloh / "Stars of Country Music" (1975)
"Devoted Enthusiast and Recreator of the Carter Family Sound"
by John Adkins / "The Carter Family" (1973)
"The Minstrels of Pine Mountain"
by David L. Taylor / Pickin' Magazine (Jul. 1977)
"Musical Ambassador for the Commonwealth of Kentucky"
by Brereton C, Jones, KY Governor, (Aug. 1995)

Acknowledgments

I dedicate this paper to all the Phipps Family.

A special thank you to Ms. Truleen Phipps Barton Morgan, one of the original members as "Helen", who provided me lots of precious pictures and materials for this paper. She also refined my poor English draft of this paper. Chuck Owens made a website of the Phipps Family. It was very helpful. Professor Ivan and Ms. Deena Tribe and Berea College offered material of the Family. Ms. Beth Harrington offered me a permission to use some pictures.

Finally, I very specially thank to my wife Junko Yamaguchi who has been allowing my pursuits for more than 40 years.

Fig.1 10-LP Collection of the Carter Family Released in Japan

Fig. 2 Movie "the Winding Stream" and Ms. Beth Harrington

Fig. 3 Tribute Records to the Carter Family

Fig. 4 the Romaniuk Family, the Canadian Carter Family,

Fig. 5 Downtown of Barbourville

Fig. 6 Lovell Baptist Church

A.P. Carter Music Park
Fig. 7 The Phipps Family Visited the Carters
(Janette Carter; "My Clinch Mountain Home", 2005)

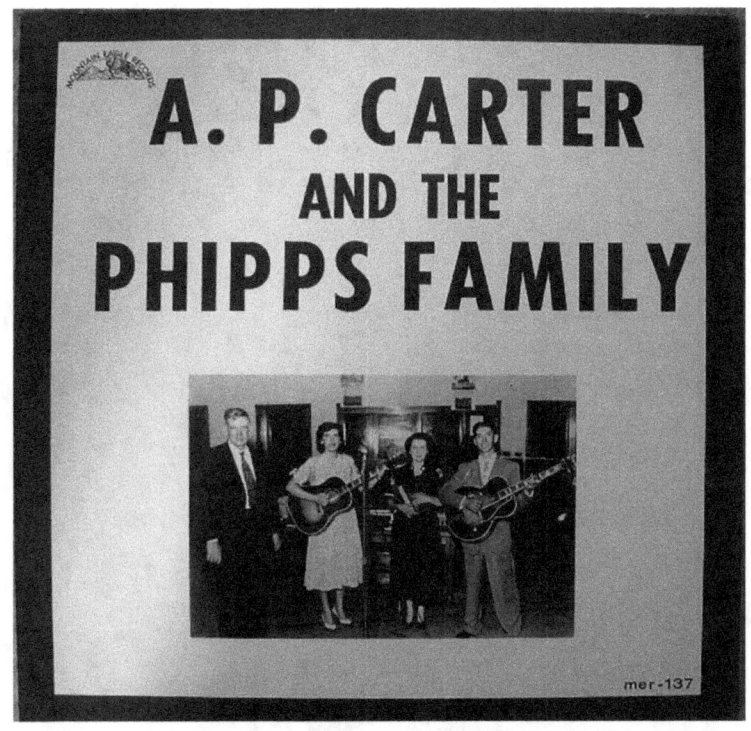

Fig. 8 A. P. Carter and the Phipps Family

Fig. 9 Eight Original Albums of the Phipps Family

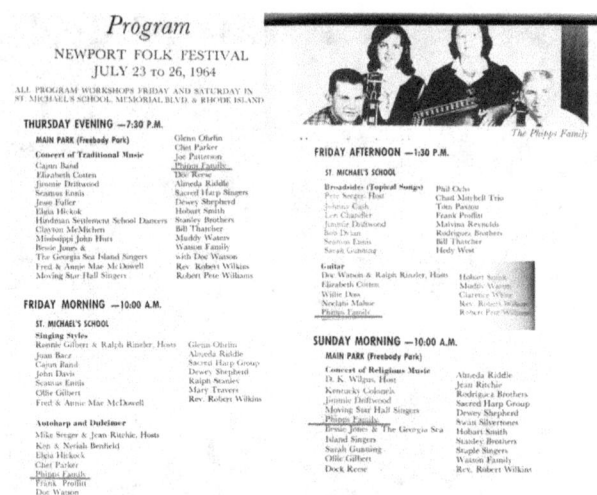

Fig. 10 Program of Newport Folk Festival 1964

Fig. 11 Teenager Performer "Helen" Truleen Phipps
(Daily News, Jul. 24, 1964)

Fig. 12 Vanguard's Album of Newport Folk Festival 1964

Fig. 13 Chicago Folk Festival 1965

Fig. 14 Leemon, Donna, Kathleen and A.L. at the National Mall in 1976

Corbin Times-Tribune, Friday, July 16, 1976 — 7

The Phipps Family
In Washington

The Phipps family from Barbourville are featured performers this week at the Festival of American Folklife in Washington, D.C. Each summer for the past 10 years, the Festival has brought together musicians, craftspeople, dancers, cooks and workers in a celebration of America's diversity. The Festival takes place on the National Mall, the 50 acre park between the Lincoln Memorial and the Washington Monument. It is presented by the Smithsonian Institution and the National Park Service.

The Phipps family was invited by Smithsonian folklorists to be part of the Regional America presentation. This week is featuring musicians, cooks, and craftsmen from the Upland South. For several decades the Phipps family has been one of the best old time singing groups in Southeastern Kentucky. Although they specialize in traditional and mountain folk music they perform everything from child ballads to early twentieth century pop. The group consists of A.L. Phipps, his wife Kathleen, their son Leemon, and daughter Donna. The family has recorded 15 albums, they have played at numerous universities and festivals and have appeared on a radio show in their area for 30 years. Much of the music that they sing has been written by Kathleen or A.L. This is the family's third appearance at the Festival of American Folklife and they are performing here this week on the Regional stage to crowds of Festival visitors each day. The Festival of American Folklife is scheduled to run 11 a.m.–5 p.m., Wednesdays through Sundays, all summer. All events are free. In the photo, taken by the reflecting pool in the Mall, are Leemon, Donna, Kathleen, and A. L. Phipps.

Fig. 15 Corbin Times-Tribune, July 16, 1976

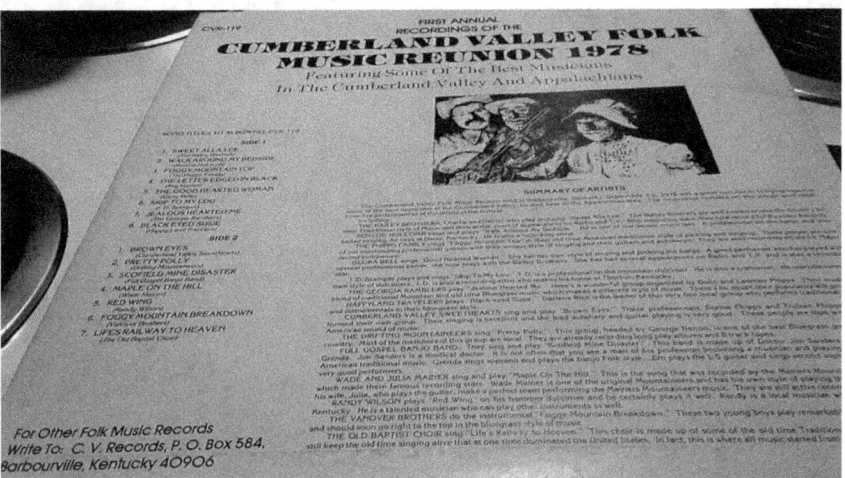

Fig. 16 Compilation Album of Cumberland Valley Folk Festival

Fig. 17 "Kathleen Passed Away" of Local Newspaper, Nov. 1994

Fig. 18 Old House of the Phipps Family

Fig. 19 Graves of A.L. and Kathleen

Fig. 20 The Singing Phipps Family

Two Brothers, Two Sisters and Their Dreams – The Story of Sleepy Hollow Ranch

By Dave Sichak
Hillbilly-Music.com

Introduction

This biography is a story of two brothers and two sisters who started their musical journey on separate paths. They later joined their efforts, literally, they got married. Together they put together a dream that became known as Sleepy Hollow Ranch.

The story is not just a biography, but also a glimpse into the history of the dream that those four people and others helped create at Sleepy Hollow Ranch and the musical interludes that made it happen.

It also is a look into some of the early hillbilly music history such as the live barn dance type shows, the nomadic ways of going to different radio stations. It also opened up an insight into something that was perhaps unique to hillbilly music (the term is used affectionately) – the parks where shows were often held on weekends for families to attend.

The Beginning – Two Sisters and Two Brothers

The Murray Sisters as they became known were the daughters of Yugoslavian immigrant parents, Peter and Eva Bogdanovich. They settled in Paw Paw, West Virginia. By 1930, the family had moved to the Milwaukee, Wisconsin area. The sisters' real names were Sophie Murray and Julie Ruth Bogdanovich. It is here that their musical careers began.

WTMJ Badger State Barn Dance
Milwaukee, WI
Postcard
Circa 1934
Murray Sisters - front row, first two on left

From the Hillbilly-Music.com Collection

In a May 1934 article, readers learn that the Murray Sisters had come to WTMJ in Milwaukee "after a long stay at Shenandoah (Iowa)" and were well known for their harmony.

In 1934, the Murray Sisters then 22 and 18, with Sophie being older, joined radio station WTMJ's Badger State Barn Dance program.

Some of the other acts on the show were Rocky Mountain Mary, the Anderson Trio and Happy Hank Jensen. One ad touts the show's entertainment as "Hill Billy Songs, Comedy, Yodelers and Dances." In those early days, the personal appearances would often be at the local movie theatres.

The Journal-Times
Racine, WI
February 13, 1934

The Capital Times
Madison, WI
August 8, 1934

The Murray Sisters
Portage Daily Register
Portage, WI
May 7, 1935

The Murray Sisters were one of the featured acts at the Sheboygan County fair in August of 1935. An article tells readers what to expect when the folks of the WTMJ Badger State Barn Dance provided the evening entertainment on Friday August 16, 1935. The local paper wrote that the barn dance troupe was a *"versatile group of hilly billies, and well-known radio entertainers. They play not only the hilly billy type of song, but also modern and old-time ballads."*

The first act mentioned was the Murray Sisters, a 'hilly billy harmony team.' They were from West Virginia and veterans of numerous radio broadcasts.

Other acts on the stage with the Murray Sisters were the Badger Ramblers, a group of four guys; the Owens Harmony Trio that sang hilly billy and old-time melodies; and Louisville Lou, a ballad singer. Another act was Hiram, a comedian, saw soloist, dancer and guitar player. Rounding out the list was Rocky Mountain Mary, a yodeler; Curly Stemper, a cowboy baritone singer; Aloma Al, steel guitar player; Doc Wenzel on the piano and accordion along with Clem, Mirandy and Rebecca, the musical family. Acting as Master of Ceremonies was Happy Hank. (Note: The term 'hilly billy' is what the newspaper article used.)

The Murray Sisters
Souvenir Program WHO Barn Dance Frolic
Circa 1939

Later in 1935, news articles were showing that the Murray Sisters were now a part of the WHO Iowa Barn Dance Frolic, making numerous appearances around the state of Iowa. One example was a six day run by the 1936 edition of the Barn Dance in Waterloo at the Iowa Theatre. The Barn Dance then included ten acts. The cast included Sheriff Quigley and Tillie Boggs (purveyors of merriment from Sunset Corners); the Three Tune Tossers (playing melodies that are different); Red and his Arkansas Ramblers (a whirlwind hillbilly band); The Murray Sisters (WHO's melody girls from Wyoming); Tom Sawyer (a one-man band who plays tunes on anything from a dollar bill to a shot gun); Dell and Scotty (the Sunflower Girls); and Grandpa Peppers (who is always cutting capers.)

It is interesting to note at times how the radio stations promoted the various acts to listeners. The descriptions were sometimes not accurate, but were more to create an image in the listener's mind. WHO, in a 1939 souvenir program, described the Murray Sisters as "Wyoming Mountain Gals, not only charming singers, but honest-to-goodness sisters. Accompanying themselves on guitar and mandolin, the Murray Sisters, Sophie and Julie, specialize in ballads of the plains and the back wood trails, old-fashioned songs with a simple heart-appeal."

They mentioned that their popularity stemmed from past appearances on vaudeville stages and various radio stations.

WHO Barn Dance Frolic
with Murray Sisters
Sumner Gazette
Sumner, IA
April 2, 1936

Murray Sisters
Sumner Gazette
Sumner, IA
April 9, 1936

WHO Iowa Barn Dance Frolic
With Murray Sisters
The Muscatine Journal
Muscatine, IA
October 26, 1935

Sleepy Hollow Cowboys and Cowgirls
Song Folio
Circa 1940

From the Hillbilly-Music.com Collection

Sleepy Hollow Cowboys and Cowgirls
and the Vagabond Cowboys
CKLW - Windsor, ON
Circa 1939

From the Hillbilly-Music.com Collection

Radio Listings
Detroit Free Press
October 11, 1939
CKLW - 3:30pm
Sleepy Hollow Ranch

By mid-1936, Pete and Sophie had married. The Newman Brothers evidently had convinced the Murray Sisters to join forces as entertainers. From Iowa, they were next seen in Pennsylvania.

On July 4, 1936, they were part of the 4th of July entertainment at Ephrata Park in Lancaster, PA. They were being heard on WCAU at the time with a half-hour daily show at 2:30 pm. The Georgia Wildcats were also part of the entertainment.

In November, 1936, an article touting their appearance at the Coal Township High School stadium at 8:00pm provided a bit of a different picture of the group's makeup. The group consisted of three brothers and two cousins and the group was known for their unique cowboy songs. Sid Newman was known as "The Deacon" and had been featured by Hollywood studios. He was a disabled World War I veteran who trained his voice while he wss recuperating. Elmer and Ken Newman were his brothers, both talented singers and musicians. Glenn Newman was described as a "snappy bass fiddler" and "Lil Abner" Newman was the comedian of the group; his sidekick was "Icky" Newman. The article continued the ruse that the Murray Sisters hailed from "the Wyoming mountains."

On December 2, 1936, the Uniontown Fire Company presented a program at the Coal Township High School Auditorium featuring the Sleepy Hollow Cowboys. In perhaps a promotion left over from the Murray Sisters Iowa days at WHO, they were billed as the Wyoming Mountain Cowgirls. The short two paragraph article stated that the Sleepy Hollow Cowboys "were a troupe of five performers, born and reared in the Everglades of Florida with a Seminole Indian tribe. They later moved to Arizona where they were educated along the lives of regular cowboys."

Intelligencer-Journal
Lancaster, PA
July 4, 1936

Shamokin News-Dispatch
Shamokin, PA
November 30, 1936

The Mercury
Pottstown, PA
April 26, 1937

The Mercury
Pottstown, PA
September 24, 1937

In April 1937, the Sleepy Hollow Cowboys and Cowgirls made their first appearance at the Boyertown High School Auditorium, presenting two shows. The shows were to benefit the American Legion Drum and Bugle Corps Uniform fund. The show times were 7:45pm and 9:30pm. Before each show, local entertainers presented a skit. The local folks were Ralph (Jeff) Dottterer, Warren (Red) Knode, Lester (Les) Kolb and William (Bill) Eagle, also known as "Parade Bill". Red and Jeff got to see the Gang at the WCAU studios on an occasion before the shows. The next day, it was reported that over 1,200 people attended the shows.

July 4th weekend saw the Cake Hotel announce a new policy by C. E. Bingaman which called for the presentation of floor shows. The opening attraction for this new policy was to be the Sleepy

Hollow Cowboys who were being heard over the NBC chains. It was advertised as Sunbury's newest night club. The Sleepy Hollow group was booked for two nights. However, no children or minors were allowed to attend the shows.

That weekend was a busy one for the Sleepy Hollow gang. They were the entertainment at St. Gabriel's Catholic Church in West Pottsgrove Township at their annual festival. It was reported that about 8,000 people saw the fireworks display and were entertained by the Sleepy Hollow Cowboys and Cowgirls prior to the $400 worth of fireworks.

The Daily Journal
Vineland, NJ
April 7, 1937

The Daily Item
Sunbury, PA
August 6, 1937

The Sleepy Hollow Cowboys came back from a broadcasting stint in Canada in mid-April 1938. They stopped off at a particular road stand - Sleepy Hollow - which was along the Lincoln Highway near St. Clair Hollow. It seems this was not the first time they had made that stop. They were returning to do broadcasts over WCAU once again. An article mentioned there were four men in the car and the mother of one of them.

The group felt at home stopping there for their group name was Sleepy Hollow Cowboys. The last time they had stopped there was in 1937. In another coincidence, it was discovered that one of the members of the Cowboys had the same surname as the Neiman brothers who ran the road stand. It was the fourth time they had stopped there. The article then tells readers that the group took their name from a a place in Minnesota.

The Mercury
Pottstown, PA
July 3, 1937

The Sunday News
Lancaster, PA
August 1, 1937

The group began to journey east. On October 11, 1939, they appeared over station CKLW in Windsor, Ontario, Canada based on our review of radio logs in the Detroit Free Press. A photo post card in our collection shows the group at CKLW and is marked

1939. It appears to have been a daily show for 15 minutes at 3:30pm. The last time the Sleepy Hollow show is listed for CKLW was on Friday, March 22, 1940. The following Monday, a Jamboree show had taken its slot. Perhaps this is when the move to what would become Sleepy Hollow Ranch on Pennsylvania Rte 663 between Quakertown and Pennsburg.

WFIL Barn Dance to WFIL Hayloft Jamboree

A couple of things were happening at once in mid-1940. On June 1, 1940, the WFIL Barn Dance appears on the radio listings, airing on Saturday nights from 8 to 9:00 pm. On June 22, 1940, the show began to originate from Sleepy Hollow Ranch, the first indication seen of the new venue. Prior to that time, that time slot showed a WFIL-WJZ (New York, NY) Barn Dance.

Promtional Ad – Premier of WFIL Barn Dance
Bristol Daily Courier
Bristol, PA
November 29, 1944

Sleepy Hollow Ranch
WFIL Barn Dance Broadcast
The Mercury
Pottstown, PA
June 22, 1940

Sleepy Hollow Ranch
WFIL Barn Dance Broadcast
The Mercury
Pottstown, PA
July 20, 1940

In December of 1944, the barn dance show began a new era over WFIL. While still called the WFIL Barn Dance initially, other ads indicate the show would become known as the Hayloft Hoedown. This would begin a long run of popularity for the show and station that would last for years. As popularity grew, it became a Saturday night staple of the ABC radio network of about 175 stations. In April of 1946, the network broadcast was increased from 15 minutes to a half-hour due to the popularity of the show. In the first ad promoting the new show in November of 1944, Elmer Newman and His Sleepy Hollow Gang were listed as the main act in the cast listing.

In May of 1945, Jack Steck took over the reigns of the show and it was renamed the **WFIL Hayloft Hoedown.** The show's second anniversary broadcast originated at the Earle Theater at 11th and Market Streets in Philadelphia. At the time it was being heard over the ABC network of over 175 stations. It was also one of the few network programs originating from Philadelphia. Originally the show took place at the Town Hall, located at Broad and Race Streets. Jack served as both producer and master of ceremonies for the show.

WFIL Barn Dance
Hayloft Hoedown
Philadelphia Inquirer
August 6, 1945

For the first few weeks of May, 1945, the WFIL Barn Dance cast performed at the Sleepy Hollow Ranch when it re-opened for the 1945 season. On Saturday May 26, 1945, the radio listings show the WFIL Hayloft Hoedown at 10:00 for a half-hour broadcast. Thus, another iteration of barn dance type programs had started over the station.

The cast of that show included Carol Wynne, known as the Girl Next Door for her delivery of Western Ballads; Lew Carter, who was a veteran of the Marine landings on Tarawa and was known as the clown prince of the show; Jack Day was the popular cowboy baritone singer; Pop Johnston held forth as the dean of barn dance fiddlers; and, the Sleepy Hollow Ranch Gang including Elmer and Pete Newman; Sophie and Julie Murray; and Monte Rosci and Pee Wee Miller (Mighty Mite of Music).

The show even had the attention of some magazines. Jenny Via offered a tip to the show concerning the Piano-Organ and accordion players on the show - Mil Spooner and Monty Rosci. Her advice was to add a good electric guitar man and form a 'Three Suns' trio that played hillbilly and western tunes. She further stated, 'Betcha an album of your recordings would command first place in anyone's music library.'

Lew Mel provided a bit of a review and insight of the show when he was invited to tag along with his friend Jack Howard during a visit to Philadelphia. He told readers that the "show has a variety of talent that could not be beat." He described the Sleepy Hollow Ranch Gang as "by far one of the smartest groups on the airwaves." He thought it was one of the finest hoedown shows possible. He wrote that he also noted the atmosphere of friendliness among the members of the cast, which seemed to give the show a bit of its popular spirit. He stated, "The group is one happy family with no one trying to out do the next fellow."

Elmer Newman
of Sleepy Hollow Ranch Gang
National Hillbilly News
August 1945
From the Hillbilly-Music.com Collection

But was Jack Steck on board with the show? In a 1946 article the general manager of WFIL, Roger Clipp, knew that a barn dance type program would be successful in Philadelphia. But Jack, who was well known in Philadelphia for his singing and comedy, tried to talk him out of it. Mr. Clipp told Mr. Steck that he was putting him in charge of the show. And as we know, the rest is history.

One of the aspects of the show not written about elsewhere was Jack Steck's idea for a Trading Post. He asked for unusual objects from the audience and if anybody had that item, the audience member would take home a prize. A television game show of the modern era also had such a gimmick.

Trio numbers were at times done by Jack Steck, Carol Wynne and Jesse Rogers. A picture of Pop Johnson, the champion fiddler. It shows his trademark outfit was wearing a top hat and tails.

Lew Carter who was the comedian of the Hayloft Hoedown went out to the Eastern Penetentiary to perform for the prisoners. A few days after he got back, a hand-made cigarette box came in the mail. It was so well done, it looked like something one would get from an expensive gift shop. Lew showed it to the folks at the station and several asked how they could get one. Lew wrote the prisoners back to thank them for the gift and told them he could probably sell five or six of them if they could send them along and he would pay the going rate for them. The answer came in a letter to Lew, *"We are making the six boxes for you. The price is high — one song."* It was signed "A Lifer."

The Hayloft Hoedown influenced the public high school educational system in Philadelphia and surrounding areas. To tap into the hillbilly trend, several schools added Barn Dance Clubs to their after-school activities. Members of those clubs were taught hillbilly dance routines and songs. The clubs held an annual dance with the entire student body invited to attend. The student "stars" made guest appearances on local radio hillbilly shows. They would also make trips to various barn dances which professional entertainers conducted in the area.

Jack Steck continued to mix it up with the Hayloft Hoedown show. In the summer he began a new policy of trying to book a name guest star at each show held at the Town Hall. The first one was on June 30, 1945 and Foy Willing and His Riders of the

Purple Sage were the guest stars. That same article mentioned that attendance at the shows was upwards to 1,500 paid admissions.

Perhaps the biggest aspect that arose from the WFIL Hayloft Hoedown show was that it began to air over the ABC network of radio stations and did so for many weeks and months. Ads have been seen touting over 225 consecutive weeks of broadcasts of the show.

The popularity of the WFIL Hayloft Hoedown caught on with the upper crust folks of Philadelphia. Jack Steck told *Billboard* magazine in 1946 that various entertainment units of the show had been booked for more than a dozen "society parties" in the fall, but he was quick to note that there was no danger of seeing the hillbilly performers dressed in white tie and tails. He stated that 'special emphasis is placed, in arranging the bookings, that the performers are to appear in folk garb — hayseed and all.

The popularity of the show caught the attention of sponsors. In 1946, it was reported that the Kold Kit Corporation would sponsor a half hour of the show at Town Hall at 10:00pm. The ABC network broadcast of the show was from 10:30pm to 11:00pm. The sponsor's contract was for 26 weeks. At the same time, the Sleepy Hollow Ranch Gang secured a sponsor for its WFIL shows - the Block Drug Company on Tuesday and Thursdays from 12:30pm to 12:55pm.

In May of 1946, the show celebrated its 100,000th person to pay admission to the Hayloft Hoedown at Town Hall. She was Mrs. Florence Woods of Drexel Hill, PA. One of the prizes she received was a lunch date with the Sleepy Hollow Ranch Gang - dressed in full stage costumes. She also made an appearance with the group on the air with them as well.

The Sleepy Hollow Ranch may have caused one to think of the cowboys on horseback in days gone by but Pancake Pete Newman intented was to change that. It was reported that in October of 1946 that he had applied for a pilot's license. Once approved, the idea was that the group would buy an airplane to enable them to travel from town to town for their personal appearances on their tours. Around that same time, the Sleepy Hollow Ranch Gang had completed some work for the Associated Transcription Company. It was also reported they were to make their first recordings for the Majestic record label in early October 1946.

It appears that the last show of the WFIL Hayloft Hoedown aired on Saturday, June 4, 1949. A Billboard ad for the Jolly Joyce Agency indicated the show had been on 225 weeks. No articles could be found about this sudden ending of the show.

WFIL Barn Dance
Town Hall
Bristol Daily Courier
Bristol, PA
January 3, 1945

WFIL Barn Dance
Town Hall
The Mercury
Pottstown, PA
March 7, 1945

Sleepy Hollow Ranch Gang
WFIL — Hayloft Hoedown
Circa 1949
L-R: Elmer Newman; Sophie Murray; Monty Rosci;
Julie Murray; Pee Wee Miller; Pete Newman

From the Hillbilly-Music.com Collection

The Sleepy Hollow Ranch Era

In the same area were other venues potentially competing for the same audience attending Sleepy Hollow Ranch shows. One was Hickory Park, located at the junction of Routes 663 and 73. Another was the Circle J Ranch at the Quakertown Fairgrounds. Another was the C Bar C Ranch at Elverson where Routes 82 and 23 met Route 401.

In 1940, the gang was heard twice a day; WEEU from 10:00am to 10:30am and then at 2:30pm to 3:00pm over WFIL.

Sleepy Hollow Ranch opened to the public on May 4, 1940 and the first act to perform was The Georgia Crackers. The Ranch would continue to open every May. The end of the season was usually in September.

The Morning Call
Allentown, PA
August 14, 1941

Mauch Chunk Times
Mauch Chunk, PA
September 12, 1941

War had broken out in Europe and the Pacific and a draft was instituted. On October 16, 1940, both Elmer and Pete Newman registered to serve in the military service. In addition, their emcee, Hank Harrigan (aka Lester Williams) and their accordion player, Monty Rosci also filled out their draft card on the same date. One gets the sense that this was a tight knit group bonded like a family.

The group had a half-hour show each day over the local station WCBA/WSAN. At various times it was aired at 3:00pm or 11:30am. During 1941, Sleepy Hollow Ranch ran ads using the type of woodsy font found in their 1940 song folio. Ads were not always seen, but still one can see the many country music performers of the era that passed through their grounds.

In that first year, there were many types of promotions to try and capture the interest of those attending the events at the Ranch. On one occasion, it was ten baskets of groceries given away. Another promotion gave away two Farnsworth Table Model Radios.

They offered FREE parking.

One show was for the benefit of the Quakertown Hospital Fund Drive. In July 1940, ten watermelons were given away as gate prizes. August of 1940 saw a "gigantic amateur contest" with cash prizes where anyone over the age of 14 could compete. November 1, 1940 promoted a big Halloween dance with cash awards for best costumes. On that same night, the Murray Sisters were to not only feature their western tunes, but also Yugoslavian songs.

The November shows advertised that all shows were held in their steam heated auditorium. In 1941, one promotional item was a free electric washing machine.

In those days, the ads promoted the appearance of the Sleepy Hollow Ranch Cowboys and Cowgirls including the Murray Sisters, Elmer and his fiddle, Pete and his guitar, Monty on the accordion, "Just Plain John singing his beautiful hymns" and Hank Harrigan "as his own busy self."

During the latter part of 1941, one can also see that the group made appearances in the surrounding area beyond the Sleepy Hollow Ranch as well. Over the years, many stars gave performances at the Sleepy Hollow Ranch. One of the more interesting names in the promotional ads was one of country music's earliest stars, Vernon Dalhart, who appeared there on Saturday and Sunday, June 28 and 29, 1941.

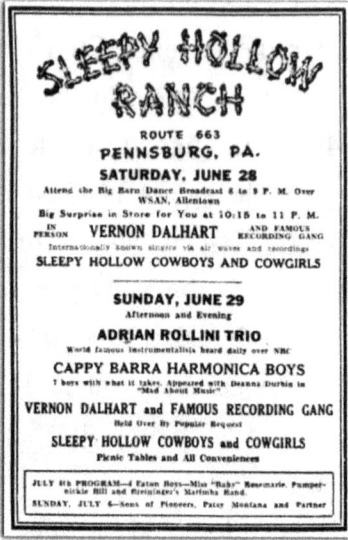

Vernon Dalhart
1981 Country Music Hall of Fame Inductee
Sleepy Hollow Ranch Appearance
The Mercury
Pottstown, PA
June 28, 1941

The Mercury
Pottstown, PA
September 6, 1941

The Morning Call
Allentown, PA
January 25, 1941

The Morning Call
Allentown, PA
May 30, 1942

The Morning Call
Allentown, PA
September 26, 1942

In 1943, due to World War II, pleasure driving was banned. But in an effort to provide entertainment, they took their show to the fans. The Sleepy Hollow Ranch Gang went on USO tours.

The Mercury
Pottstown, PA
June 24, 1944

The Morning Call
Allentown, PA
June 30, 1944

The Morning Call
Allentown, PA
May 5, 1945

The Morning Call
Allentown, PA
June 2, 1945

Philadelphia Inquirer
June 15, 1946

Philadelphia Inquirer
June 22, 1946

SLEEPY HOLLOW RANCH

RT. 663—BETWEEN PENNSBURG and QUAKERTOWN, PA.

GRAND RE-OPENING
SUNDAY, MAY 4th

ELTON BRIT
WORLD'S HIGHEST YODELER STAR OF RADIO SHOW

TENNESSEE JED
HEARD DAILY OVER ABC NETWORK

SLEEPY HOLLOW RANCH GANG
STARS OF WFIL-ABC HAYLOFT HOEDOWN; ALSO DAILY OVER WFIL 12:30 NOON

GEORGIA YODELERS
DAILY OVER WTTM

SMOKEY and HENRY
FAMOUS BLACKFACE COMEDIANS

SHOWS EVERY SUNDAY
RAIN OR SHINE

ADULTS, 50c plus tax
CHILDREN, Half Price

COMING MAY 30th—RODEO

The Morning Call
Allentown, PA
May 3, 1947

SLEEPY HOLLOW RANCH

Route 663 between Pennsburg and Quakertown, Pennsylvania
SHOWS EVERY SUNDAY, RAIN OR SHINE

TOMORROW
PAPPY HOWARD and His
CONNECTICUT KERNELS
SLEEPY HOLLOW RANCH GANG
ABC—WFIL NETWORK STARS
Appearing every Sat. nite on WFIL's Hayloft Hoedown at Town Hall. Also heard daily on WFIL at 12:30 N MON. PLUS of OUTSTANDING WESTERN ATTRACTIONS

COMING SUNDAY, MAY 25th
LULU BELLE & SCOTTY

Admission Every Sunday 50c plus tax
Children Half Price
To reach Sleepy Hollow Ranch: P. & W. Lines from 69th Street or Reading Terminal Lines to Quakertown. FREE bus Sundays & Holidays from Lehigh Valley station, Quakertown to Sleepy Hollow Ranch, every hour starting 1:15 P. M. If driving, Route 309, turn left in Quakertown on Route 663.

Philadelphia Inquirer
Philadelphia, PA
May 17, 1947

SLEEPY HOLLOW RANCH
On Route 663
Between Pennsburg and Quakertown

ANNOUNCING 1949 SEASON
May 1 through Sept. 25

SUNDAY, MAY 1

ABC HAYLOFT HOEDOWN STARS
5 Years on the ABC Coast-to-Coast Network

SLEEPY HOLLOW RANCH GANG
Heard on WFIL—Monday Thru Fri., 4:30 p. m.
Sat., 12:30 p. m.

PLUS Other Outstanding Acts!

See and Hear Your Favorite
Radio, Stage and Screen Stars

SHOWS EVERY SUNDAY—Rain or Shine

The Mercury
Pottstown, PA
April 30, 1949

Sleepy Hollow Ranch
On Route 663 between Pennsburg & Quakertown, Pa.
Sunday, June 26
Afternoon & Evening

RED CAPS

SLEEPY HOLLOW RANCH GANG

101 RANCH BOYS

Show Every Sunday, Rain or Shine

Special Charter Bus Service from Widener Bldg. Arcade, South Penn Square, to Sleepy Hollow Ranch, at 1 P. M. and 3 P. M. Round Trip Fare Including Admission Price $2.50.

Philadelphia Inquirer
June 24, 1949

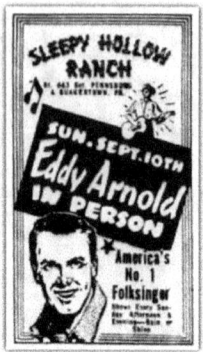

Philadelphia Inquirer
Philadelphia, PA
September 8, 1950

Philadelphia Inquirer
Philadelphia, PA
September 15, 1950

Philadelphia Inquirer
May 17, 1952

Philadelphia Inquirer
August 2, 1952

The Mercury
Pottstown, PA
May 13, 1955

The Morning Call
Allentown, PA
May 27, 1955

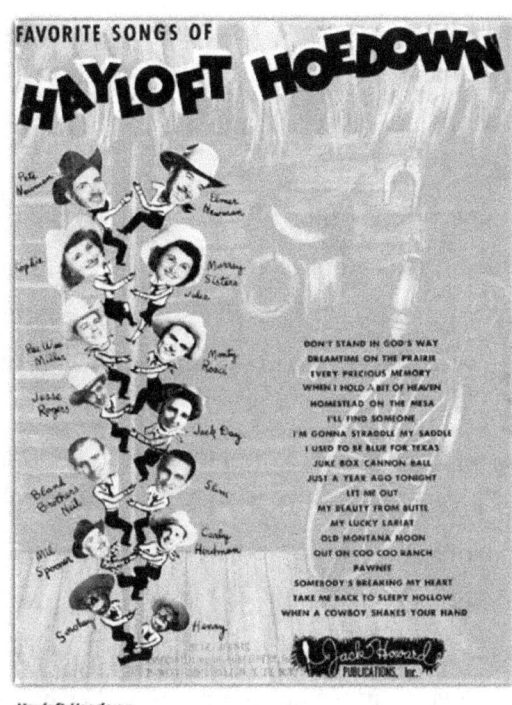

Hayloft Hoedown
Song Folio
Circa 1948
From the Hillbilly-Music.com Collection

Pancake Time - Pete Newman
WAEB Radio Promotional Ad
The Morning Call
Allentown, PA
July 17, 1949

The year of 1949 was one of the busier and perhaps lucrative ones for the gang. There was the new recording contract with a major label and the two Newman brothers had their own radio shows over local stations.

Allentown's new radio station, WAEB, was promoting "Pancake Time" at 6:30am - a Monday through Saturday morning radio show.

Around that same time, WFIL-TV announced a new program. It was to be called "Wiffil Ranch." The premise was that it would give viewers a taste of life of the cowboys of the Old West. It made its debut on July 18, 1949. Pancake Pete Newman was to host the half-hour show that would air at 6:00pm. The first film featured was "Phantom of the West."

Pete was to tell the viewing audience about "Western people and customs." It appears the target audience may have included the kids. The show was to organize a group known as "Pony Express Riders." The kids were to be asked to write Pancake Pete at the WFIL-TV studios.

Little items buried in articles revealed personal tidbits about a member or two in the group. Penny Britt (the wife of Elton Britt) told readers in one article that Julie and Elmer named their cocker spaniel after Rex Allen because both Rex and the dog were 'blondes'.

Sometimes it was not always about being on stage. *Cash Box reported in January of 1953 that Pancake Pete Newman had an hour long show that aired over WNAR in Norristown, PA and WSAN in Allentown, PA, spinning records from his own library at Sleepy Hollow Ranch.*

In early 1953 *Cash Box reported that the gang was taking a two week break to do some remodeling work at the Ranch. A new arena was built in a different location to provide a larger ring and seating capacity, as well as other general overhaul work.*

A feature story on the Sleepy Hollow Story in *Billboard* in June of 1954 provided some insight into Ranch operations and history. The article noted that before the park opened in 1940, the Sleepy Hollow Ranch Gang had been sponsored by Drug Trade Products of Chicago for ten years.

In 1954, there were eight members of the Newman family active in the management and entertainment at Sleepy Hollow Ranch. Ken (Pancake Pete) Newman and Sophie Murray's children MaryEva and Dan were one side of the family. Dan (Elmer) Newman and Julie Murray's children Danny and Charlie were the other side of the family. Kenny and Danny were the older children and developed into performers. Mary Eva and Charlie also tried their hands at entertainment. The other members of the entertainment family were Monty Rosci, the accordionist and Hank Harrigan, a West Virginia native, who had been with the group since 1940.

Entertainment offerings to the public were free dancing and kiddie rides. They had just received a license to sell liquor in December 1953. The admission fee in 1954 was 50 cents for adults and a 25 cents for children ten to 16. Rodeos and midget auto racing were a part of the entertainment during the season and the separate admission was $1.50 and 50 cents. The normal admission fee did include the entertainment which usually consisted of up to a half dozen acts that alternated during the day and night. Picnic space and parking was free. The parking lot could hold 1,500 cars.

The ranch opened on Sundays at 10 am and the first stage show is at 1 pm. The shows ran in half-hour intervals at that time. Booking the acts at the Ranch was handled by the Jolly Joyce Agency along with Harry Cooke, Earl Kurtze and Dotty Nunnemaker.

Stars such as Eddy Arnold would net 70 per cent of the gross. Another 10 per cent was to cover the cost of newspaper, advertising and operating expenses. Other revenue streams for the Ranch were the leasing of rides and concession space, giving them 25 per cent of the gross. At that time, the Ranch had two kiddie rides. The Ranch also ran its own restaurant, soft drink stand and bingo concession.

With the 1954 season, the group was thinking of expanding to two weekend shows (Saturday and Sunday).

The Sleepy Hollow Inn was open year-round and free square dancing was offered on Wednesday, Friday and Saturday nights, with no admission fee.

The Musical Winds Began To Change

Like many barn dance and hillbilly music shows of the era, the Sleepy Hollow Ranch entertainment scene felt the impact of the wave of rockabilly and rock and roll. The acts appearing at the Ranch were a different mix, catering to a new generation of music fans. Bill Haley and the Comets were an example of this change. Bill's popularity was such that he made several appearances at the Ranch.

The years of 1958 and 1959 saw Bill Haley appearing once again along with such groups as The Comets and The Premiers.

In 1960, a few ads indicate the shifting musical scene. One ad touts The Roof Rockers (promoted as rock 'n roll) as well as Wanda Jackson who was perhaps a bit rockabilly at the time. But during that same time, stars such as Little Jimmy Dickens and Ozark Jubilee personalities were to appear.

Local Sponsor: Freese's Farmers Market, Auction & More

Sponsors always seem to find a way into the history of the artists of that older era. During the research of this group and venue, one such sponsor stood out a bit. It was Freese's Farmer's Market and Auction. For about a year around 1950, they ran ads that featured not only their store, but would have country music acts appearing at the store to draw fans as well. The store featured auctions, a Farmer's Market, social party, used cars, furniture showrooms and Nettles' Restaurant. It was located on North State Street in Pottstown, PA. There were a variety of acts booked for these Friday evening specials, both known and lesser-known. On special occasions, the Sleepy Hollow Ranch Gang were the featured entertainment. Such was the case on May 20, 1950 for Freese's 12th Anniversary.

Freese's was not your normal grocery store. One ad mentioned that they could accommodate up to 33,000 cars at no charge. Another ad tells the reader they were literally a large farmer's market. They had over 110 stalls under one roof. The shopper could find everything from smoked meats from five well known butchers, dressed poultry, farm eggs, at least ten popular fruit and vegetable stall holders, Lehigh and Lancaster County potatoes, Swiss and sharp cheese, fresh oysters and clams, homemade baked goods, candies, cigars, tobaccos, potato chips, cider, vinegar, ice cream, waffles, sodas, birch beer, cookies, novelties, toys, hardware, records, gold fish, white mice, auto accessories, medicines, liniments, jewelry, new cooking utensils, electric appliances, religious books, cut flowers and potted plants, clothes, storm windows and screens. One could even buy a car from a local dealer. You could buy wholesale or retail. In addition to the Nettle's restaurant that served full course home cooked meals, there were six other restaurants. Nettle's Restaurant was owned and operated by Harvey and Grandy Nettles; the couple had been married almost 70 years when Grandy passed away in 2012. Daniel Freese owned Freese's Market and Auction which he began to build section by section in 1939. He sold the property to Berman Truck Mart in 1971. He died at the age of 86 in 1975.

The Mercury
Pottstown, PA
Freese's Ad Featuring Sleepy Hollow Ranch Gang
May 19, 1949

The Mercury
Pottstown, PA
August 18, 1949

The Mercury
Pottstown, PA
April 20, 1949

The Mercury
Pottstown, PA
January 6, 1950

The Mercury
Pottstown, PA
January 20, 1950

Swing Yer Partner (1953) (TV Show)

Philadelphia Inquirer
Philadelphia, PA
August 30, 1953
— Swing Yer Partner

The TV Listings show that in the fall of 1953, the Sleepy Hollow Ranch Gang were part of a television show that aired late nights over Channel 6 (WFIL) called "Swing Yer Partner".

It appeared to be a hoedown type of show. Another article in 1954 mentioned that the Rambling Hoedowners played square dance music on the show. No other information was found about this apparent short-lived show.

However, searches show that the show was also broadcast over WFIL radio (AM 560) at the same time as the television show. It is this author's guess that the show aired from the Sleepy Hollow Inn where square dancing was offered several nights a week.

Philadelphia Inquirer
Philadelphia, PA
July 26, 1953
Swing Yer Partner
— TV Broadcast

Philadelphia Inquirer
Philadelphia, PA
August 7, 1953
Swing Yer Partner
— Radio Broadcast

Delaware Valley Barn Dance (TV Show)

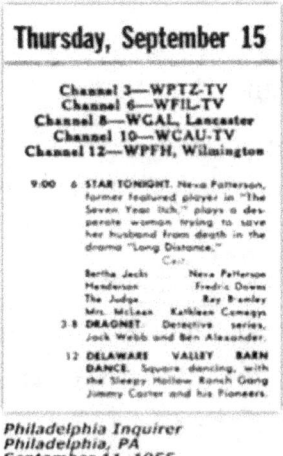

Philadelphia Inquirer
Philadelphia, PA
September 11, 1955
TV Listings for Week
(Note: Image is combination of three screen shots for presentation purposes.)

In the fall of 1955, the Sleepy Hollow Ranch Gang became part of a television show called the **Delaware Valley Barn Dance** on channel 12. The Half-hour show aired on Thursday nights at 9:00pm on channel 12 - WPFH - out of Wilmington, Delaware.

It featured the Sleepy Hollow Ranch Gang, Jimmy Carter and his Pioneers and square dancing. Based on the television listings reviewed, the show appears to have run its course in June of 1956.

The last few weeks of the show saw the TV listings list the show as 'barn dance'. The last listing was June 23, 1956 on a Saturday night.

The TV Listings never mentioned any guest stars or if there were other members of the cast. But some hints were found in newspaper articles that seem to indicate that the Ertman Sisters were a part of the show as well as Barbara Shirley.

Other research found that James (Jimmy) Carter, a former DJ on radio station WEEZ in Brookhaven passed away at the age of 47 in February 1967 after a brief illness. He lived in Chester, Pennsylvania. Another 'ad' for King Jack's Super Market featured Jimmy and his band appearing at the store and seemed to indicate King Jack's was a sponsor of the show.

Notable Personal Appearance — Eddy Arnold

Of all the acts that appeared at Sleepy Hollow Ranch over the years from 1940 through 1963, the most popular appears to have been Eddy Arnold. Hank Harrigan recalled in a 1986 interview that Eddy pulled in about 8,000 people in 1944. An article in the National Hillbilly News indicated he surpassed that in 1947 with a crowd over 11,000.

The Ranch arranged for three more Sunday bookings of Arnold. Based on the ads in 1947, the June 22, 1947 show may have been the one with the large crowd. This was a time in Eddy's career where he hosted the Checkerboard Jamboree show over WSM. Notice the listing of Roy Wiggins, Eddy's steel player at the time, in one of the ads.

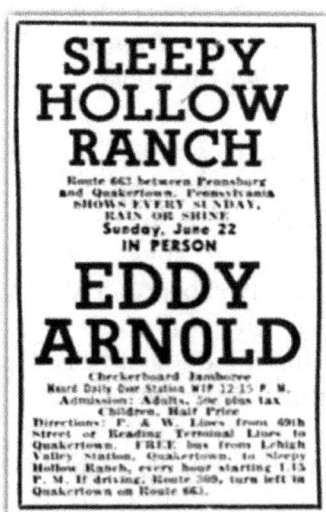

Eddy Arnold
Sleepy Hollow Ranch —
June 22, 1947
Philadelphia Inquirer
June 21, 1947

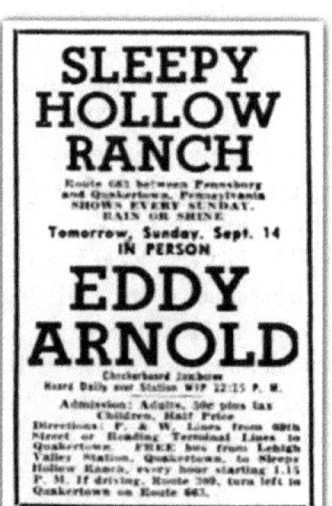

Eddy Arnold
Sleepy Hollow Ranch —
September 14, 1947
Philadelphia Inquirer
September 13, 1947

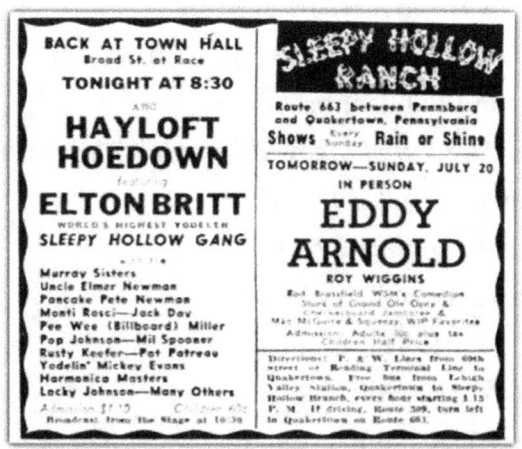

Eddy Arnold
Sleepy Hollow Ranch — July 20, 1947
Philadelphia Inquirer
July 19, 1947

Eddy Arnold
Sleepy Hollow Ranch — August 17, 1947
Philadelphia Inquirer
August 16, 1947

Songwriting Credits

It seems Elmer Newman got the itch to try songwriting around 1946 and over a period of three months wrote 17 songs and five of them were recorded.

Our collection includes numerous song folios and magazines with song lyrics. Here are songs that are credited to one of the Sleepy Hollow Ranch Gang members:

1. ***Within This Broken Heart of Mine***
   Jimmy Walker, Slim Stuart and Elmer Newman
   (Jack Howard Publications - 1947)
2. ***I Courted The Sunshine And Married The Rain***
   Elmer Newman and Billy Wilson
3. ***I've Lived A Lifetime For You***
   Elmer Newman and Ray Whitley
   (Bourne Inc. - 1947)
4. ***It's Hard To Say Goodbye***
   Elmer Newman and Pancake Pete Newman
   (Jack Howard Publications, Inc. - 1946)
5. ***Don't Stand In God's Way***
   Elmer Newman and Bob Newman
   (Jack Howard Publications, Inc. - 1948)
1. ***I'm Gonna Straddle My Saddle***
   Dr. Louis Menakar, Ted Donofrio and Pancake Pete Newman
   (Jack Howard Publications - 1948)

Recording History / Information

Pancake Pete Newman fell ill in early 1947. His doctor ordered him to go to Florida to recuperate. The expectation was that he would stay there for about a month. As soon as he returned, the Sleepy Hollow Ranch Gang was scheduled to record four sides for the Majestic label.

Research indicates the group recorded for Majestic in July of 1946 and December of 1947.

In the 1940's, the group made several recordings with the Majestic label. One review in *Cash Box in July 1947 was for "I'm Lonesome Now" b/w "I Was Never Nearer Heaven In My Life" on Majestic 11012. Cash Box told readers, "The Sleepy Hollow Ranch Gang step out to offer ops a pair of sides that may attract phono play in spots that go for lots of wailing. The topside tune "I'm Lonesome Now," shows piper Elmer Newman in the tonsil department, as he runs thru this tear-jerker in slow tempo. Usual string accompaniment fills the bill throughout, with vocal efforts hogging the lime. On the backing with the Murray Sisters doing "I Was Never Nearer Heaven In My Life,» the ensemble blends well as they offer more moody stuff. You take it from here.»*

The Courier-Post
Camden, NJ
May 21, 1948

In 1946, a new record label, Cowboy Records, was being led by Jack Howard of Philadelphia and songwriter James E. Myers ("Side Saddle Joe", "Westward Bound").

A short blurb in a magazine indicated the label had recorded eight sides with the Sleepy Hollow Ranch Gang and eight sides with the Santa Fe Rangers. The Sleepy Hollow Gang recordings included recordings by Monty Rosci doing accordion solos.

In January 1949, it was reported that the group had signed a three year deal with the RCA Victor label. Cash Box reviewed one of their latest offerings —

"Till The End Of The World" b/w "Three Wishes" on RCA Victor 21-0036. *Cash Box* wrote: *"Here's one platter that has just about everything. The Sleepy Hollow Ranch Gang open the topside with some lively melody, grand lyrics and great backgrounding to make "Till The End Of The World» one of the best westerns cut in many a moon. The flip, «Three Wishes,» is just as good and sounds just as lively, lilting and happy as the topside. Both sides have moneymaker pressed right into them.*

Peach Picking Time Down In Georgia
Vocal by Pancake Pete Newman
Majestic
11006 B
Circa 1946

Keep On The Sunnyside
Sleepy Hollow Ranch Gang
Varsity
8081
Circa 1950

It's Hard To Say Good-Bye
Pancake Pete Newman
with the Sleepy Hollow Ranch
Cowboys and Cowgirls
Cowboy Records
Cowboy CR-103-B
Circa 1946

Til The End Of The World
Sleepy Hollow Ranch Gang
Vocal by The Murray Sisters
RCA Victor 21-0036-A
Circa 1949

November 3, 1963 — A Fire Burns The Ranch

> **Sleepy Hollow Ranch Leveled by $50,000 Fire**
>
> The Morning Call
> Allentown, PA
> November 4, 1963

Early Sunday morning November 3, 1963, Sleepy Hollow Ranch met a fiery end. The fire was discovered by a passing motorist around 5:40am Sunday morning. By the time the first fire company arrived, the bunkhouse type building as engulfed in flames. In all, firemen from five volunteer depqrtments in Bucks and Montgomery Counties (Pennsburg, Milford Township, East Greenville, Red Hill and Green Lane) battled the blaze.

The motorist woke up one of the owners - Daniel Newman (who lived next to the ranch). He ran 300 yards to a neighbor's house to notify the Pennsburg Fire Department.

Over 100 firemen were on the scene. Fire Chief Harold Boardman of Milford Township said the firemen had enough water but the fire had a 'good head start.'

The news reported that the Newman's had insurance, but probably not sufficient to cover the estimated $50,000 in losses. The insurance covered the combination of the dance hall, restaurant and bar.

The fire also burned two of the four concession stands near the burning building, but firemen were able to put out the flames before those were badly damaged. A small fire in the rear of the property in a wooded area was also put out.

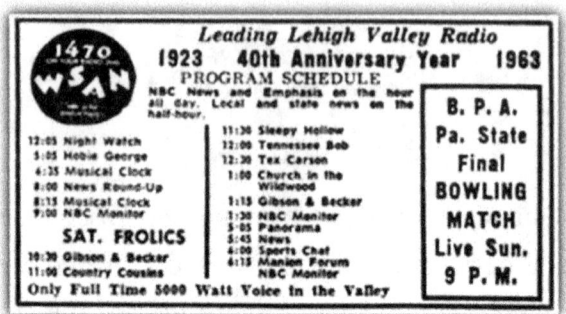

The Morning Call
Allentown, PA
November 9, 1963

According to a news report, Sleepy Hollow Ranch was closed around 2:30am Sunday morning by one of the bartenders. He told Fire Marshal William D. Underkuffler of Upper Bucks County that when he left, he saw no sign of a fire. An accompanying picture showed the venue had been leveled. The 100 by 80 foot one-story frame building was gone.

The gang at Sleepy Hollow had a Saturday morning radio show over WSAN, which was celebrating its 40th anniversary in 1963.

In May, 1985, the 11.9 acre property was put up for sale. It included a modern three bedroom home with an apartment above; a basement with a large recreation room, built-in bar and fireplace. Also included were garages and horse stables. The sale included 7 rustic log cabin concession stands and a 45x45 rotunda. Acres of parking. A 150x250 rodeo arena with a seating capacity of 2,000. Liquor (bar) license was also part of the offering.

A 1986 article recounting the history of the park indicates that Pete and Sophie purchased the 23 acre tract that was in Milford

Township that included a five-room house for $2,200, supposedly shortly after being married in 1936. Later, the two couples formed an equal partnership and began building the ranch with the help of about 100 employees.

Revival Concerts — August 17, 1986 & August 20, 1989

The Milford Historical and Preservation Society put together a reunion concert of sorts to conjur up memories of the days of old when the Sleepy Hollow Ranch Gang were hosting many of country music's great performers. They former members of the 'family' came from far and wide to attend. Hank Harrigan (his real name was Lester Williams) brought his accordion with him from Florida where he was living in retirement. Monty Rosci, by then a retired jeweler living in Haverstown, drove up for the reunion. Julie Newman, one of the two Murray Sisters, drove in from her home in Richland Township to join her son Charlie who brought a banjo and steel guitar.

Monty Rosci enjoyed the scene, pointing to the large crowd assembled in front of a temporary stage. He noted, "See the people here. They love things like this."

Julie was having a ball relating that many said her voice is still the same though she knows it wasn't, but enjoyed the compliments all the same. She said folks kept coming up to her and asking, "Remember me?".

Even though rain dampened the audience that day, the band played two concerts to crowds of 3,000 each time. Their concert may have given some of the younger fans a taste of the music that was played in a by gone era.

A few years later, another "Sleepy Hollow" day was held and over 5,000 people showed up on the farm of Robert and Linda Duck to the Uppder Bucks. But there were hoops to go through to enable the historical society and the Ducks to hold the concert, but in the end, the concert was held. Old Sleepy Hollow regulars showed up - Hank Harrigan who was an announcer, Monty Rosci was on the scene once again along with Julie Newman.

As one might expect, other events were held similar to what was held in the past - horseback riders competing in riding events, conventional races such as the barrel race. The Sleepy Hollow Gang, the Newman Brothers and other old-timers took the stage for the second performance at 7:00pm to close the day. Mr. Duck said that in 1986, the Milford Historical Society netted $8,000. He was hopeful they raised more this go around.

Family Information:

1. Kenneth ("Pete") Newman (B: 1917 D: 2000)
2. Sophie Murray (B: 1913 D: 2010)
   1. Married: June 1936
1. Daniel ("Elmer") Newman (B: 1907 D: 1969)
2. Julie Murray (B: 1915 D: 2012)
   1. Married: October 1937

Appeared At Sleepy Hollow – 1940 through 1960

The following listings are based on perusal of promotional ads seen in local newspapers in the years mentioned. Not all weeks could be documented. Ads may not have run in a few years as well.

But the reader will note the variety of entertainment the Ranch booked beyond country music.

WFIL Barn Dance Broadcast	Smiley (Frog) Burnette and his Gang
Four Harlem Rhythmaires (Harlem›s greatest Jive Harmony Singers)	The Four Dudes (CBS Stars - barbershop quartet)
Three Loose Nuts	The Gibsons (comedy bicycle team)
Percy Kinsig and Gypsy Sweetheart	Captain Schremmer (ventriloquist, juggling w/Punch &ammp; Judy Show
Calgary Kid (Allan Erwin?)	
Delmore Brothers	Sons of the Purple Sage
Mort Lawrence (old city slicker)	Carrie Lee and Her Sunset Rangers
Buck Nation and Tex Ann with Cowboy Caravan	Annie Benton and his Eastern Gentlemen (dance band)
Willis Meyers and his Bar X Ranch Boys	Elton Britt
Zeke Manners and His Gang	Hank Briggs and the Seven Dudes
Horsehoe Mike and Cowboy Joe with Buckeye Four	Five Radio Rubes
	Percy Einsig (Pennsylvania Dutch Singer)
Smokey Styer, blackface comedian	
Breininger's Marimba Band	Ferry the Frog (Renowned Contortionist)
Dopey Duncan	
Tumbleweed Ludy	The Plainsmen
Ramblin' Red Foley	The Four Marshalls
Sons of the Pioneers	The Grant Family (four clever tin-type imitators)
	Ben Alley (WFIL artist)

Acts appearing at Sleepy Hollow Ranch 1941

Uncle Josh, Mary Lou and the Gang	Pop Johnson's Old-Timers
Willis Myers and his Bar-X Ranch Boys	Tumbleweed Ludy
	Shorty and His Radio Rascals
Texas Jim Robertson	Eddie Peabody, the Banjo King
Georgia Crackers	Eddie Conner's Trio
Vernon Dalhart	Hugh Cross and His Radio Pals
Adrian Rollini Trio	Shug Fisher
Cappy Barra Harmonica Boys	Major Bowes' All-Star Unit
Sons of the Pioneers	Cousin Malcom Claire (Spareribs - Black Face Comedian from WLS)
Patsy Montana and Her Partners	Doll Brothers
The Doring Sisters (From NBC Plantation Party)	Tom Emerson and His Mountaineers
	Hoosier Hot Shots
The 4 Polka Dots (NBC Harmonica Group)	Breinninger's Military Marimba Band
Whitey Ford (Duke of Paducah)	Zeb Carver and His Country Cousins
Lulu Belle and Scotty	Happy Johnny and Gang
Hank Briggs and his Swing Billies	Betty Jay and the Plainsmen from WBAL - Baltimore, MD
Slim and the Gloomchasers	Gene Austin
Darling Sisters	Sherrill Sisters (comediennes)
Gracie and Harris (World Champion Jitterbug Dancers)	Slim Mitchell (cowboy singer)
New York Vaudeville Acts	Denver Darling and his Gang from Village Barn
Zeke Manners and His Gang	
Four Eton Boys (Former Model Minstrels)	
3 Nit-Wits (Knock about Comedy)	

Hugh Cross and his Radio Pals	Dopey Duncan and the Melody Rangers
Shug Fisher	
Lulu Belle and Scotty	Brown Twins (Sensational Tap Dancers)
Shad-Rac Boys	
Stars of Plantation Party	Happy Johnny and the Plainsmen (From WBAL - Baltimore)
Duke of Paducah (Whitey Ford)	Smokey & Henry (Black Face Comedians)
Cousin Lee, Sarah Lee and the Gang	
Two Texans (From Denver, CO)	Hank Lawson and the Knights of the Road
	Uncle Jack and Mary Lou and their Gang
	William The Magician (Bringing his Spooks)

Mac McGuire and his Harmony Rangers (WCAU)	Pop Johnson and his Old Timers (Lots of comedy, singing and dancing)
Smilin' Dave and his Buckaroos	Reg Kehoe and his All-Girl Marimba Band (Steel Pier - Atlantic City))
Harmonica Kings	
Willis Myers Bar-X Ranch Boys (WSAN)	Dick Thomas
	Betty Jay and the Plainsmen
Breininger's Military Marimba Band	MALE Bathing Beauty Contest
	Big Amateur Contest
Cactus Rex (WTTM - Trenton)	Kidoodlers (NBC Novelty Act)
The Arkansas Woodchopper	Graybill's Animal Circus - Pnies, Dogs, Boxing Cats
Musical Aces and Two Queens	
Martinez Animal Circus	Elton Britt
Sammy Weeks	Riff Robbbin Trio
Skunk Hollow Trio (Hillbilly Novelty Act)	Broadway Buckaroos
	Pat Buttram (The Winston County Flash)
Jesse Rodgers	
Ranch Pals	The Three Loose Nuts (w/Jelly Bean Anderson, Brother of Rochester)
Roy Acuff and his Smoky Mountain Boys	
	Meredith and Snoozer, The Dog With the Almost Human Brain
Ford Rush (The Singin' High Sheriff)	
Smokey and Henry (Black Face Comedians)	
Hoosier Hot Shots	

Lulu Belle and Scotty Chester Valley Boys (WFIL - Harmonica Wizards) Tumbleweed Rangers (Direct from overseas USO Tour) Meredith and Snoozer (The Dog with the Human Brain) Hoosier Hot Shots Jesse Rogers Joe Edison - emcee (WEEU)	Three Loose Nuts (w/Jelly Bean Anderson, Brother of Rochester) WLS Gloomchasters with Shorty Long Pappy Howard and Champion Hill Billies (From Cleveland) Happy Johnny and Gang (From Baltimore) Barbary Coast Boys (Songs & Comedy of Gay 90's)
Rex Allen Pappy Howard & His Kernels (From Cleveland) Jimmy Walker and All-Western Stars Slim Stuart (Stewart?) and the Saddle Sweethearts Polly Jenkins and Musical Pals Santa Fe Rangers (WFIL - Shorty Long, Rusty Keefer, Jack Day & Pee Wee Miller) Red Foley Down Homers Jack Andrews and "Henry" (Greatest High Schooled Brahma Bull) All-American Championship Rodeo Tex Ritter and his Prairie Pals The Arknasas Woodchopper Chester Valley Boys	Hank Harrigan and Lew Carter Billy Wilson (The Cowboy Poet) Joe Edison (Ton of Fun Emcee) Curley Bradley Tom Mix Georgia Yodelers (From WTTM - Trenton, NJ) Johnny Olsen (Ladies Be Seated) Jesse Rogers Pioneer Band (Allentown, PA) Barbary Coast Boys Harry Ranch and His Kernels of Korn Jack Dawson Jack Steck Carol Wynne (The Girl Next Door)

Eddy Arnold Jesse Rogers Doc Hopkins Roy Wiggins Rod Brasfield Mac McGuire and Squeezy (WIP) All-American Championship Rodeo Elton Britt Dick Thomas (Sioux City Sue) The Georgia Crackers (Hank, Slim & Bob Newman)	Red Caps Rex Allen Texas Jim Robertson Lulu Belle and Scotty Pappy Howard and His Connecticut Kernels Slim Stuart and the Plainsmen Tennessee Jed (ABC Radio Star) Georgia Yodelers (WTTM) Smokey and Henry (Famous Black Face Comedians)
ABC Hayloft Hoedown Stars Eddy Arnold Lulu Belle and Scotty Sons of the Pioneers Tom Mix Curley Bradley Dick Thomas	Buckeye Four 101 Ranch Boys Red Caps Jimmy Wakely and His Saddle Pals w/Sonny (Horse) Jesse Rogers Jack Day Slim Stuart and the Plainsmen
Smiley Burnette Jack Day and the Singin' River Boys Championship Rodeo Eddy Arnold Sunset Carson and his $20,000 Horse	Steve Gibson & The Five Red Caps Johnny Olsen and Ladies Be Seated Hawkshaw Hawkins DeZurik Sisters (Cackle Sisters) Nelson King (WCKY DJ)

Dopey Duncan and the Tophands Pee Wee Miller and the Santa Fe Rangers Carl Smith Hank Snow Cozy Morley (Corn Cob Humor) Carter Sisters with June Carter 101 Ranch Boys	Bill Haley and the Saddlemen Johnny Olsen TV Show Lawson's Original Bums Elton Britt Tim Holt Ray Whitley Hawkshaw HawkinsBingo, the Movie Chimpanzee
Pat Buttram Hawkshaw Hawkins Homer and Jethro Ray Whitley	Rex Trailer Dick Thomas Eckert Family Jimmy Wakely
Bill Haley and the Comets Carl Smith Jimmy Dean Rex Trailer and Goldrush Curly Herdman Red Foley Rex Allen Little Jimmy Dickens and the Country Boys Slim Whitman Jesse Rogers and Sally Starr Texas Jim Robertson Homer and Jethro	Mac McGuire Hank Snow Jimmy Wakely Jack Valentine (Star of Action in the Afternoon) Ferguson Trio Georgia Crackers Lone Pine and Betty Cody Elton Britt Charioteers Tootsie Hippodrome TV Show Reidel, The Magician

Bill Haley and the Comets Jack Valentine and the Ferguson Trio Texas Tommy with his pony and dog act Smiley Burnette Mac McGuire Curly Gibson	Jesse Rogers Sally Starr Curly Herdman Marvin Rainwater Dick Thomas
Marvin Rainwater Rusty and Doug (Kershaw) George Jones Curly Herdman	Lou Graham Sunshine Boys (Gospel Quartet) Harmonica Rascals
Sunshine Boys Cook Brothers (From WWVA Jamboree) Buck Benson and his Radio Troupe The Charioteers (Quartet from Bing Crosby Shows) Tommy Schaffer Bill Haley and the Comets	Shorty Long Jesse Rogers Olsen & Johnson (Hellzapoppin' Revue) Al Rex and His Meteors (Formerly with Billy Haley) Igo (The TV Ghoul) Sally Starr
Grandpa Jones and his Grandchildren Buck Benson and his Country Neighbors The Premiers (Rock 'n' Roll Group)	Bill Haley and the Comets The Cook Brothers (WWVA Jamboree)
Wanda Jackson The Cook Brothers Ozark Jubilee Personalities	Suzi Arden The Roof Rockers (Rock 'n' Roll) Little Jimmy Dickens

Credits & Sources

1920 United States Federal Census

1930 United States Federal Census

The Journal Times; Uptown Theatre Ad; February 13, 1934; Racine, WI

Badger State Barn Dance Featured At The Oshkosh; May 19, 1934; Oshkosh Northwestern; Oshkosh, WI

County Fair, Which Opens Thursday, To Have Many Worth While Features; August 13, 1935; Sheboygan Press; Sheboygan, WI

WHO Barn Dance Frolics At Iowa For Six-Day Run; September 29, 1935; The Courier; Waterloo,IA

Mountain Music, City Slickers, Irish Film; September 30, 1935; The Courier; Waterloo,IA

WHO Barn Dance Frolic Coming; October 19, 1935; Muscatine Journal; Muscatine,IA

Radio Stars At Strand Theater; October 26, 1935; Muscatine Journal; Muscatine,IA

On The Air; July 2, 1936; The Mercury; Pottstown, PA

7 Stars of Air Waves To Give Program here; November 30, 1936; Shamokin News-Dispatch; Shamokin, PA

Fire Company To Offer Program; December 2, 1936; Shamokin News-Dispatch; Shamokin, PA

Legion Drum Corpos Books Cowboy Troupe; April 4, 1937; The Mercury; Pottstown, PA

Veterans To Visit Broadcasting Studio; April 24, 1937; The Mercury; Pottstown, PA

Cowboys Appear In Benefit Tonight; April 27, 1937; The Mercury; Pottstown, PA

More Than 1200 Hear Radio Cowboy Troupe; April 28, 1937; The Mercury; Pottstown, PA

To Present Floor Shows At Cake Hotel Grille; July 3, 1937; The Daily Item; Sunbury, PA

Fireworks Display Closes Festival; July 5, 1937; The Mercury; Pottstown, PA

Cowboys Stop Off At Roadstand Again; April 15, 1938; Latrobe Bulletin; Latrobe, PA

Folk and Western Reviews; July 14, 1947; Cash Box; New York, NY

Folk and Western Reviews; April 23, 1949; Cash Box; New York, NY

The Cash Box Folk And Western Roundup; January 1, 1953; Cash Box; New York, NY

The Cash Box Folk And Western Roundup; January 31, 1953; Cash Box; New York, NY

What The Radio Offers Today; October 11, 1939; Detroit Free Press; Detroit, MI

What The Radio Offers Today; March 22, 1940; Detroit Free Press; Detroit, MI

What The Radio Offers Today; March 25, 1940; Detroit Free Press; Detroit, MI

Hayloft Hoedown; Lew Mel; September 1945; National Hillbilly News; Poster Show Print Co; Huntington, WV

American Folk Tunes; July 14, 1945; The Billboard; Cincinnati, OH

American Folk Tunes; November 10, 1945; The Billboard; Cincinnati, OH

American Folk Tunes; April 20, 1946; The Billboard; Cincinnati, OH

American Folk Tunes; April 27, 1946; The Billboard; Cincinnati, OH

American Folk Tunes; May 11, 1946; The Billboard; Cincinnati, OH

American Folk Tunes; May 25, 1946; The Billboard; Cincinnati, OH

American Folk Tunes; August 24, 1946; The Billboard; Cincinnati, OH

American Folk Tunes; September 14, 1946; The Billboard; Cincinnati, OH

American Folk Tunes; October 5, 1946; The Billboard; Cincinnati, OH

American Folk Tunes; March 1, 1947; The Billboard; Cincinnati, OH

A New Recording Company; June 1946; National Hillbilly News; Poster Show Print Co; Huntington, WV

Arnold Pulls'em In July / August 1947; National Hillbilly News; Poster Show Print Co; Huntington, WV

Philly Record Co. Signing Top Names; January / February 1948; National Hillbilly News; Mr. & Mrs. Orville Via; Huntington, WV

On The Inside With Jenny Via; January / February 1948; National Hillbilly News; Mr. & Mrs. Orville Via; Huntington, WV

America's Fastest Growing Western - Hillbilly Network Show - Hayloft Hoedown; Arlie Kinkade; July 1946; National Hillbilly News; Mr. & Mrs. Orville Via; Huntington, WV

Cast Marks Second Year of 'Hoedown'; May 25, 1947; Philadelphia, Inquirer; Philadelphia, PA

It's Happening Here; Frank Brookhouser; January 12, 1949; Philadelphia, Inquirer; Philadelphia, PA

This, That 'n' The Other; May / June 1949; National Hillbilly News; Mr. & Mrs. Orville Via; Huntington, WV

'Wiffil Ranch› Set For Debut On TV; July 18, 1949; Philadelphia, Inquirer; Philadelphia, PA

Sleepy Hollow Gang Record Two Tunes; March / April 1950; National Hillbilly News; Mr. & Mrs. Orville Via; Huntington, WV

Country Chatter and Platters; Penny Britt; December 1950; Country Song Roundup Issue No. 9; Charlton Pub. Co.; Derby, CT

Eats, Drinks, Names Country Park Formula - Sleepy Hollow Story; June 26, 1954; The Billboard; Cincinnati, OH

Complete Television Programs For Today; June 23, 1956; Philadelphia, Inquirer; Philadelphia, PA

Dr. Smith To Emcee Show; June 16, 1961; The Daily Intelligencer; Doylestown, PA

Sleepy Hollow Ranch Leveled By $50,000 Fire; November 4, 1963; The Morning Call; Allentown, PA

Fire Damages Sleepy Hollow; November 7, 1963; News Herald; Perkasie, PA

Nationally Known Sleepy Hollow Ranch; May 17, 1964; Phildelphia Inquirer; Philadelphia, PA

Action Line; July 24, 1971; Philadelphia, Inquirer; Philadelphia, PA

Revival Walkes Sleepy Hollow Gang; Popular Country and Western Band Reunites in Milford Twp.; August 18, 1986; The Morning Call; Allentown, PA

Country Sound Back In U. Bucks; Chuck Ayers;; August 21, 1989; The Morning Call; Allentown, PA

Milton Estes:
A Forgotten Star

Don Cusic
Belmont University

Preface

In November, 2010, I received an email from Micki Estes with an unpublished manuscript that I downloaded and read. It was a manuscript about her father titled *Milton Estes: The Phantom of the Opry*. In her email she said "I would appreciate any critique you may offer" and included her phone number and email address.

I replied that I thought the work warranted a good, academic article and perhaps a book by an academic publisher—but it would take a lot more research. She was not receptive to those suggestions because she was determined that this manuscript was a money making book. I knew, although I did not tell her, that the manuscript needed extensive editing and rewriting. I then put it in a file and forgot about it.

In 2015 I was searching through my files and came across the file on Milton Estes. I pulled it out, looked it over and sent an email to Micki, telling here that I thought this would be an interesting article in the *International Country Music Journal* and for those who attend the annual International Country Music Conference. She quickly rejected that idea and, during a phone call, told me that she had spent eight years on this project and her family had advised her not to "give it away for nothing." She said she had done more research and had material to add to the original manuscript. I told her I thought there might be the possibility of a book from an academic publisher, but I doubted if there would be any money in an advance or, really, any large sum of money at all.

Her family seemed convinced that the project was worthy of a commercial book and, if published, would make a lot of money. I did not pursue this further.

In the summer of 2017 I was at the British Archive of Country Music in Dover, England, and ran across a CD of Milton Estes that had been released by Cattle, a reissue label in London. Since the British law on copyrights protected recordings for 50 years (not 70 years as later amended) the material was Public Domain in England but not in the U.S. There are a number of small labels in the U.K. that reissue material that is Public Domain. According to Dave Barnes with the British Archive of Country Music, the releases from his label average about 200 units sold—so there isn't a lot of money involved.

On that same day at the British Archive of Country Music, Dave Barnes copied a Milton Estes songbook for me. I had thought about the manuscript from time to time and continued to believe it had potential to be a good article for the *International Country Music Journal*.

In 2018, I learned that Micki Estes had died on May 11, 2016. I contacted her daughter, told her of my interest in the manuscript and she said that her husband would be in contact. I never heard from him.

The body of this work is based on Micki Estes' unpublished manuscript as well as research that I have done. In my book on Eddy Arnold, I first learned of Milton Estes when he was with Pee Wee King's band. Estes was never a "star" but was popular for a new short years and then "disappeared" from the country music community.

Introduction

The key factor in Nashville becoming a major recording center—according to Owen Bradley—was Ernest Tubb's decision—at Paul Cohen's request--to record in Nashville. Prior to that request, Tubb's first two recording sessions were in San Antonio, then he recorded in Houston, Los Angeles, Dallas, Chicago and New York. In 1947 Tubb had recorded in Chicago on February 10 and in Los Angeles on March 24. Then came the request from Paul Cohen, head of Decca's country division, to record in Nashville. Ernest Tubb was on the Grand Ole Opry and lived in Nashville so recording there would be easier than going to Los Angeles, Chicago or New York.

Discussing the reason that Nashville became a major recording center, Owen Bradley said, "If Ernest had said no, we wouldn't have done it, He was that big." (Pugh 130 and Hawkins 226). (In 1947 a *Billboard* article stated that Tubb had received over $50,000 in royalties from Decca during the first six months of that year.)

That historic recording session took play on August 11, 1947.

In 1945, at the end of World War II, Nashville did not have a single record company or recording studio, although radio stations had studios. The following year, Nashville had it's first record label, Bullet, an independent started by Jim Bulleit (prounounced "boo-lay) and it's first recording studio, The Castle Recording Laboratory.

The Castle Studio was started by three WSM engineers, Aaron Shelton, Carl Jenkins and George Reynolds, who had recorded artists in WSM's radio studios. The first major label recording occurred in December, 1944, when Eddy Arnold recorded four songs for RCA Victor. Prior to that, there were field recording sessions by Victor Records in 1928, but it was the only major label field recording done in Nashville and nothing memorable emerged.

The Eddy Arnold session ignited the idea in Aaron Shelton for a commercial recording studio and WSM allowed the use of their studios because the station would receive goodwill and fees from studio bookings.

In 1946, the three engineers set up Castle Recording Laboratories (the name came from WSM's logo, which billed itself the "Air Castle of the South). In 1946 or 1947 the engineers moved to the Tulane Hotel at 206 Eighth Avenue North (on the corner of Eighth and Church Street), a short distance from WSM's offices. The engineers took a Scully lathe to a large, wood-paneled room on the mezzanine level of the Tulane and set up shop.

Bullet Records began by recording and releasing a number of records in the white gospel, black gospel, Rhythm and Blues, country and pop genres. In January, 1947, Francis Craig recorded "Near You," which was released in April and became Nashville's first million selling record, remaining on the top of *Billboard's pop chart for 17 consecutive weeks.*

There is no doubt that those factors had an impact on Paul Cohen when he suggested to Ernest Tubb that he record in Nashville.

On that August 11 session, which began at 9:30 in the morning and finished at one in the afternoon, Ernest Tubb recorded "That Wild and Wicked Look In Your Eye," "A Lonely Heart Knows," "Don't Your Face Look Red" and "Answer to Midnight." "That Wild and Wicked Look in Your Eye" was a "B" side that reached number nine on the *Billboard* chart in 1948.

The same day that Ernest Tubb made his first recordings in Nashville at the Castle Studio, Milton Estes also recorded four songs, "Whoa Sailor," "Swing Wide Your Gate of Love," "When the Fire Comes Down" and "Too Many Women." It was not Estes first recordings in Nashville; earlier he had recorded two songs for Bullet, "That's Why I Worry" and "Say You'll Be Mine" with the vocal by Jimmy Selph. It was released as a single but did not chart.. The Decca recordings were released on two singles but neither charted. (In fact, Milton Estes never had a chart single during his career.)

Also on August 11, Bob Pressley recorded four songs for Decca.

The next day, Red Foley and Jimmie & Leon Short each recorded four songs. On August 13, Tubb recorded three more songs and on August 18, Red Foley recorded four songs. When Paul Cohen came to Nashville, he generally wanted to hold several recording sessions. Ernest Tubb and Red Foley were Decca's big acts, but Cohen must have seen potential in Milton Estes.

Cohen returned to Nashville in December, 1947, for more recording sessions at the Castle Studio. He recorded Salty Holmes, Dick Thomas and His Nashville Ramblers, Bob Pressley, the Pine

Ridge Quartet, Jimmie & Leon Short, four sessions with Ernest Tubb and five sessions with Red Foley over a period of a week (although a session on Foley occurred on December 24).

During that series of recordings, on December 19, Milton Estes and His Musical Millers recorded eight songs: "New Wabash Cannonball," "New Filipino Baby," "Answer to Drivin' Nails in My Coffin," "Happy Birthday Polka," "The Almighty Dollar," "The Waltz I Waltzed With You," "Seems Like Yesterday" and "Out in Pioneer Town." During that same day, Red Foley and the Pine Ridge Quartet also recorded.

None of the songs Milton Estes recorded charted, although all but one song was released.

In February, 2020, I decided to look at the Milton Estes file again and pulled it out. As I read it I realized that although Micki Estes was not a professional writer, she was a diligent and dogged researcher about uncovering stories of her father. As I looked at the manuscript I was tempted to put it back in the file drawer because I knew it needed a lot of work with extensive editing and re-writes. However, the story of Milton Estes, told in Micki's manuscript was simply too intriguing to ignore so I began days of edits and re-writes. I have tried to keep the "spirit" of Micki's manuscript while I edited and re-wrote

There are shifts in the manuscript from first person to third person and back again. Frankly, the manuscript would benefit from more research but I wanted to see this story told and didn't know when I would have the time to do it again. The COVID pandemic made this work possible because the country virtually shut down in March, 2020 and that enabled me to spend time on this article.

The result is the following manuscript based heavily on Micki Estes memoir of her father.

At the end of this manuscript I compiled all of the information about Milton Estes' professional career that I could find.

The story of Milton Estes is a fascinating, though tragic story and gives a glimpse of the life of a country musicians during the 1940s, of Nashville and the Grand Ole Opry but also the story of a family connected to the Opry and their life off stage.

In a "Forward" to the manuscript, Micki Ellis pointed out "a world famous photograph" in Jack Hurst's book, *Nashville's Grand Ole Opry* that is a picture of Milton Estes standing next to Hank Williams but "only the face in semi-profile is visible."

She thanked Ronnie Pugh and Otto Kittsinger for their help in researching her manuscript. Micki and her brother, Denny, had done interviews and other research and worked on this project together. Denny completed five chapter outlines and gave them to Micki but four days later he died in an automobile accident. That caused Mickie to stop work for about two years. However, she picked it up again and began to compile what she had found. This is the manuscript that I received.

The Life of Milton Estes: Compiled by Micki Estes

Milton Estes and his band, The Musical Millers, were much more than successful representatives of Royal-Barry, Carter Mills and The Martha White Flour Company during his time as a performer on the Grand Ole Opry.

Milton's early musical influences were gospel through church and singing schools, but he had an eclectic taste because he loved all music and learned the different types, such as dance bands, polkas, pop and so-called modern music, but above all, he enjoyed true harmony. He simply adored any kind of harmony singing. He was particularly fond of the so-called "blood blends" of families who could produce all four parts, and was a lifelong advocate of harmony singing. He set out to make his way in the world as a performer, and played and sang whatever it took to get him onstage. He also was comfortable doing any kind of acting or skit performance, as well as comedy. Comedy was a special favorite and he used it every chance he got. When he was called upon to form quartets, he was fully familiar with harmony singing. He was a long time fan of the Grand Ole Opry and country music became his life's focus, but he was at home with any kind of performance.

The Musical Millers Band included some of the better known "side-men" of that time. Almost any one of them could have gone on their own as a "solo act" in those days. Orel (Curly) Rhodes, better known then as "Cousin Odie", was an outstanding comic, a very good singer, and a much better than average bass fiddle player. Curly's on-stage counterpart in the comedy department was Clell Summey, who was outstanding at comedy as well as playing the Hawaiian steel guitar,(not the pedal instruments so widely used today) Clell Summey's stage name was "Cousin Jody"

There were several fiddle players at various times in the Musical Millers. Dale Potter, Tommy Jackson. Benny Martin, Chubby Wise, and someone early on known as "Ripplin" Reubin all played fiddle in Milton's band. Reuben is pictured in photos and songbooks but his true name remains a mystery.

There was also an outstanding accordion player, Elbert "Eggy" McEwan, who doubled as a "wry wit," He was probably better known as a practical joker with no peer. The other band members knew, when he was around him, to stay on their toes at all times.

Wayne Fleming played twin-necked steel guitar and the band's front man and featured singer was Jimmie Selph, who was a multi-talented singer and prolific songwriter.

There were also several ladies who contributed much to the band at various times. Their stage names were always, "Martha White."

The time period of this story stretches from his beginnings in 1914 to the middle thirties and well into the middle fifties.

Milton Estes' career on the Grand Ole Opry ran the gamut from amusing, to not so amusing, and in a few instances held tragic and sad stories. Milton had several vices, but drug use was not one of them. However, liquor, women, and an ever-present desire to be fishing when he should have been working, were among his known vices.

A long-time fixture in Nashville's famed Printer's Alley was Nelson Rhodes, who served as major domo/doorman/greeter at every club in the Alley at one time or another since the1940s. . Since you could not buy spirits by the glass in Nashville, the traditional loophole for patrons of those clubs was to keep their own bottle behind the bar so they could be served without the club breaking the law. Milton and others, which included Hank Williams, frequented all the clubs in the Alley. Nelson remembered that Hank and Milton spent many an evening draped across the barstools imbibing from their private stock, kept in brown paper sacks behind the bar. Nelson remembered that Milton was always polite, a good tipper, and never got loud or sloppy, but that he could sure "put away" the booze. He remembered Milton as a snappy dresser who always paid his bar bills. Nelson was far too polite to inquire as to what brand was inside each customer's sack, but he smiled fondly and stated "Oh yes, I remember Mr. Milton well. He drank with Hank."

Beginnings

Some genealogical tracing has unearthed the possibility that the Estes family tree may have a connection to an Italian count, Alfonso d'Este, Duke of Ferrara, who was married to the infamous Lucretia Borgia. Further investigation reveals that Lucretia (illegitimate daughter of Pope Alexander VI) was politically married to various wealthy and powerful men, which was the way it was back then. Her husbands had a habit of dying and leaving their holdings to her, which her father controlled . The Count was Lucretia's third husband, and it was apparently a legitimate love match even though it began as a political arrangement. This union produced five children. That connection is a romantic and amusing notion, but no one in our family paid much attention to that except as merely a sidebar to our roots. Generations later some of our ancestors came to America seeking fame and fortune and made their way to Kentucky, Virginia and Tennessee.

Stefano Estes was the first Estes to immigrate to the United States. He settled in Claiborne County, Tennessee, where he was a coal miner and part-time music teacher. Not much else is known of him except that his son was Steve Estes, father of Milton Estes who was also a coal miner and musician, taught by his father Stefano.

Steve Estes was a coal miner but, like Loretta Lynn's father, was also a farmer who tilled the soil to keep food on the family table. He was known for being charming, affable, and he loved to spin tall tales. He served time in the military, and claimed to have been one of Teddy Roosevelt's Rough Riders who charged up San Juan Hill, where he was wounded. No actual records are in the Estes family attesting to that fact, but a large antique framed portrait of Steve in full military uniform from that time is one of the treasured possessions in the Estes family. That is evidence that he was in the army but the story of him being one of Teddy Roosevelt's Rough Rider is debatable. However, it never hurts to have a war hero in the family

Milton Escoe Estes was born in Arthur, Tennessee on May 9, 1914, His mother was Artie Myers Estes and his father was Steve Estes. The couple had a daughter, Milton's sister, Allie, who was two year's older. Not much is known of Artie's early life except that she was from a large family that settled in and around Arthur in Claiborne County, Tennessee. Myers Grove was named for her family. Myers Grove still exists, mostly as a farming community nestled in the foothills near the Cumberland Gap in Tennessee, with a cemetery and church where Milton is buried not far from his mother.

Allie, Milton and their cousin, Josh, son of Artie's sister Nancy, lived a Huck Finn type of lifestyle. They were free to roam the green hills and be typical kids, doing chores first, then filling their days with fun and, oftentimes, mischief. The Powell River near their home was especially enticing, and provided them not only with recreation but as a source of food from a trotline. For the uninitiated, a trotline is a long piece of weighted fishing line or heavy twine stretched across a river or pond, with many baited hooks hanging from it. A successful trotline must be tended and harvested regularly and bait replaced as needed. This responsibility rested on the shoulders of those three musketeers who were not yet teenagers. They certainly knew how to mix business with pleasure.

One spring day, following several days of heavy downpours, the trio set out to harvest the trotline and do a little swimming as well. Not noticing that the river was at or near flood stage, and the current was much stronger than usual, they got into a homemade boat, determined to do their duty. Cousin Josh, who was two years than Allie, was the first to notice that the river was moving much too fast, and, as Allie told the tale for years, it looked like a river for whitewater rafting. They rode the swollen river until they decided it was time someone should go for help. Milton volunteered and dived in, but disappeared under water and, when he surfaced, the boat had overtaken him after banging hard into his head. Down he went a second time, and Josh and Allie feared he was gone for good but he surfaced again, sputtering and thrashing. Josh leaned over the side of the boat and grabbed him by his hair. They floated downstream for over half a mile and finally came to rest on the opposite bank where the river made a sharp turn.

Josh climbed over the side of the boat and dragged Milton, by his hair, to the shore. Next came the hard part, as far as those three were concerned. They had been told to never go swimming while checking the trotline. Although Milt had been the only one in the water, all three were soaking wet from their rescue attempts, and they were half a mile from where they should have been. How to get the boat back to its starting place? The trotline!

Josh, was on the riverbank and walked back upstream to the trotline, cut it loose, and then used the line to pull himself hand over hand, to the other side of the river. Once there he cut the other end loose, tied it to a large piece of wood, and floated the trotline downstream to where Allie, Milt, and the boat were waiting. The two attached the trotline to the boat and pulled the boat back upstream to the original spot where their adventure began.

None of them could think of a good excuse for not having the trotline intact as it should have been and they still had to confess that not only had they been swimming, but they had almost lost Milton. After satisfying themselves that their offspring were alive and of sound limb, a parental "whooping" was administered by Steve. The trotline only yielded six fish that day!

On another occasion, they were playing hide and seek and Milton was searching for the perfect hiding place when he accidentally fell into the site where the old outhouse was located before it was replaced with a larger one. He was up to his neck, yelling at the top of his lungs before being rescued, albeit from afar, with the longest ropes to be found!. The cleanup took days, and mirrors a similar incident related by Roni Stoneman of the

Stoneman Family. She, too, fell into an outhouse. If you grow up in the country, that's the chance you take, I guess.

While life went on for Allie and Milton, things were not going smoothly for Artie and Steve. Steve was a philanderer and had many paramours until, finally, Artie decided enough was enough and divorced him. By this time, the family had moved to the Yellow Hill Community, across the state line in Kentucky near Middlesboro. Artie worked in a factory in Middlesboro to support herself and Allie, who also worked in the factory as soon as she was old enough. By that time, Milton had left home after many arguments and much butting of heads with Steve, from whom he was estranged during most of Steve's remaining life. Steve was married and divorced several times. Milton never revealed the reasons for being at odds with his father, and neither Allie nor Artie ever spoke about it, but father and son did reconcile shortly before Steve's death.

Steve was an amateur musician who was the son of a music teacher who gave instructions in the area around Tazewell and Myers Grove. Milton learned music early on. While a teenager, he attended the Sizemore Conservatory in Wheeling, West Virginia, after dropping out of formal schooling at home. He received a teaching certificate at Sizemore which he never used. He had previously attended every singing school that came around, learning to read the shaped notes prevalent in church hymnals at the time.

During his adolescent years, Milton became friends with John Cawood, whom he met after the family moved to Yellow Hill. The two went everywhere together and shared a talent and love for making music and singing. However, in their mining camp surroundings, there were few calls for paying jobs. Most of their outings were to schoolhouses or churches for pie suppers, usually ending with a square dance. Milton became especially adept at calling sets for square dances, a talent he used in later years on The Grand Ole Opry. Many times their only pay at those singings was some good local home cooking. Later, Milton wrote a gospel song, "Singing All Day and Dinner on the Ground," (with Joe Allison and Governor Jimmie Davis), inspired, no doubt, by memories of those outings.

Milton soon learned that girls are attracted to musicians so it wasn't long before he was using his talent to get on the good side of an attractive female. He was the first to arrive at any church or schoolhouse gathering where music and young ladies would be, and used his musical talent and personal charm to his advantage. John said that when it was time to go home, more often than not he would have to look for Milton, who would be found holding hands and sweet talking one of the pretty girls at the singing!

John later became a radio personality and country/gospel DJ on WMIK in Middlesboro, where he also headed his local gospel quartet.

At that same radio station, my brother Denny had the privilege years later of working with John when he first began his own radio career.

Milton could play the guitar, mandolin, bass, fiddle, and piano. He could play anything with strings, and could read music, although he professed that it was not enough to hurt his playing. He had learned music arranging through formal musical training. I have personally witnessed him sitting at the kitchen table, with no instrument in sight, writing music the same as you or I would write a letter.

After his conservatory years, Milton searched for a way to earn a living that was fun and not too difficult. His natural ability to connect with people, and his charisma and charm served him well, and he was soon traveling on the vaudeville circuits, engaged in any theatrical job he could find, all the while gaining skills as an entertainer.

While in Cincinnati, Milton met Jim Ballard, an entertainer in that area, who put Milton to work in several of his venues. It was on Ballard's advice that Milton began to seek more stage jobs and he soon found them in places like the Renfro Valley Barn Dance (near Lexington, Kentucky), and the WLS Barn Dance in Chicago. He even ventured as far away as New York City where he dipped his toes in vaudeville.

An Entertainer is Born

During the 1930s—the Great Depression years—Milton was affiliated with medicine shows, tent shows and theatrical troupes that criss-crossed the country, playing show dates in every possible venue. Local theatres and schools provided ready venues for reaching less populated areas where entertainment was not regularly available. For a time he was with the DeForiest Shows, and later with the Bisbee Shows, where he filled in as advance man, traveling to towns early to promote the coming show, post bills and sell advance tickets. In June, 1932, while with DeForiest, he wrote a letter to Joy Brown, a young lady in Gainesboro, Tennessee whom he was trying to "court."

The courtship was not successful because she was 14 and her parents felt she was too young, but Joy Brown kept the letter, which read, in part "Would you like to get some inside information on actors and show people? Well, here are a few of the facts, some good features and some bad ones. We have a good time going from place to place and always meeting new people and forgetting most of them as soon as we are gone and meet some more. .... We are looked upon by some people as being a very low class of people but that is not true. You may find some bad people in show business, yet there are so many people who are not. [S]ometimes we go into a town and not knowing anyone we at once begin trying to meet someone and ... we do not meet with the approval of the better class of people and immediately we are branded."

Even at this stage of his life, he was not naïve to the lifestyle he wanted, and set out to get it.

Micki Estes showed the letter to Richard Kokochak, "a certified graphologist specializing in jury selection" who was "fully credentialed in the art/science of handwriting analysis." Kokochak compared the handwriting on the 1932 letter with his handwriting from a letter written shortly before his death in 1963. The graphologist knew "absolutely nothing about Milton or the circumstances involved. Here are some of the conclusions he drew:

"I see him as a troubadour of his time."

"Milt is looking for some in-between time with Joy. It is Milt's firm belief he can attain the impossible. (Curiously, was there a class or status distinction between Milt and Joy at the time of the letter?)"

"Milt is a romantic, but he is also made up of romantic stories. Such is the predicament of the troubadour—How to tell the story without engaging himself. Milt does it by romanticizing what he does. However, this is contrasted by the background of the times, the mid-1930s which are not so romantic. The troubadour enchants us by his experience on the road and those who stood on the sidelines and listened heard only one version."

"The troubadour myth casts Milt into the role of the God of Love, wandering. The troubadour is of higher rank than the musician, performer, and actor who merely speak his words. The troubadour "invents" the words. I see this as the conflict that exists in Milton the man. The conflict that exists between who he is and who he could be. It is the universal conflict of the poet."

"The uniformity of the earlier letter implies clarity of thinking and organization. This indicates objectivity, harmony, coordination, and timing, all necessary ingredients in music making. Uniformity suggests one who is self-disciplined and self-controlled. His "inner machine" is finely tuned which is positive to his integrity. Rhythm will sometimes neutralize otherwise negative characteristics. At the time of this writing Milt appears to be on an even keel both socially and emotionally."

"He also has disguised letter formations in which certain letters can be mistaken for other letters. This is often seen in the writing of persons who are contrary, tricky, amoral, or who demonstrate active resistance to accepted and legal norms of behavior. I see this manifest itself in Milt as Hermes, the God of Communication, the Messenger. Hermes was a silver-tongued liar. He invented the lyre. I see the shape of a clef mark or lyre in the capital I in the word 'I'm.'"

"[A] self-starter who sees an opportunity and goes for it."

"I see many musical formations in his letters. Many of his capital T's remind me of guitars or banjoes. I see sharp signs in the loops of his f's, which means "brilliant" or "higher than."

"He must have been a silvery tongued idealist who was good at telling the story everyone wants to hear.'

"I notice the difference in his signature thirty years later that he had allowed his imagination to color the incidents of the day.... He never lost his lute.'"

Believe what you wlll about any kind of analysis or character definition from any source, but this analysis of Milton the Man seems to be a remarkable zeroing-in on the face Milton showed to the world.

Later, while with Bisbee's Shows, Milton had the good fortune to work with both Boob and Rod Brasfield, and he became good friends with them. He also took on the skills of a show producer, learning what it took to make a show successful. Most of it came naturally and underscored his instincts at pleasing an audience

Milton was a natural entertainer and learned a lot on the vaudeville circuit. He especially loved comedy, and paid special attention to the routines he saw, and learned to mimic them, often with his own spins and embellishments. This aspect of his theatrical training led him to even greater things. He performed various "hobo" skits as part of his radio personas, i.e., Cicero Sneezeweed and Bozo, just to name two. Corny as it seems now, at the time it was the way to go, and when he no longer had time to do the characters, he made sure there was comic relief in any show he produced.

Mary Rosaline Gore

Mary Rosaline Gore was born in Livingston, Tennessee, the tenth and last child of Marion Colquette Gore and Delia Dillon Gore. Two months before her birth, her father, Marion Gore, was struck and killed by a train in a job-related accident. This last child went unnamed for the first three months of her life, because Delia had promised her older son, Elmer, who was in France in World War I, the privilege of choosing a name for the baby. Battlefield communication was slow, and it was three months before Mary Rosaline received her name.

Three children in the family had died in infancy, and two older boys and two girls had left home --- thus leaving Delia to raise young Rose, as she was called, and the other two siblings, Lois, age six, and Carson, who remained at home. Fourteen-year-old Carson found employment at a shoe shop in nearby Livingston, which helped supplement their meager sharecropping income. Older sons Cordell and Elmer had left home several years before, and daughters Velma and Lola had married and moved to nearby towns. Lois and Rose were frequently left alone while Carson and Delia were in the fields, working to provide food for the table. These were rough years for everyone, but they managed.

Cordell, the eldest, was definitely the wanderer of the family, and was not heard from very often. One Christmas Eve Cordell unexpectedly returned home (he never said where he had been all those years). He had never met his younger sisters until then. On learning that toddler Rose and young Lois would have no Christmas because there was no money, he asked his Mom if she had any cash. She reluctantly parted with her one remaining dollar bill when he asked for it, figuring that a single dollar would not buy enough to call it Christmas. Young Carson's meager wages were long since gone paying for needed supplies for the sparse larder.

Cordell set out for town, and Delia prayed he would not drink away their money, as she knew he was prone to do. He was gone the entire day, and into the evening. Delia tucked the girls in and, long after they were asleep, she heard singing from far off down the country lane. The singing grew nearer and she recognized the voice as Cordell's. He fell into the creek and cursed loudly, but stayed his course to the back door, arriving with three bags filled with toys, food, candy, and other Christmas goodies. So startled was his Mom that she could only say, "Just tell me you didn't steal any of it." He laughingly explained that he used the dollar to get into a floating crap game and parlayed his winnings to buy Christmas gifts for all, getting drunk in the process.

Cordell left home right after Christmas and did not surface again for over 30 years, when he was discovered living in California. Delia always missed her eldest living son but could do nothing to keep him near.

Rose and Lois grew up more or less in a normal atmosphere once the family moved to Livingston proper where the girls attended school. After a few years, they moved to Oneida, Tennessee where the married daughters had settled. Rose and Lois did their parts to add to the family coffers by finding work in the local sock mill. In Oneida we find Rose at a crossroads in her young life.

In the spring of 1934, while acting as advance man with Bisbee's Shows, Milton was in Oneida where a chance encounter with 16-year-old Mary Rosaline Gore changed both of their lives forever. While walking home from work, Rose was spotted by Milton, who was fastening a show poster to a street lamp. From his lofty perch he liked what he saw, and quickly came down and tried to make her acquaintance. Being a well brought up girl, she refused to speak to a stranger. She was more or less "promised" to another young man, so she had no interest in a stranger.

However, faint heart never won fair lady, and Milton devised a scheme to meet her. He became a "stalker," for lack of a better term, and followed her at a distance to see where she was going.

He returned the next day to her home while she was at work, left some free show tickets and became fast friends with her mom, older married sister Lola, and her husband, Oscar Price. So charming was he that he was invited to stay for dinner. Imagine Rose's surprise to walk in on the new best friends!

There is an old adage which says "pet the cow to catch the calf,:" which Milton had expertly done with Rose's family. He persisted in his courtship even after the show moved on, returning to Oneida at every chance. Sadly, there remain no love letters or any correspondence between them. Rose finally broke off with her boyfriend and became engaged to Milton. She went to beauty school in nearby Knoxville with her cousin, Inez, which she attended after saving enough money from her sock mill job.

After earning her diploma in March, 1935, from the Southern School of Beauty Culture of Knoxville, she opened the first beauty parlor in Tazewell, Tennessee, which was near Middlesboro, Kentucky, where Milton's family now lived. The courtship continued, and on November 29, 1935, the two were married at Tazewell, with both mothers and sister Allie in attendance.

Rose didn't stay in the beauty parlor business for long, choosing instead to go on the road with the tent show and her new husband. She even served a turn as a magician's assistant, participating in a girl-disappearing-in-a-trunk routine. The magician's wife began the trick onstage by getting into the trunk, and abracadabra – disappeared totally, only to "reappear" with Rose running down the aisle from the rear of the tent. Rose and the wife resembled one another so that identical clothing and the element of surprise and speed completed the trick. Rose never enjoyed the limelight but went along to be with Milton.

To get off the road, Milton forsook the tent shows for a more stable job and, in early 1935, went to work with Red and Raymond at WSB in Atlanta. Red and Raymond were a popular father-son duo, heard daily on WSB, and did personal appearances in the area. It was while in Atlanta that fellow musician Joe Zinkan and his wife, Lois, and Daddy and Mama became friends. That friendship continued through many years. It was also while in Atlanta in early 1936 that Mama suffered a miscarriage and they decided to return home to be near family.

Daddy and Mama would alternate living with his family and her family during those early years. Milton took a job as a strolling musician in Middlesboro, entertaining at a club which was actually a speakeasy during Prohibition. It was owned by a local "crime family" and served bootleg booze. It provided all forms of "entertainment," both in the bar room and behind closed doors in the hotel upstairs. Milton strolled among the tables with his guitar singing requests. He was a very popular feature of the club, and generous tips came in handy. One of the bosses was the same size as Milton and frequently took him to his home and opened an expensively furnished closet with the invitation to take what he wanted, Milton was always in top fashion, very well dressed, a trait he continued throughout his life.

Nightly fights at the club were the norm, and many times Milton literally feared for his life. An escape from the speakeasy job came one night after Milton witnessed two of the "family" henchmen holding a man forcefully between them while another "family" member shot him dead in cold blood. The crime was never prosecuted, but Milton decided to move to a safer line of work.

Milton Joins Pee Wee King

George Rockwell, the father of American Nazi Party founder George Lincoln Rockwell, was the creator of a very funny and famous routine where, using an empty banana stalk, lectured as a medical doctor with the assistance of a beautiful nurse-assistant, ala Nurse Goodbody.

George Rockwell was never a Nazi, and was estranged from his son, George Lincoln Rockwell.

"Doc" Rockwell's banana routine was so funny and well known that it was imitated up and down the vaudeville circuit.

Milton saw it and gave it his own spin. and it became one of the highlights of his part of any show.

In 1935, Pee Wee King and the Log Cabin Boys played a theatre in Middlesboro where Milton was the locally-hired emcee and opening act. Milton did the banana routine, and Pee Wee laughed so hard that he fell off his chair. After the show he hired Milton on the spot to go with the Log Cabin Boys to WNOX in Knoxville, about 60 miles south. That move "suited Mama and Daddy just fine."

In December, 1935, Milton joined Pee Wee and the Log Cabin Boys at WNOX in Knoxville, with other artists on Lowell Blanchard's Mid-day Merry Go Round. WNOX paid their performers, which was a departure from other radio stations that merely allowed them "free advertising" for personal appearances. A steady radio income, along with income from personal appearances with Pee Wee, came with the WNOX job, which lasted for about a year.

J. L. Frank was Pee Wee King's manager and booking agent as well as his father-in- law. Frank had been Gene Autry's manager until the singer left Chicago for Hollywood. An able and shrewd promoter, who was a successful show producer with a magic touch, Frank guided many artists into prominence. J. L. Frank urged the Grand Ole Opry management to start charging admission at a time when the show was outgrowing every venue it used. While at the Dixie Tabernacle, and shortly before the move to the War Memorial Building, the minimum price of 25 cents per ticket was instituted.

J. L. Frank was inducted into the Country Music Hall of Fame in 1967 for his role in making country music and its artists the success it is today.

J. L. Frank arranged for Pee Wee King and the Golden West Cowboys, the name of his new group, to leave Knoxville for WHAS in Louisville in January, 1937. There was a devastating flood in Louisville that January and February, and the group took to higher ground and waited it out. They were miserable and Rose was pregnant with Denny. They survived the flood and things went well for the band. Dennis Milton Estes arrived on the scene on May 19, 1937.

In those days, new mothers and infants stayed in the hospital for at least a week, and a somewhat daunting hospital bill was coming due. To commemorate Denny's arrival, Mama told us the story of how Daddy penned the song "My Little Buckaroo" and promptly sold it to J. L. Frank for the massive sum of $35 (the amount of the hospital bill). Frank got the song to Gene Autry, who recorded it and it sold well, although it had another composer's name on it! Had Daddy told this story, I might not believe it, but coming from Mama, who never knowingly told an untruth, I know it happened just that way.

Being a consummate showman and entertainer, Pee Wee and J. L. Frank hired only those they considered to be the very best at what they did. Thus, Milton was put to work as a "feature" entertainer, where his talents were utilized as a musician, singer, songwriter, emcee, comedian, and any other job that needed filling. Milton instantly became a hit. By joining the Golden West Cowboys, he joined the ranks of other extremely talented singers and performers, such as Redd Stewart, Cowboy Copas, Eddy Arnold, Texas Daisy, Orel "Curly" Rhodes (brother of Texas Daisy), Minnie Pearl, Clell Summey, and Joe Zinkan, to name but a few. The lives of those and other later famous musicians and entertainers would be interwoven throughout most of their careers, and their paths would cross, and recross countless times. Curly and Clell became known as Cousin Odie and Cousin Jody when Milton was hired by Cohen Williams to promote Martha White Flour. Cousin Jody achieved fame years later on the TV show "Hee Haw."

While pregnant with Denny in Louisville, Mama missed her family, so Daddy arranged to have Mama's 11-year-old niece, Eileen Price (sister Lola's daughter) come for short visits. With only eight years difference in their ages, Eileen was more like a sister than a niece. Several times a young Eddy Arnold stopped by Oneida on his way back to Louisville from family visits in Tennessee, to drive her to Louisville. Eddy could be assured of being well fed on those stops because Lola was a terrific cook and hostess and her husband, Oscar, was a great host and joke teller.

It was a Lola's table that Eddy developed a fondness for peanut butter and tomato sandwiches, while being regaled with my Uncle Oscar's jokes. Eddy loved those jokes, and Eileen remembers he would laugh so hard that no sound would come out and he would struggle to breathe. Anyone who knew Eddy can vouch for this type of laugh fest.

Eddy told of how much help Milton was to the Golden West Cowboys in all areas of performing. He said that Milton taught him the harmonies to all their trio songs.

There were several automobile mishaps and many times the Golden West Cowboys played dates on crutches and in bandages, prompting Milton to dub them "The Walking Wounded."

In 1937 Pee Wee King and the Golden West Cowboys joined the Grand Ole Opry in Nashville . Milton was King's emcee and a featured performer. I've heard that King and his band brought about a subtle change to the Opry, although this change was hardly subtle. It was a real knock-'em-down, slap-'em-in-the-face type change that most everyone agreed was really needed. To add an air of professionalism to the group, they rehearsed their entire show often, to the point where they would come onstage playing the intro to their first number and then proceed without lapses.

They would begin their portion of the Opry with Redd Stewart, Eddy Arnold, Milton, or whichever solo artist was in the spotlight, as a seamless piece of sheer entertainment. No tuning up onstage or deciding which tune to play – it was done smoothly from start to "chase" or exit music. This was not to take away from any of the other entertainers and musicians on the Opry, many of whom only came into town for the Saturday night show and hadn't seen each other since the last show, whereas the Golden West Cowboys performed together daily. The Opry is never rehearsed as a complete show, but by today's standards it is important that each artist be up to snuff on his or her part before appearing.

The Golden West Cowboys brought an air of total preparedness to the stage, and dressed in western costume, thereby setting a tone later used to good advantage by a lot of acts appearing on the Opry. Those acts made a name for themselves and a fortune, for Nudie suits! The Cowboys were never rhinestoned or sequined, but at least they matched in Western design and color.

The Golden West Cowboys were tremendously popular and played many personal appearances. It was while doing a personal appearance in New Hope, Alabama on Friday, May 13, 1938, that they received a phone call inviting them to Hollywood to appear in a movie with Gene Autry. They left for the West Coast the following Wednesday. It was a grueling trip that was accomplished by driving night and day, stopping only to eat, fuel up, and change drivers.

They spent four weeks filming *Gold Mine in the Sky,* which featured Autry and Smiley Burnett. The story line was nearly the same as most western films of the day: a white-hatted cowboy comes to the rescue of a damsel in distress (whether or not she knew she was in distress) with lots of bunk house music, horseback chases, and fist fights where the hero's white hat NEVER gets knocked off his head. It ends with the cowboy kissing his horse and riding off in the sunset.

Gold Mine in the Sky was no different, but it was charming and a showcase for the musical talents of the group. Milton had lots of face time in the movie but no dialogue and no individual screen credit.

I still enjoy watching the film because it is true to the genre of western movies so loved by generations. Daddy said that making movies was easy and fun for a while, but he would not want to do it forever. Also appearing in *Gold Mine* were The Stafford Sisters, with a young Jo Stafford singing her part of the trio from the left side of the formation. Years later, Jo made a huge hit with her recording of "You Belong to Me" written by Pee Wee and Redd Stewart.

It was during his stint with the Golden West Cowboys that Milton came to be a lifelong fan of close harmony singing like that done by the sister act The Dinning Sisters. That group had been at

WLS's National Barn Dance, and consisted of sisters who truly had what is known as the "blood blend" of harmony.

It was after Denny was born in 1937, and shortly before I came along in 1939, that a young girl came to our door in Nashville, asking for Daddy. Mama was pregnant with me, and the girl was also pregnant. Mama never named the woman but told us that she claimed to have had a relationship with Daddy, not knowing that he was married, and now was carrying his child.

There they stood, belly to belly, discussing the same man and what to do about the situation. The girl met Daddy when the group played a show in her town (Mama never said where) and formed a liaison. She seemed a decent person, realized that the situation was hopeless for her, so she apologized and left.

Mama never knew what happened to the girl or the child, but she heard the child was a boy. The incident brought about a brief separation between Mama and Daddy. He went with the Delmore Brothers to Raleigh, and she went to her sister's in Oneida. They reconciled shortly after when he returned to Nashville in late 1938. In later years Denny and I talked about this, wishing we knew who our half brother was so we would each have another sibling.

The Delmore Brothers and Raleigh

After returning to Nashville from Hollywood, in September,1938, Milton decided to go with the Delmore Brothers to WPTF in Raleigh, along with Joe Zinkan, who had also been with Pee Wee's band. The Delmore Brothers were at WPTF a short time (from mid-September until December 1938) before moving to Charlotte, North Carolina. Their work habits had placed their tenure at WPTF in jeopardy (and at other radio stations during their career), so Daddy chose not to stay in Raleigh, but returned to Nashville and WSM.

Mama stayed behind because of her pregnancy with me, living with her sister in Oneida, and with Grandma Artie in Middlesboro. Daddy worked again for Pee Wee King and doubled as an Opry announcer for WSM. Meanwhile, Grandma Artie became ill with breast cancer so there were many trips back to Middlesboro.

Twenty-five years after Daddy went with the Delmore Brothers to Raleigh, Alton Delmore wrote a book *Truth is Stranger Than Publicity*. Charles Wolfe, a professor at Middle Tennessee State University and author of several books on country music, edited the book. In a footnote there is a mistake about the arrival of the Delmores in Raleigh in 1938. Wolfe stated that Milton and Joe Zinkan had been brought from the Opry to Raleigh to form the nucleus of the band to work at WPTF. He states that this band was "intact" for two years. Wolfe is mistaken because Daddy was back in Nashville on WSM in 1939 only three months after being in Raleigh and by the time of my birth in April, 1939.

The Delmore book states that during the time of their transition from the Opry to WPTF an unidentified member of the band "double crossed" them and took over their work at Raleigh. Since Daddy was with Pee Wee King at that time on the Opry, it might be natural to presume it was Milton Estes.

I went to the Country Music Foundation's Archive and read the original manuscript written by Alton Delmore about his account of what happened and subsequently talked with many of the people who knew one or both of the parties about the account. From that, I pieced together a timeline of Daddy's time with the Delmore Brothers.

The Delmores left the Opry at the end of September. Alton Delmore stated that "[o}ne of Pee Wee's main men begged" the Delmores to take him with them to Raleigh, and stated that person "was on his last legs" and was about to have a "nervous breakdown" so they agreed to take him with them to Raleigh. Delmore indicated that this person (never identified by name, simply alluded to in statements) would be "dealt with later" in his book. No chapter on this person has ever been found in Delmore's papers that identified him.)

That person gave notice to J. L. Frank and, according to Delmore, Frank allegedly became furious with him for leaving Pee Wee's employ and fired him without letting him work out a two weeks' notice.

Delmore stated that "this person" went to Raleigh in those two weeks to seek out lodging, etc. to pave the way for their arrival. I spoke to those who knew Mr. Frank, and they unequivocally said he would not have become "furious" with anyone, and probably would never have done what Delmore claimed.

The presumption is that it was probably Milton who went to Raleigh from Nashville two weeks before the Delmores. If this was the case, WPTF station management probably did talk to him. Since he was accustomed to taking charge and producing shows, it would have been natural for him to suppose the Delmores would want to have things in place, especially since that was why that person was to go to Raleigh early to scout out housing, etc.

In the Delmore book, it states they arrived in Raleigh on that first day, admittedly "nervous" and in "bad shape" after having driven all night from Nashville, drinking large amounts of whiskey along the way. They were scheduled to do a morning show and then a noon show. On their first day, after their programs, a meeting was held with WPTF management and all remarks were addressed to "this person." That may have been because of the "bad shape" (their words) of the Delmores.

It was claimed that "this person" told a theatre manager at a personal appearance that he was the "star" of the show. This would have been absurd on its face because the Delmores were the act and not Milton Estes.

If WPTF management continued to deal with Milton and not the Delmores directly, it may have been because of the attitude and condition of the Delmores in that three to four month period. Throughout the Delmore book there are references to how management at every station where they worked was "out to get them" or that they "looked down their noses" at them, and generally developed a mindset that management was not something they enjoyed dealing with. They had been an entire day late for their initial audition in Nashville for a spot on the Opry. That, plus their admitted reputation of being drunken rowdies who destroyed hotel rooms and other drunken behavior sets a behavior pattern, at least in my mind.

In December, 1938, the Delmores reportedly showed up for a show and found it usurped by this person. What time did they show up and in what condition? That was the end of the Delmores on WPTF.

I have been unable to find anyone who heard the Delmore accusation until it appeared in Delmore's book. Not one person, even Joe Zinkan, ever mentioned any problem.

As for "a nervous breakdown" or "being on his last legs," that simply does not fit the persona of Milton Estes either as a person or as an entertainer. According to Grant Turner, Milton had "mastered the art of relaxation."

I feel that inasmuch as the Delmore manuscript was written 25 years after the fact, and given their admitted drunken demeanor and reputation, coupled with their paranoid feelings toward any kind of station management, that Delmore wanted to fix the blame on someone besides themselves for any failure at their radio station engagement. After a short period of time, from September to December 1938, they were history at WPTF.

I spoke with Lionel Delmore, son of Alton and he was most gracious and friendly on the phone and stated that he looked forward to sitting down and talking with me. He said that he remembered Milton, and was extremely cooperative. Unfortunately, he became ill with cancer and died before we could get together. I feel that if he had been aware of any wrongdoing on Milton's part toward his father and uncle, he would not have been so willing to talk with me.

Returns to Nashville and the Grand Ole Opry

Deciding that it was just not worth the trouble, and with Mama being pregnant with me, Daddy went back to the Opry as an announcer and re-joined Pee Wee's band. Grandma Artie had become ill with cancer, and a lot of time was spent going back and forth to Kentucky. Daddy was back in Nashville, where I was born on April 2, 1939.

It happened when Mama, Daddy and Denny were spending a nice Spring Sunday at Pee Wee's home. I had the opportunity to view some snapshots that Pee Wee King donated to the Hall of Fame Archives, and among them were several shots of Daddy mugging for the camera at what appears to be a picnic or backyard gathering. In some of the snapshots was Mama, who appeared to be pregnant. None of the photos had dates, but it may have been at this gathering when Mama went into labor and delivered me three weeks prematurely.

J.L. Frank and his wife, as well as Pee Wee's wife, Lydia, and others, were enjoying the early spring weather. In the course of the afternoon, Mama told Lydia that she felt something was not quite right with her eight and a half months pregnancy so the ladies retired to the bedroom to check things out. Lydia had given birth to Marietta Jo, Frank, Jr., and a set of twins so she knew the drill pretty well. Mama's water had broken and Lydia felt that it was time to get to the hospital, and went to inform the others.

Daddy had been through Denny's birth so he was a seasoned veteran and wasn't too alarmed but Pee Wee, despite having children, had never been present for the birth of any of his children since he had been on the road at the times of their births.

Pee Wee went absolutely berserk and started barking panicked orders to "do something" and cursing, waving his arms, and insisting on a police escort. He managed to get a motorcycle escort, much to Mama's humiliation, and we all arrived at St. Thomas Hospital amidst the ravings of an apparent madman! Lydia's assessment was correct, and something was definitely amiss. Since St. Thomas was a Roman Catholic affiliated hospital, the doctors examined Mama and then forms were brought for Daddy to sign authorizing the sacrifice of the mother in order to save the infant.

At that point, Daddy went slightly loony as well, and the rest of the ensemble almost got out of control, but one doctor said he thought he could rescue both and he did just that. So, on April 2, 1939, Marilyn Alice Estes made her entrance into the world despite being a breech birth with the umbilical cord wrapped precariously around her neck. A relief to all, to say the least.

The nurses mistakenly thought that Pee Wee was the father because of his behavior but Mr. Frank smoothed things over by buying a box of chocolates for each nurse on the shift. Mama needed a blood transfusion, and the Golden West Cowboys lined up to do their part. It turned out that only Curly Rhodes was a match, and forever after that he said I had his blood flowing in my veins! However, Pee Wee got things a little confused and remembered himself as being the blood donor. Lydia tried to set him straight numerous times, but he always claimed I was "blood" kin, and professed to be my Godfather.

That's OK with me, since not everyone can have a Country Music Hall of Famer for a Godfather. Daddy and Mama brought me home to an apartment on Acklen Avenue, near Vanderbilt University.

A few months after my birth, Grandma Artie's condition worsened, and during the next year we were back and forth to Middlesboro to help care for her until her death in June, 1940.

With a growing family to support, Daddy was looking around for opportunities to improve his lot. He had become acquainted with Wally Fowler when Fowler was at WSM during the late 1930s as part of the John Daniel Quartet. Upon learning the financial side of quartet singing, conversations with Fowler led Daddy to get in touch with the Stamps-Baxter organization in Dallas with an eye to putting his natural talents and love for harmony singing to good use. His early experience with singing schools and conservatory training made him a definite asset to Stamps-Baxter. Wally Fowler and Daddy reconnected years later when Fowler staged the "All Night Sings" with the Oak Ridge Quartet in Nashville. Stamps-Baxter was first to come up with the concept of the "all night sings" and they became an instant success. The Musical Millers Quartet appeared on the first of Wally Fowler's "All Night Sings" on November 4, 1948. Daddy also lent his voice to the Oak Ridge Boys Quartet whenever anyone was sick or on vacation, since he could sing all four parts. Milton and Fowler were known to bend a few elbows along the way as well.

Singing Gospel

The Stamps-Baxter Music and Printing Company was one of the biggest songbook publishers and promoters of gospel music in the country. Virgil Oliver Stamps and J. R. Baxter, Jr. had formed the company in Dallas, Texas in 1926.

Daddy went to the Stamps Baxter singing school in Dallas shortly after Grandma Artie died in June, 1940. After completing Stamps Baxter training, he was sent from Dallas to WFTX in

Wichita Falls with the first Lone Star Quartet. This group was formed as a temporary group but neither Daddy nor the others knew that at the time. The Stamps-Baxter concept of the use of multiple groups had been successfully established by this time and so the entire group was dismissed except for Daddy, who was then sent to another location to form another Lone Star Quartet. Daddy had the ability to listen to a group while they were singing and show them or write for them several different arrangements in order to improve their sound, the song, or its manner of presentation. His natural ability as a show producer and as a showman stood him in good stead.

The Stamps-Baxter system provided a salary, car, travel expenses, and also provided a percentage of sales from Stamps-Baxter songbooks and whatever merchandise they chose to promote. Milton was a master at arranging and scoring music and had a natural and uncanny ability to hear, and sing, all four quartet parts. He insisted that those who auditioned had to be able to sing *a cappella,* since most quartets had very little musical accompaniment except a piano or possibly a guitar.

Drawing on contacts he had made in Raleigh with the Delmores, Milton was sent to Raleigh in early November, 1941, to form another Lone Star Quartet and audition for a spot on WPTF. They were hired and the Estes family settled in Raleigh where Daddy not only appeared with the Lone Star Quartet, but emceed "The Tobacco Hour" and began expanding his career to utilize his natural talents and abilities as emcee and show producer.

Family Life

Throughout the early years of their marriage, Daddy and Mama lived in a series of boarding houses. Before apartment houses or motels were commonplace, boarding houses were the norm. My earliest memories of Daddy and Mama were when we were at a "Mrs. Porter's" in Raleigh. Large old houses were broken up into rooms or "apartments" which rented to singles, with the larger spaces going to families, although there was one large room with a kitchenette and, if you were lucky, its own bath. Most had communal bathrooms that were shared by all the tenants, and woe unto you if you left it in a mess!

Those not fortunate to have cooking facilities ate in the dining room at regular mealtimes. The places without dining facilities were rented because several single rooms and maybe one or two "apartments" could be put to good use by married couples doing the cooking and the single ones sharing the table and kicking in their share for groceries. They took turns grocery shopping, too, since supermarkets were few and far between.

At any given time in any number of cities, Mom and the other wives cooked for the band. The boarding houses were utilized in most of the cities where Daddy worked, and Mama did her share of kitchen duty. Some of those who shared our table at different locations along the way were Archie Campbell (he raved over Mama's biscuits) Curley Rhodes and Clell Summey.

The boarding house system was a Godsend in our early years. Mama did our laundry in the bathtub, sometimes without a washboard. She could always count on a babysitter, and Denny and I were doted upon by the other boarders. I firmly believe this interaction played a large part in making us both very outgoing and sociable kids. When acts moved on to a new radio station, finding a boarding house was their first priority.

In 1945, Delia Upchurch had a large home at 620 Boscobel Street in Nashville and decided to take in boarders. Her first boarder was Shorty Boyd, and then came Don Davis, steel guitarist for Pee Wee King' band. Don persuaded her to not only rent rooms, but to throw in meals as well. For $7 a week we had a bed and shared bath, breakfast for 75 cents and dinner for 85 cents. We were in that large fraternity of musicians with likes, talents and ambitions.

She became known as "Mom" to her boarders, and like any good mother, sometimes had to keep her "kids" in line. Members of her large "family" through the years included a Who's Who of country music: Daddy and Mama (while Denny and I were in Middlesboro with Allie and Lester), several of the Musical Millers (Wayne Fleming, Dale Potter), Grandpa Jones, the entire Carter Family, Carl Smith, Joel Price, Faron Young, Gordon Terry, Lightning' Chance, Walter Haynes, Buck Trent, George McCormick, Buddy Spicer, Donna Darlene, Luke Brandon, Hank Cochran, Stonewall Jackson, Paul Sharon, Stan Hitchcock, Jimmy Elrod, Pete Wade, Rudy Lyle, Joe Edwards, Larry Kirby, Strolling' Tom Pritchard, Grady Martin, Lloyd Green, Ray Edenton, Blackie Bennett, Hank Garland, Donnie Young (Johnny Paycheck), Darrell McCall, Benny Williams and Howard White, just to name a few. Stars, sidemen and songwriters all shared the frat house which "Mom" supervised. As long as they were in the music industry and behaved themselves, they were welcome in that stone and stucco home.

In Mrs. Porter's boarding house during out first few months in Raleigh my first conscious memory is of me standing barefoot and in training panties on the front porch at the boarding house, balancing myself with one hand on Daddy's knee, and bouncing up and down to the rhythm of his guitar while he sang:

Won't you come along with me
> Down the Mississippi
> We'll take a boat to the land of dreams
> Float down the river down to New Orleans

I clapped my hands with the others when the song ended.

It was while we were in Wichita Falls that Mama first became ill and, after our move to Raleigh, she was diagnosed with cancer and hospitalized. She, of course, was too ill to keep up with Denny and me, so Eileen was sent for and proved to be a godsend.

Since Eileen would be living with us, we needed more space as a family so we moved around the corner from the boarding house to 409 North Bloodworth Street, a large two-story white frame house with four bedrooms, a large dining room, big kitchen, and two bathrooms. Since Mama was hospitalized, 18-year-old Eileen did the actual moving from the boarding house. Granny Gore arrived and she pitched in too.

Eileen recalled that shortly after the move, while Mama was still in the hospital, Daddy picked her up from secretarial school, drove home,, walked in, stopped her at the living room and ordered her to stay there. Then he, Granny, Ollie the cook/nanny/housekeeper, and us kids emerged from the kitchen with the very first birthday cake she ever had. Daddy had arranged the celebration, complete with a hand picked gift of a new purse to match her coat. We all sang "Happy Birthday" and within 15 minutes he was off for a personal appearance. She says it was her most memorable birthday.

Mama's diagnosis of cancer came at a time when that was a death sentence. Cancer treatment was in its pioneer days, and Mama was the first woman at Duke University Hospital to undergo radium treatments. The effectiveness of this treatment was unknown at the time, but having done all they knew how to do, her doctors told her to go home and get her affairs in order, find someone to raise her kids and wait for the end within six months. The prognosis was grim, but they did not know how stubborn Mama could be about things that truly mattered. She chose not to follow their advice.

Daddy hired Ollie, (whose surname sadly no one remembers), a wonderful black woman to keep house and cook while Eileen and Granny Gore tended to the kids. When Granny was there, she and Ollie got along well, and divided their duties between Mama and us kids. Ollie was uneducated and could not read or write, but she knew how to take care of a family. She did the grocery shopping by the pictures on the cans, and could whip up gourmet meals at the drop of a can opener! Her biscuits were superb, and Denny remembered never being sent off to school two blocks away without one of those mouth-watering creations slathered in butter and jam!

We both learned a lot about life from Ollie and, when the time came to leave her, we were all devastated because she would not leave her family and travel with us to Nashville.

Not many of us remember the World War II years when oleo margarine first came on the market. Along with gasoline, most things required rationing stamps so leather, meat, butter, and a lot of other things were scarce. Oleo margarine came in a one pound white block, with a packet of flavoring and food coloring included so the entire block could be mixed until it was yellow like butter.

Granny Gore was intent on taking care of Mama and Daddy so she arose every morning when Daddy did and made him a cup of coffee before he left for his early morning radio show. Granny hustled Daddy off for his show, and when Ollie arrived, they poured their own cup and turned on the radio to listen while they started the day.

At a time when most entertaining was done at home, the Estes family had a state-of-the-art Radio/Victrola which was used during the evening to play the latest dance records and listen to radio shows with our guests. The Victrola featured a knob that activated an automatic record changer so that a stack of 78 RPM records could be loaded. Continual changing of discs was a thing of the past. The Victrola would replay the last record over and over until it was turned off or reprogrammed.

One day, Granny cautiously knocked on Mama's door and hesitantly informed her that something was wrong –- Daddy must not have made it to work because the station had played "Don't Sit Under the Apple Tree" ten times and he was still not there!

Since we were new arrivals in the neighborhood, our neighbors knew nothing about us. They only saw two kids, a young lady, Eileen, whom they mistakenly thought was our mother since Mom was still bedridden. They did not see Dad because his comings and goings were early mornings or late evenings after personal appearances. Most of our new neighbors were astounded and shocked when any of Eileen's boyfriends came to visit her. Eileen was quite beautiful, and she had little trouble finding beaus, most of whom were in the navy or army at that time.

One of Mama's doctors, early in her illness, made weekly house calls. The mailman would often be invited in for a cup of coffee and a piece of Ollie's pie, so it seemed like there were a lot of men coming and going at 409 North Bloodworth. Eileen laughed about some of the icy stares she received, and smiled inwardly at their obvious thoughts about all those men coming and going, and with those sweet little children around, too!

Before Mama could get out of bed and venture into the yard or porch, the neighbors did not know the true story. Once, Denny and I had retrieved some empty beer bottles from the trash and refilled them with Kool Aid and sat on the front curb drinking the Kool-Air from the beer bottles. One concerned neighbor could stand it no longer, and confronted Eileen with an angry "Mrs. Estes, do y'all know that yore little babies are sittin' out there on the curb swiggin' beer? Just what are y'all gonna to do about it?" Eileen invited her inside to investigate the situation, and after carefully tasting the contents together they had a good laugh and became friends. She was introduced to Mama and they, too, became friends.

Every day Daddy would drop Eileen off at secretarial school on his way to his noontime show, and often a strange female would also "hitch" a ride. Eileen later figured out that this was one of Daddy's cheating affairs. .

Eileen laughingly recalled that whenever Pee Wee King was in Raleigh for a show, he would visit with Daddy and Mama, and always found time to take her to lunch at The Green Lantern cafeteria on her break from school. People stared and he told Eileen that it was because people would always remember seeing him in western attire escorting a very pretty, very tall young lady. Pee Wee was five feet six inches while Eileen was just under six feet tall.

Mama knew that all was not well in her relationship with Daddy, and she was overwhelmed with dread at the prospect of dying, not for her own death, but the thought of leaving her two babies with Daddy. It seemed like more than she could endure. She prayed a lot about her predicament.

Not being one to negotiate with God (she felt this was not the right thing to do since you do not bargain with The Big Guy) she reached deep within herself and came up with a plan to grow as strong as she could so that we would at least remember a mother who was not weak, gaunt, and bedridden.

Ollie was instructed by the doctors to feed Mama Jello, custards, milk toast, and bland foods. Mama not only grew weaker on this fare but she was constantly hungry, so she summoned Ollie to her bedside and told her that from then on she would eat whatever the family ate – beans, greens, corn bread, biscuits, meat and potatoes. If that kind of diet killed her, so be it – but she vowed not to die hungry with a wasted look that her kids would always remember. Ollie did as she was told.

Mama's strength improved to the point that at her next checkup (which none of the medics anticipated), her doctor, Annie Payne (great name for a doctor, huh?) came to the waiting room door and asked where Mrs. Estes was. When Mama stood up and approached her, Dr. Payne's mouth dropped open and stayed that way for about two minutes. Rose had rallied and felt and looked much better. Mama steadily improved, and for the balance of her life--over 50 years--she credited her survival to the "cornbread cure."

Eileen came to Raleigh to help Mama during this most difficult time of her life and she became a large part of Daddy's professional life as well. She had secured a scholarship in Tennessee to attend secretarial college, but when Mama fell ill, she managed to transfer the scholarship to a school in Raleigh. She attended classes then came home to Mama, did her homework and helped Denny and me to book shows. She was charged with reading and answering Daddy's large bags of fan mail, which was good practice for a secretary. The fan mail read like letters from home, and a lot of them told about crops, daily lives, and anything under the sun, just as they would write a relative or friend. Such was the charisma and charm Daddy exhibited, even through the radio waves. People trusted him, loved him, and felt close to him.

After I returned to Nashville from Michigan, I spoke with Melvin Sloan, leader of the Grand Ole Opry's Square Dancers, and brother of Ralph Sloan, who stated that when he heard Daddy on the radio, he felt like he was talking directly to him and him alone. He felt like Daddy was an old friend, which was proof of Daddy's charisma that transcended the airwaves.

Eileen recalled that gifts came to Daddy from his listeners and fans: a jar of jam, box of cookies, cakes, handmade trinkets, and all manner of offerings. Denny recalled the time one fan delivered to one of Daddy's personal appearances a fully trained English Setter after he heard that hunting was a sport Daddy enjoyed. The quartet and the dog drove back to Raleigh and got as far as our front door when the dog balked. Pushing and dragging was in vain so he ended up tied to a tree in the back yard.

Daddy phoned the fan, who laughingly explained that as a pup the man's wife would use a broom to keep him out the house, swatting at him if he even came near the door. Aside from being an outdoor dog, he turned out to be a crackerjack hunter.

World War II was raging and gasoline rationing was important to the war effort. Booklets of gas stamps were issued and if you had no stamps, you got no gas. The quartet pooled their resources to get enough stamps to keep personal appearances going, using Daddy's 1940 Pontiac Chieftain furnished by Stamps-Baxter. The car had room for all of them and seemed to defy gas rationing. Even quartet members who owned no automobile seemed to magically acquire gas stamps. Once Denny and I got in real trouble when we took a book of ration stamps and played "post office" by sticking them all over the garage wall. That was the first "whoopin" I ever had, and I remember it to this day.

Denny's experience with the car caused him a bit of anguish. One time, while playing "driving daddy's car," he noticed that a small insect had become trapped inside the glass covering over the speedometer. With his newly acquired tiny pocket knife Denny tried to use the tiny blade to pry off the glass and release the poor thing, but it only broke the knife tip, which fell behind the glass with the bug. Denny lay awake several nights waiting to be punished for his misdeed, but Daddy probably never noticed the problem, so nothing ever came of the incident. The old car probably went to its grave with the knife blade and bug in the speedometer.

The Lone Star Quartet

The Lone Star Quartet was tremendously popular at WPTF where Daddy also performed on a noontime radio show called "The Tobacco Hour" which featured The Tobacco Tags band. He also was emcee of their Saturday night radio show. The format of the noontime show was a dress rehearsal for his later stint on WSM's "Noontime Neighbors." His association with the Tobacco Tags later gave him the idea to craft the Martha White Jingle, which was based on an old public domain song recorded by many artists through the years.

The stories of Daddy's exceptional talent were not just rumors. Every musician ever associated with him in those early and later years also had an exceptional and unique talent. No wonder so many of the quartet and band members became the Super Sidemen associated with the Nashville Sound years later.

Many gospel quartets in those days sang with little musical accompaniment, usually only a piano or guitar, and often simply *a capella* It was, and is, difficult to sing this way but Daddy was extremely good at it. Whenever he auditioned singers for various parts of his quartets, the one ability that he always insisted on for a signer was to be able to sing a capella Denny once witnessed an incident at our home in Raleigh, when a bass singer whose name isn't known to me, auditioned for the Lone Star Quartet. His range was incredible, and Daddy asked him to follow his lead on the piano, then struck a middle bass note. The singer responded and they went lower, lower, and still lower, with each progression being exactly on key and in perfect pitch. Daddy asked if he could go even lower, he nodded, and then not only sang the lowest note on the piano but went a full note lower! It seemed that the whole house vibrated. He was hired.

Only the best could be in the Lone Stars. Some of the quartet members were Carl Raines, Clark Blanch, "Little" Johnny New, and piano player Charlie Fryer to name a few. They were all exceptional talents.

While in Raleigh, Daddy received notice that he was to be examined by, and possibly inducted into the U.S. Army. Germany had already surrendered, and Daddy was being examined at the induction station when word came that Japan had also surrendered. The war was over. Daddy, along with the two hundred other near inductees at Raleigh, was told to "just go home and wait." They waited, but the call back from the army never came. .

We remained in Raleigh until Daddy decided to return to WSM, initially as an Opry emcee. Daddy was back in Nashville in October, 1945, with early morning shows at WSM and the first Opry broadcast for Martha White Flour in January, 1946.

I have examined countless photographs of the Grand Ole Opry cast onstage, and looked at all the faces with a magnifying glass. Not once have I found a picture of Daddy onstage, with the exception of a photo published, oddly enough, in a cookbook for Martha White Flour. While not an official WSM Opry cast photo, it shows him at the microphone center stage, with Rod Brasfield, Grant Turner, Cousin Jody, Dale Potter, Eggy McEwan, Ernest Tubb, and Annie Lou and Danny. Mama explained that his absence from group pictures is probably because he was off fishing somewhere and could not be bothered to show up.

Back to Nashville and the Opry

The return to Nashville in October 1945, began Daddy's climb up the WSM/Opry ladder as a star and personality in his own right. His affiliation with Martha White was a dream come true for a young entertainer seeking his place in the world. He would be allowed to grow along with the fortunes of Martha White, and he put together a team to get him, his music, and his sponsor center stage wherever there was an opportunity. So far as we have been able to discover, he never had a manager; he preferred to chart and rule his own course, although he did utilize Jim Denny and the WSM Artist Bureau to book shows for him and the Musical Millers.

Grant Turner said that WSM Station and Opry Manager, Harry Stone had a lot to do with building shows. Jack Stapp worked with him on that, but Harry Stone was the one who put shows together, and the two probably said "Let's get Milton to come to WSM."

In the December, 1945, edition of *The Grinders Switch Gazette* was an announcement. "Look who's back," it said. "In October, 1945, Milton came back to WSM [from Raleigh, NC] as staff M.C. You will hear him on the air every morning from 6 to 7 CST, and from 12:30 to 1:00 P.M. on the "Noontime Neighbors Show."

Waylon Jennings' words "I've seen the world with a 5-piece band lookin' at the backside of me" comes to mind when I remember that in all the time Daddy was on the Opry, neither Denny nor I ever viewed a show from out front. I was 22 years old before I viewed the Opry from the audience side of the footlights and witnessed the tremendously spellbinding and entertaining production it is.

Martha White Flower

Cohen Williams was a visionary. He had a vision of how to run a flour business and that included the best way to get his product in front of the public. When he took over the reins of the Royal Flour Company, based in Lebanon, Tennessee, he already knew about the success of the Burris Mills venture in Texas that bought radio time and hired a band, Pappy O'Daniel's Light Crust Doughboys. He decided he could do even better by hiring the right entertainment and putting that entertainment on WSM clear channel 650 in Nashville. He began a search for the right entertainer to do that.

Cohen was an avid country music fan and knew what he wanted to help him sell his flour. The Royal Flour Company had sponsored some Opry shows, but when it became Royal Barry Carter Mills, the company changed its name to Martha White. On a suggestion from Jack Stapp, Cohen listened to Daddy on several occasions on the radio and in person and became convinced that Milton Estes was the right person for the job so he hired Daddy to carry forth his dream of building the Martha White Flour Company.

Daddy entered into an arrangement with Cohen Williams to form a band to be known as the Musical Millers, with Daddy as the Old Flour Peddler. The financial arrangement was unusual in that day and age because the band members were paid directly by the company and Daddy could keep all the proceeds from any personal appearances by him and the band as long as the Musical Millers upheld the Opry tradition of appearing the required number of weeks yearly on the Opry.

Grant Turner, whom I consider to be the Dean of Opry Announcers, came to WSM in 1944. He met Daddy when he returned to WSM in 1945, and announced his early morning shows. Grant told me that Tom Hansard was one of the producers of "Noontime Neighbors." That show was a big production, produced in segments. Milton produced the country music part of the show, and Owen Bradley did the pop music part, leading a 26-piece orchestra. Milton was emcee and handled all of the musical parts of the show and then gave the reins to John McDonald, Farm Director of WSM, who presented the farm news. John McDonald was popular, and his farm reports were not just hog and bushel reports. One of his best loved topics was the many uses of corncobs.

WSM relied on the demographics of its rural audience in guiding how "Noontime Neighbors" went, and focused on things the listening audience wanted to hear. Their mail told them what their audience preferred.

Milton was an avid fisherman and referred to "Noontime Neighbors" as "The Fishing Show." There were daily reports on "catches" that became a regular spot on "Noontime Neighbors."

Grant was the announcer for the early six a.m. show for Martha White.. "How Many Biscuits Can You Eat This Morning" was their theme song for quite a while. Daddy took the Martha White version from an old time fiddle tune.

Martha White Lindsey was the daughter of Richard Lindsey, Sr., who founded Royal Flour Mills in 1899 and he named his flour after his then three-year old daughter. When the Williams family acquired the company in 1941, they changed the name of the company to Martha White and kept Martha's sweet face as the logo for their product.

From the first early morning broadcast in 1946, the jingle "How Many Biscuits Can You Eat This Morning?" became a household melody throughout the South and over the WSM airwaves. The jingle was based on an old-time folk/fiddle song of the same name, which was composed sometime before 1924 and originally attributed to Gwin Foster. The song was re-recorded in 1939 by Foster with the Tobacco Tags backing him. Since Daddy worked with the Tobacco Tags in Raleigh, he was already familiar with the song.

The song was in public domain by the time we got to Nashville, and had been recorded by countless folk and old-time singers, including Dr. Humphrey Bates. Uncle Dave Macon, Stringbean, and others throughout the years.

I remember sitting at the kitchen table in the War Memorial apartment while Daddy put this jingle together from that tune. He would strum the guitar and sing some words, then write them down, then repeat the process. When it came to the part of the jingle "Always bake with Martha White, 'Goodness Gracious It's Good' that was my cue to say "goodness gracious it's good." I had such fun helping Daddy write that jingle! It became synonymous with Martha White and Milton Estes. The jingle then went to the ad agency handling the Martha White account for $25 a week. I doubt that Daddy ever gave a second thought to claiming authorship since it was part of his deal with Cohen Williams to promote Martha White flour at every turn.

Years later, Will (Bill) Graham of the Noble Drury advertising agency took credit for having "crafted" the jingle. Graham at one time was a publicist for WSM who had written numerous press releases about Daddy and other WSM artists. Much has been said about the Flatt and Scruggs "You Bake Right With Martha White" song that they used and even recorded on one of their albums but only the old timers to remembered the original jingle popularized by Daddy.

Daddy wanted to have me do a voice over of the phrase to be used on all the radio spots, but Mama put her foot down and simply would not allow it.

Grant Turner remembered that the Musical Millers accordion player was Eggy McEwan, who later played at the legendary restaurant "Jimmy Kelly's" as a strolling musician. Jimmy Kelly's 216 Club was the original club and Daddy's favorite watering hole for much elbow-bending. It was located at that time virtually in the shadow of the WSM studios. Eggy spent much time clubbing with Daddy, but he did not fish.

Milton Estes favorite hobby was fishing and Turner remembered that Milton "fished at Rudy's on Trace Creek. Rudy's wife did the cooking at a fish camp there. They would stay at Rudy's two or three days or at least once a week. He always had good boats and equipment. There was a sports shop 'Tommy's' on Gallatin Road in Madison, and a lot of stars bought their boats there. Milton bought an aluminum boat when they came out. I went with him once to Trace Creek. The motor developed trouble which made me nervous but Milton loved it [time spent on the water]. Trace Creek was west of Waverly off old Highway 70 then you go north to a road that leads to the creek."

Turner continued, "During that time it became clear that he would rather be fishing, and the Martha White agency complained about it. According to Cohen Williams, they were paying him $50,000 per year. Milton threw it all away because he got to where he didn't want to work."

Milton Estes was a showman and a great show producer. He blazed the trail with giveaways of flour and corn meal at shows. He and the band traveled by Chrysler limo, and gave away coupons for prizes. They carried a sample sack to the shows to do the "commercials."

"The thing I always thought about Milton was that he was totally relaxed," recalled Grant Turner. " He could come to a microphone and he was never tense or nervous. Milton could just carry the show through, and if anything went wrong, you'd never know it. That was probably his strongest point. He was totally organized and he knew exactly what was coming next. He was a wonderful emcee, and knew where he was at any point in the show. He was not an announcer; he did not read commercials. I never heard him read one commercial, but on the air he would make comments like 'We gave away so many bags of Martha White Flour last night' and that kind of thing. The [WSM] announcers doubled as emcees to a certain extent, then the talent emceed his portion of the Opry. If some were unable to act as emcee the announcers picked it up but Milton handled it all. And he could really sing! However, he mastered the art of relaxation to the extent that he worked himself out of a job or two. But he could handle a show perfectly because he had that know-how and experience."

Mama always said that Daddy was a master at getting the audience involved in his shows at whatever school house or court house they played. He would get individuals onstage and interview them and do various things to make the person look and feel good about being a part of the show. He just had a knack with people and could put them totally at ease. This carried over to his radio and Opry work, too.

Grant recalled some incidents from their personal appearances. "Once they were returning from north of Carthage, Tennessee and two small towns stuck in his mind; one was called Defeated and the other was Difficult. On a country road late at night some neighborhood boys wanted to roust them and hassled them, but on the main road, Highway 70 out of Carthage, they were stopped by a patrolman. When he stopped them he looked inside, shining his flashlight on everyone, and Cousin Jody was asleep. The officer said 'You are all drunk! That man is the drunkest I've ever seen!' They talked their way out of it. Without his teeth Jody looked drunk. His nose and chin would meet without his teeth in. Once a photo circulated in which Jody was not labeled as an entertainer, and he wanted to sue for slander."

"Milton and Eggy McEwan hung around together a lot," continued Turner. "They drank and needed help. I heard stories that Milton pawned Eggy's accordion to buy liquor and Eggy woke up and looked for it and they had to search to redeem it. The music community treated it as a joke that booze would preempt working tools."

Daddy had a rule that none of the band could drink while "on duty" and he did not drink either. Afterwards, the band members could get drunker than Hooter Brown, but not while working with him for Martha White.

Milton wasn't a tall fellow but he commanded an audience just like a big man, or like a "big businessman." He was rugged and had a good color with a perpetual tan because he was outdoors so much."

Daddy was originally on WSM radio in the early morning. The response was as Cohen Williams knew it would be and Opry time swiftly followed so that, by 1946, Daddy's radio appearances grew to 26 times weekly, doing early morning and noontime shows. He was also required to be the entertainment at corporate functions for the flour salesmen and companies of Martha White and, in general, became the first paid spokesman for a product, long before Ed McMahan educated us on life insurance and Publishers Clearing House. Charismatic and always amiable, Daddy was the perfect spokesman.

Grant Turner and Joe Allison both stated that "All of WSM was abuzz about how much money he was making -- $1700 a week, which in 1947 was a fortune!" Both Allison and Turner said the halls at WSM literally rang with the news every time Daddy's name came up.

Years later, when I started to research this book, I was dismayed that no paper trail could be found anywhere to verify his arrangement with Martha White. Williams' daughter, Connie King Brothers, was also concerned that neither of us could track down anyone who had documents about the arrangement. It was not until Louise Scruggs, wife of Earl Scruggs and the business manager for Flatt and Scruggs verified that Cohen Williams preferred to do business with a handshake only, and that they never had a written contract. Lance Leroy, long-time booking agent for Flatt and Scruggs, verified what Louise Scruggs had said, that Cohen Williams liked to operate on a handshake so that if either party became dissatisfied, there would be no drawn-out "goodbyes."

Williams knew he had the right person in Daddy, who was now billed as Milton Estes, "The Old Flour Peddler" along with his band, "The Musical Millers." The band members, were auditioned and hired by Daddy, but were all paid by Martha White Flour. They were to do the live early morning programs, with an additional half hour segment every Saturday night on the Martha White portion of the Grand Ole Opry. That particular Opry segment was broadcast nationally by NBC. At that time the Opry did not have the Friday night shows.

Daddy's first year's salary was to be $48,000 and that was to be his own money. Consider that this was in 1946, so that was a fantastic amount of money for most people. Many of the major league's better baseball players were paid less than a third of that amount. The band members, and all of their traveling expenses, were paid by Martha White Flour. The Musical Millers first steel guitar player, Wayne Fleming, said that his weekly check was $50 from Martha White, not from Daddy. Daddy was to keep all of the personal appearance receipts, as long as he and the Musical Millers promoted Martha White Flour on all their road shows. To say this arrangement proved to be successful for all is a classic understatement. Daddy really threw himself into this job, and drove the band members to improve "every time we go out."

According to Connie King Brothers, the daughter of Cohen Williams, Cohen often told her that Daddy was the very best at convincing people to buy any product that he had ever known. By his own admission, Williams was always delighted with his choice over the period of years that followed. Ms. Brothers also said that Williams would closely listen to *all* of Daddy's radio programs and was more than delighted with what he heard. Cohen himself was an advocate of authentic country music and did not like amplified instruments. He made one exception for Clell Summey's electric steel guitar, but did not approve of drums or other percussion instruments in country bands.

Ms. Brothers recalled that "Milton was a flashy dresser, always in good taste. He loved good clothes and, if I'm not mistaken, he wore a grey felt hat that had a rolled up brim," She continued, "When things started going downhill for Milton, my Daddy began looking around for someone else but, you know, my Daddy never said a word about Milton drinking, he just never would bring that home. He never mentioned that. But that doesn't take away from what all he did. Talent comes out naturally with people who have real talent – and he did. He always knew what he wanted from his band. He was great at predicting outcomes and he picked up on things immediately to make the best show possible. "

When my brother Denny last spoke with Williams, in the Spring of 1968, Cohen still spoke in the most glowing terms about his association, and of his own *personal* relationship, with Daddy. There were several times, however, when Daddy would, or would not do something, which infuriated the brass at WSM. He would be a no-show for days at a time, and management at WSM would fire him. Then Cohen Williams would intercede on Daddy's behalf and smooth things over. In spite of all those times, Cohen never lost his faith in Daddy, and strongly defended him in all matters until the very end. Daddy never went to Cohen Williams for help when any of those troubles occurred but Ms. Brothers told us that on more than one occasion, her Dad had stepped in, and in one instance had even 'angrily threatened' to 'immediately' cancel all of Martha White's advertising on both WSM, and on The Grand Ole Opry."

He did this, according to Ms. Brothers, to force Harry Stone (WSM's manager) to back off and rehire Daddy. Edwin Craig, the president of the National Life and Accident Insurance Company, which owned WSM and the Grand Ole Opry, was the ultimate decision-maker on Daddy's behalf, and he had a close relationship with Daddy. If things got too heated and ended in Daddy's suspension or outright dismissal, Daddy would call Mr. Craig, who would in turn call management and tell them to put him back on. They always did until the bitter end when the management became a united front and refused to reinstate him."

Hatch Show Print in Nashville houses printing plates dating back to the origin of the Ryman Auditorium and even further. They printed show bills and posters for whatever event was appearing in Nashville or was coming to town. After my return to Nashville to live, I happened to drive by the Hatch location on Fourth Avenue, where Alan Jackson's tour bus was parked at the curb. I decided to go in and inquire about Daddy's printing plates, with a view to purchasing them. I was warmly greeted by the manager, who produced a clipboard with a thick accumulation of yellow legal pad paper and went down a list until he found Daddy's name. He explained that since Hatch was now under National Historical protection, they could not sell the plates, but yes, indeed, they have them. Through several physical moves of their facility, the plates are intact, and they have graciously given me several prints.

Any publicity photos for Martha White were taken by their ad agency, and the plates were probably produced from those. There is a photo in Jack Hurst's book showing Daddy with a moustache, which is totally awful in my opinion, but I saw it on city buses and billboards while it was being used. Apparently he didn't like the "look" too much either, because (thankfully) it wasn't utilized too long.

Family Life From Raleigh to Nashville

In 1945, after returning to Nashville, Daddy and Mama made plans to move the family from Raleigh. In what became a summertime routine, Denny and I were taken to Allie's in Middlesboro for a long visit until plans in Nashville could be finalized. Mama and Daddy stayed at Mom Upchurch's boarding house, where they accompanied Grandpa Jones and Ramona to Kentucky to be married. Mama and Daddy always felt comfortable leaving us in the care of Allie and Lester. They had no children of their own, and it was like having a second Mom and Dad. They were indulgent and spoiled us, but not to the point where we were impossible to live with. We had the same rules and privileges that we had with Mama and Daddy. The advantages were tremendous to us as kids, and I know it helped Mama a lot, and gave her breathing space to be with Daddy and escape the cramped apartment.

In Raleigh, I was enrolled in first grade and wanted to be more like Denny and learn to read. However, three months into the school year, we pulled up stakes and went back to Middlesboro so Daddy and Mama could go to Nashville and set up our new life there. I was enrolled in first grade in Middlesboro in the late fall, just long enough for me to remember coloring pumpkins for the Thanksgiving holiday (I made them pink because that was prettier than orange) and Santa Claus and Christmas trees for that season, only to be bundled up with all our stuff right after Christmas and leave for Nashville where I was enrolled in first grade at Howard School on Second Avenue. Mama recalled that none of the teachers wanted either Denny or me in their classes because we had been in two schools in less than six months so that must mean we were brain damaged or "slow." The teachers eventually drew straws to see who "lost" and took us in our respective classes. Mama said the teachers were pleasantly surprised to get bright, well adjusted students despite our career of moving about.

Things were not totally settled when we arrived in Nashville during the early winter days of 1946. It was cold, wet and miserable. We stayed for a week or so in a motel/trailer park (they were called tourist courts in those days), on Dickerson Pike. Also in residence at the motel were Clell and Sarah Summey . Clell became famous as "Cousin Jody" playing his famous non-pedal steel guitar, affectionately nicknamed a "biscuit board." Later,, Cousin Jody appeared on the Opry as a single act, and appeared in package shows along with backups such as Smiley and Kitty Wilson. He was one of the acts on the Gannaway movie series, and later became a great addition to the "Hee Haw" TV series. He had worked with Daddy when he was with Pee Wee King, and was half of "Odie and Jody," the comedy team of the Musical Millers.

Our little family stayed at the motel/trailer park until we moved downtown to The War Memorial Apartment Hotel, located at Seventh and Charlotte, diagonally across from the State Capitol Building and at the opposite end of the same block as the National Life Building, which housed WSM on the fifth floor.

Our small apartment in the War Memorial Apartments, consisted of one large room. It was a sort of combination living room-dining room-bedroom with one double bed (a Murphy bed, that folded into the wall), two cots (for us kids), a small bathroom, and a very small kitchenette. However, it was only one block away from the WSM studios and Daddy's new work and he promised us that it was only a temporary home.

It also was a block and a half from the "red light district" across from the State Capitol on Seventh Avenue. We, of course, were forbidden to even walk on that side of the street (we didn't know why), but we could play on the grounds of the Capitol, which we did almost daily, weather permitting. We climbed on the statues and cannons and gamboled on the green lawn. There were no other children in residence, so outside of school we spent a lot of time together.

Denny and I also had the run of downtown Nashville, which in those days was not nearly as large as it is today. When we were "out" Mama threatened us with a fate worse than death if we did not stay together at all times, so we roamed the Arcade and Fifth Avenue dime stores, literally "joined at the hip" since we were always together.

If we were gone more than an hour, we could expect Mama to be hoofing it up the street with fire in her eyes but we were so central to downtown as it was then, that we could safely come and go the three to four short blocks away from the apartment building. Another playground was the basement of the apartment building, where we played hide and seek amid the furniture storage and laundry areas and vast array of rooms. There was a small grocery store located in one corner of the basement on the Charlotte Avenue side, and we made zillions of trips there to buy candy and gum which, we learned, could be charged to our room account.

We knew our exploring time would be short lived, so we made the most of it. We lasted about eight months before Mama put her foot down and insisted that we have proper housing where kids could lead a normal life. Mama told me later that if left to his own devices, Daddy would have stayed in that hotel forever. He didn't really care about being a home owner, but he finally caved to her pressure.

Since Mama did not drive, she began spending large chunks of her days getting into cars with realtors who whisked her away to show her nearly every home in Nashville that was for sale. She didn't care whether the desk clerks thought it strange that men collected her from the lobby of the hotel and left with her for several hours during the day. She was always back by the time school let out. She eventually found suitable housing for us based on the budget given to her by Daddy, and so 3615 Baxter Avenue in Inglewood was our new home. We each had our own bedroom, a back yard, and the Jere Baxter School playground was right across the street from our front lawn. We made friends quickly with the kids in our neighborhood, and our house quickly became kid headquarters since it was located so close to the playground.

When we were at the Memorial Hotel Apartments, a lot of socializing went on amongst WSM workers, script writers, and anyone else who happened to be around. There were a lot of colorful characters and Mama and Daddy were popular with all of them. A lot of parties went on, both planned and impromptu, at our residence, or at WSM functions.

At one of the parties, a public relations man for one of the Opry performers or sponsors dropped by. His name was "Tiny" Grayson and he was a giant of a man, nearly seven feet tall, a real saint of a man but, unfortunately, a very homely man to look at (sorry, but true). All of the Opry brats seemed to love him though, and he in turn loved kids in general. He was so tall, that in order to be able to drive his car, "Tiny" had to have the front seat removed so he drove it sitting in the back seat.

But back to that party. "Tiny" Grayson had walked up behind the wife of one of those Southern industrialists in attendance while she happened to be standing alone at the bar. When "Tiny" reached past her to pick up a glass of Champagne, the slightly tipsy woman took one quick, terrified look at "Tiny" and screamed "Oh My God! I don't think I can ever drink enough of this stuff to make you go away." By that time, "Tiny" had long been accustomed to adverse reactions to his appearance, so he was somewhat amused by this particular encounter. He laughingly, and repeatedly, related the incident to anyone, and everyone, over and over again, for a long time following the incident.

That amusing incident happened about six months prior to what I feel to this day has to be the cruelest practical joke ever played on anyone at any time. For WSM's Christmas party that year, all of the entertainers drew names from a cowboy hat to exchange gifts at the party. I won't tell which Hank played a very bad joke on the other Hank, but one of the Hanks had a terrible thirst for liquor that everyone knew about. The other Hank, (he had the same thirst that very few knew about) bought for the first Hank a fifth of Jack Daniel's whiskey. He then went to a Nashville locksmith, who sold novelty combination locks styled as stoppers and had it installed into the neck of the gift bottle! Hank Number One then wrapped it in very pretty Christmas paper and placed it under the tree.

When all the gifts had been handed out, Hank Number Two unwrapped his, and then spent the rest of the evening at the party trying to figure out the combination to that lock. He finally gave up on opening the bottle normally and broke the neck off the bottle by striking it against the door. He then poured what was left of the whiskey into a tall glass, shouted "Merry Christmas" and drained it straight down !

There was a lot of practical joking at WSM. One of the most often related was an incident involving the YWCA and a pair of binoculars utilized by staff announcer Louis Buck. The windows from one of the WSM newsrooms overlooked the YWCA and Buck and his fellow voyeurs frequently watched young ladies in the various rooms of the Y. One holiday weekend, when most of the young women were not in residence at the Y, Buck trained his spyglass on other Nashville buildings. The Hermitage Hotel was across the corner from the YWCA and, in his scanning, Buck discovered a man in his room engaging in sexual self-gratification. Buck called to others at the station and they enjoyed the "show" for a time, then decided to play a trick on the unsuspecting man. Through deduction and a phone call to the front desk of the hotel, they ascertained which room was occupied, and then telephoned that room. They watched as the phone was picked up by the man and Buck said in his most mellifluous tone: God's watching you! The man threw the receiver across the room, much to the loud laughter of those in the WSM studios.

That tale was told by Daddy to Mama and although neither Denny nor I understood what we were hearing at the time. It finally became funny when we understood what transpired.

Another time, announcer Tom Hanserd was the victim of a prank when the engineers set him up to read the news into a dead microphone while the real news was being read in another studio by another announcer. In mid-sentence the unsuspecting Tom heard a voice saying "Get back. You're too close. You're spitting on me. Back off." Tom was sure this was going out over the airwaves and sweated bullets until an engineer came and let him off the hook.

Such was the camaraderie that existed at WSM in those early days.

In our new home, Mama set about furnishing the house and settling in. Mama had great taste in clothing and furnishings, and could have been a decorator had she chosen to do so. Once, while viewing the TV series "The West Wing," I noticed several sofas, chairs and lamps which looked identical to those Mama had selected for our home. I am certain the furnishings in The White

House are authentic, but nonetheless they reflect Mama's good taste in my opinion.

Some tweaking in our new house was needed here and there, not the least of which was the matter of security and proper locks on the doors. The house had a basement, albeit not fully finished, with a stairway leading up to a 3-foot landing which had a door on either side, one into the kitchen and one into Denny's bedroom. Neither of those two doors had a lock. Mama reasoned that while upstairs we were safe enough if the front and back doors were locked but what if someone got into the basement and came up to murder us in our sleep? So she asked Daddy if he would install sliding bolts on the doors so we could feel safer. No problem, said he, and promptly installed sliding bolts on the two doors in question – on the stairway side! After his mistake was pointed out, he got mad and left home for two days! No more "honey do" lists for Daddy.

Those double doors to the basement resulted in the loss of my belief in Santa Claus. Denny, of course, had already had this revelation, but had not spoiled it for me. One year we had each asked for bicycles from Santa, and after we went to bed, Daddy and Uncle Lester went to the basement to assemble them. Lots of Christmas cheer was flowing, and before long it was so cheerful that as they started to go upstairs, they fell backward down the stairs with a terrible noise and fits of hilarious laughter. Denny and I were sharing his room because of all our holiday guests, and we sprung from our beds to see what was the matter. From our position at the top of those stairs we saw the two besotted elves, and that was the end of Santa for me.

Daddy and Uncle Lester were always fast friends and, from the time of our births, we were special to Allie and Lester. One of Allie's favorite Christmas memories was the year four-year old Denny got an electric train from Santa and Daddy and Uncle Lester got down on the floor to set it up for him. Once finished, they would not let him play with it, saying "Get back, Denny, you'll break it" and hogged the train set for most of the day.

At holiday time our house was always filled with guests and family members and was generally a grand time, A lot of good food, drink, and socializing abounded. Favorite Christmas memories to us involved our housefuls of guests.

One year our guests were Allie and Uncle Lester, Granny Gore, Mama's sister Lois and her husband Ray, and their 12-year old son, Lloyd. We loved houseguests and the more the merrier was our philosophy at holiday time. That Christmas Eve when Denny and I hung our stockings on the mantle and went to bed, the adults began discussing the fact that Lloyd was at a terrible age – too old for Santa and too young to be left out of the stocking phase of Christmas. After much holiday cheer and scheming, it was decided that Lloyd, too, should have his own stocking and one of Allie's nylons was pressed into service. It was tacked to the mantle and the task of filling it began. The job became problematical when the more they stuffed in the stocking, the longer it stretched. They finally resorted to stuffing in all the candy and fruit in the house, using magazines and anything with bulk, until it finally came to rest on the hearth and stretched almost eight feet across the floor! The next morning, Lloyd doubled over with laughter at the sight, and told that tale every Christmas holiday.

At Christmas and on birthdays Denny and I enjoyed the benefits of the good life when Daddy was alive and we always got every item we asked for, and then some. We enjoyed some unique toys, and really had a ball with our material wealth. Mama didn't always reap the same benefits gift-wise because by this time Daddy was totally into himself. One Christmas Eve he presented her with a boxed Schaeffer ball point pen and pencil set he had picked up on his way home for the night. She no doubt was crushed that he had not put more thought into her gift, but she never let on. I thought it was a rather cheesy gift for her since our tree was nearly covered with gifts for me and Denny. Still, we were kids who really were "rewarded" or "bought off" by the tremendous amount of money that was showered on us. In the end we had more fun playing with our friends and not thinking about the money part of things.

When Micki began working on this manuscript, she approached Bill Anderson who asked, during his "Backstage at the Opry" TV show, if anyone had any information about Milton Estes to let him know. As a result of that request, a letter from Durward Willoughby came in.

Micki stated that he wrote about the 1948 and 1949 period when he was their neighbor and newspaper boy. Mickie stated that Durward had first-hand knowledge of Daddy's automobiles since he worked at Inglewood Garage, owned by J. B. "Shorty" Robinson. Interestingly, Shorty lived next door to Bunny Biggs of the Jamup & Honey Opry comedy team. The garage was three or four miles north of the Nashville City Limits sign at Cahal Avenue. (The population sign read 147,000 at that time!)

The Inglewood Garage did a lot of work on vehicles used by several Opry personalities, including Daddy. In those days many of the Opry stars made their road tours in nine passenger "limos." Part of his job was searching for parts to keep the cars running. Shorty would tell Durwood to "get your ass in the wind, but don't get caught," thereby earning Durward the nickname "Speedy." According to Speedy, Daddy was one of the few who had a Chrysler limo (most had Cadillacs). Shorty's garage favored GM autos, but Speedy said he thought Chryslers were easier to work on and required less maintenance. Part of his duties included acting as courtesy car driver, taking customers to work and picking them up. Many times he took Daddy downtown to WSM in the big black Chrysler. They would wave us past the gate at the parking lot. Boy, was I in tall cotton! Driving that big Chrysler at WSM!" Speedy also rememberd dropping off Daddy's fiddle player, Dale Potter, at WSM while his new '48 Plymouth Coupe was serviced.

Speedy knew airplane mechanics and worked at Colmill Flying Service at Cornelia Fort Airpark. On those service drives, they would talk about their mutual fondness for Willis Vic, the flight instructor. Daddy earned his pilot's license and took us for rides frequently and used the plane to promote his shows as well. In April, 1947, Bill Graham wrote in *Record Roundup* magazine "One of the hottest show promotions of the month is credited to Milton Estes, who got air-minded to plug his personal appearance at Columbia, Tennessee, this month. A qualified pilot, Milton chartered a plane and ballyhooed his show with the Saturday afternoon crowd by circling over the city with a loud-speaker system in his plane. As he told the neck-craning populace about his show, he further plugged the appearance by releasing thousands of throw-aways over the city."

Daddy loved to take risks and felt confident in doing whatever he wanted to do while at the controls of the plane. One favorite trick was to fly low over the Cumberland River and dip the wheels in the water and then climb out rapidly. I was along for the ride one day when he did that, and after the stunt I came home and gleefully told Mama how we had "washed the wheels." I was henceforth banned from flying with Daddy, which made me heartbroken.

Once, while flying with Denny, Daddy's plane developed engine trouble and was forced to land in a pea patch. The successful landing was not without damage, however, as the vines from the peas totally wrecked the underside and wheels of the plane, but the farmer took both of them to his house where his wife fed them an excellent lunch. That lunch included cornbread made with Martha White meal. Phone calls were made to rescue Daddy and Denny and restitution for the destroyed crop was made to the farmer.

That was the last ride that Denny took with Daddy in an airplane.

Sadly, Willis was killed in an air crash near Camden, Tennessee, the same area where Patsy Cline, Hawkshaw Hawkins and Cowboy Copas lost their lives. After Willis died, Daddy never flew again.

Fishing was Daddy's true love. He fished with whoever would go with him, and if there were no takers, he would go alone, spending hours on the water. He didn't really care if he caught anything, although he was quite skilled as an angler. Everyone had a Milton Estes fishing story to tell. Grant Turner told where Milton liked to fish but, truth be told, he would fish in a bucket if that's all there was handy.

One Sunday Daddy was supposed to sing a solo at our church, and I decided to ride over with him ahead of Mama and Denny. Instead of going five blocks to church, Daddy headed the car to Waverly and the boat dock, where we spent the day fishing in our Sunday finery. When we arrived home well after dark, there was literally hell to pay from Mama.

Golf was another hobby Daddy enjoyed and, while it was fun, it was also a way to keep his hand in with the Martha White executives and top sales people. I recall many times going with him and my brother Denny to some country club for Daddy to play golf. I would wheedle money from him to go horseback riding at the stables next door, while Denny traipsed around the links acting as caddy and earning pocket money from tips.

Milton Estes became a member of the Grand Ole Opry in June, 1946. In her unpublished manuscript, Micki Estes describes "a look at the incredible rich, colorful crazy quilt which made up Daddy's years at WSM and the Grand Ole Opry. These were some of the people with whom he worked, admired, and became friends. I do not mean to single out any one person or artist as being more popular or influential to Daddy, but merely to give insight into the wonderful community that made up our world at that time."

She continued:

Today it is a widely-held belief that one must have a hit record or two before being made a member of the Grand Ole Opry but, during the early years of the Opry, the recording industry had not yet become the power that it became and enjoys today. Since the beginning of the Opry, many of its early stars did not even record their music, including Uncle Jimmy Thompson, The Fruit Jar Drinkers, Gulley Jumpers, and even Roy Acuff early on. The airwaves ruled the live Opry shows. Such was the case with Pee Wee King, and most of the early Opry members. In the early days it was the popularity of an artist that was the key to Opry membership. The amount of fan mail often made the difference in whether a performer became a member or not.

Upon his return to WSM, Daddy quickly moved to the front of the pack.

Since the beginning of his career, Daddy had performed with the very best musicians, featured artists, and stars, and would accept none but the best to be in his band or be with him on stage for any show that he assembled. Milton Estes admired and respected those with talent.

When he was asked to put together the Martha White showcase band, his experience with tent shows and touring with J. L. Frank and Pee Wee King taught him what went over best with an audience. His band, the Musical Millers, was the Best of the Best.

Jimmy Selph was the featured performer or "front man." Selph was a terrific singer and prolific songwriter and was at the front of the band when Daddy oversaw the Musical Millers show. Jimmy went on to become one of the leading side men in Nashville and had a great career as a session musician. He and Daddy co-wrote lots of songs and he later sold his entire song catalog to Sony Publishing. I do not know what his and Daddy's relationship was toward the end, but Jimmy stated, after several requests from me, that he preferred not to talk about it.

The first steel guitarist with the Musical Millers was Wayne Fleming, who played pedal steel. He worked with the Musical Millers and in my several phone conversations with him at his home in Roanoke, Virginia, he gave me insight into the salary structure and working conditions with Daddy. He, too, lived at Ma Upchurch's boarding house and stated that he was paid $50 per week, which in his words was a "fortune" at that time. He said that the checks came from the Martha White Company, not from Daddy. His dream was to be a Texas Troubadour with Ernest Tubb and when an opening came with Tubb, he realized his dream of becoming a Texas Troubadour.

James Clell Summey played "biscuit board" steel guitar. Clell later gained fame as "Cousin Jody." Curley Rhodes and Clell formed the comedy team of Odie and Jody in the Musical Millers group. They were rube comics who dressed in funny costumes and did corny humor loved by audiences during the Musical Millers personal appearances. Clell had worked with Daddy at various times in Knoxville and in Raleigh. His wife, Sarah, was one of Mama's closest friends.

Orville "Curley" Rhodes was the original bass fiddle player and half of the comic relief on the show. Curley had also been with Pee Wee King. He was single when the Musical Millers were formed but, after meeting Mary Claire, secretary to Jim Denny at WSM, the two began a courtship and married. Sarah Summey and Mary Claire spent many Sunday afternoons with Mama while the guys were at a personal appearance. Mary Claire often said to Mama later that if Daddy had just taken stock options from Martha

White in the divorce settlement, our family would have fared quite well. But at the time, who knew?

Cousin Jody is responsible for my real love and avocation – comedy. While Curley and his new bride, Mary Claire, were on their honeymoon, Daddy performed at a Sunday Dunbar Cave show. Daddy had decided to forego the Odie and Jody portion of the show for lack of a partner. At the last minute Daddy decided that I could do the straight man lines so the act could proceed. I said OK, not fully understanding what was about to happen but I agreed because Daddy asked me to. Jody rehearsed me and we went on with this:

Micki: It can't be done!
Jody: It can be done!
Micki: It can't be done!
Jody: It can be done!
Micki: No, it can't! (Stamping my Mary Janed foot)
Daddy: Hold on a minute, stop arguing. What can't be done?
Jody: Milk a cow with a monkey wrench!

The audience roared with laughter, probably not from the old joke but from a little girl arguing with the costumed Jody. I experienced my first wave of laughter coming across the footlights, and I never got over it. I was eight years old.

Elbert "Eggy" McEwan was an accordionist like Pee Wee King, and he and Daddy hit it off right away. He loved being a prankster and practical joker and he zinged many an unsuspecting "victim" to kept his own funny bone alive. In the military, Eggy had been a crewman on the backup aircraft to the "Enola Gay" that dropped the atomic bomb on Hiroshima. Eggy said that none of the crew of either aircraft knew which would deliver the dreadful payload until almost over the target. He said he was glad not to have been on the plane that actually unleashed so much horror. Eggy and his wife were childless, much to my and Denny's dismay, but they did have a cocker spaniel Eggy acquired in the Philippine Islands that he brought back to the states. "Flaps" flew every mission with Eggy after Hiroshima, and understood no English except "eat" and "want to play flashlight?"

While "Ripplin' Reuben" was the first Musical Miller fiddle player, not much is known about how long he stayed or even who he was.

Tommy Jackson was a great fiddle player who worked with the Musical Millers for quite a while. He, too, went on to become one of the Super Side Men when the Nashville Sound was born. Tommy was a nice young man who had good insight into what Daddy was doing and how he was treating Mama. While Daddy was never physically abusive, and wasn't home much to argue and be verbally abusive, Tommy saw Daddy's behavior at shows and personal appearances with the groupies and hangers-on of that time and felt it was not right. Tommy could have been employed by any artist or band in Nashville, but he enjoyed being a Musical Miller.

Mama was not naïve to the situation when Daddy was not at home. She told me years later that Tommy would flirt with her outrageously at any occasion where she and Daddy and Tommy were present because Tommy knew Daddy didn't like it. Mama and Tommy often conspired together to get Daddy's goat in this respect, and often it was the highlight of any gathering for Mama to gain the upper hand, so to speak.

Dale Potter was a fresh-faced kid who played the hottest fiddle to come down the pike. As a youngster listening to Bob Will on the radio, he dreamed of playing the fiddle like he heard on the radio. The harmony of the instrument stayed in his heart and mind, and when he got his own fiddle and began learning, no one bothered to tell him he had been listening to two fiddles in Bob Wills band so he set about learning how to make the twin sound before he knew it was a twin fiddle sound. He succeeded in creating the sound, and became one of the hottest fiddlers in Nashville.

By this time Daddy brought on board The Carter Family and Dale fell in love with Anita Carter. Dale lived at Ma Upchurch's boarding house, and was roommates with Don Davis, steel guitarist for Pee Wee King and later for Cowboy Copas. Dale and Anita Carter married while he was a Musical Miller but then he was drafted into the Korean war. He and Anita divorced while he was away, and she married Don Davis, his roommate.

Other notable fiddlers to rotate through the Musical Millers band were the legendary Benny Martin and Chubby Wise

The decision was made to have "Martha White" as a singer in the band so, during the late 1940s, Daddy and Cohen began looking for a female vocalist. They found the first, Dottie Dillard, in the corridors of WSM.

Dottie told me that in 1947 she had sung on radio and with big bands around Nashville, including those led by Owen Bradley and Frances Craig. Dottie said that she agreed to take the job to be on the Martha White early morning radio shows even though she was a bit dubious, since she was accustomed to singing at night with the big bands. She recalled that after she agreed, Cohen Williams took her to Harvey's Department Store on Church Street and purchased her Martha White frock. She remembered seeing the newly installed escalator at Harvey's--the first in Nashville—and the sign that said "No Bare Feet Allowed."

Cohen selected Dottie's "Martha White" dress and paid the magnificent sum of $2.98 for it. Publicity photos from the WSM Grand Ole Opry Museum files show her wearing the dress and mugging with Milton and the Musical Millers. She thought Daddy was a consummate showman, and enjoyed her brief association with the Musical Millers. She reluctantly gave up the job after only a short time because she found herself burning the candle at both ends and it became too much for her.

In 1950, Ramona Reed became the singing "Martha White." Ramona was a good singer and was in the band at the same time Dale Potter was Daddy's fiddle player. Dale tried to set Don Davis up with Ramona when she first came to town but it didn't quite work out. Ramona did not stay long; she later sang with Bob Wills and the Texas Playboys.

The last singing "Martha White" was May Hawks, who was from Cookeville, Tennessee, about 90 miles east of Nashville. May and her husband moved to Detroit where she began her singing career on WJR in Detroit and also in Saginaw, Michigan, where Jimmy Dickens saw her perform. Dickens heard that the Martha White folks were looking for a girl singer and recommended her. After an audition with Estes, she got the job.

The singers who sang as Martha White did not last long. For whatever reason, girl singers didn't go over at that point in time, even after Daddy brought the Carter Family to the show. According to Effert Burke, chief salesman for Martha White Flour Company and privy to many corporate decisions, the fan mail did not favor June or even Mother Maybelle and there were a lot of letters complaining about them. We must remember that this was a time when female singers with a group of men were not perceived as having wholesome images, whether deserved or not.

The acceptable girl singers were Kitty Wells, Wilma Lee Cooper, Dot Swan, Annie Lou (and Danny) and (Clyde and) Marie Dilehay, who traveled with their husbands.

Interaction With Other Entertainers

Following are observations of Daddy's interaction with other members of the Opry during his time at the Opry, presented from Denny's and my points of view.

Roy Acuff

Roy and his wife, Mildred were the power couple in Nashville when Daddy and Mama arrived, and their warmth and hospitality were enjoyed by all Opry members. Roy and Mildred, who, had married in Middlesboro, Kentucky, formed the core of the Opry Family, and their circle of friends included all who were on the Opry and WSM.

I remember going to the Acuff home on Log Cabin Road, where the house was a log house, but definitely not a "cabin." Their Sunday open houses were legendary and were so widely attended that it seemed like everyone was backstage at the Opry. The house was tastefully furnished and had memorabilia from Roy's travels.

There was a "stuffed" horse "tethered" at the corner of one of the massive stone fireplaces and the house was so large that it took two furnaces to supply heat for the cold winters.

There were Sunday socials with artists and musicians all over Nashville when personal appearances allowed, with every band member of every band hosting at least one gathering. We had our share of open houses as well, and the camaraderie was genuine. The holiday open houses and parties were especially well attended with lots of eating and drinking.

Roy was always a great friend of Daddy and was always available with bail money whenever he needed to be sprung from the jailhouse.

Hank Williams

I remember hearing Daddy and Mama discuss Hank Williams' latest "health problem," which was substance abuse, and his latest stay in the rehab facility in Madison. Hank wrote "House of Gold" for Daddy, who was the first to record the song, on December 30, 1949. for the Coral label.. According to Mama, he would have preferred Hank write him a ballad, but he was still glad to record the song. .Daddy always felt at odds with the positive reactions whenever he sang a sacred song. Those songs brought Daddy the most fan mail. His renditions of "Hold Fast to the Right," "Old Time Religion," "30 Pieces of Silver," and "E-A-S-T-E-R" were his most requested numbers before "House of Gold.".

I remember seeing Hank and Audrey in the halls at WSM and one time they brought Bocephus along. He was in Hank's arms because he was not yet toddling. I remember seeing Audrey in a leopard skin coat, which I thought was the most beautiful garment I had ever seen.

Daddy and Hank drank together on numerous occasions and had a great like and respect for one another. In the Nashville music business you often write songs with your friends. Daddy never co-wrote any songs with Hank but he did co-write with a cohort of Hank's, Vic McAlpin. Vic was a prolific songwriter and had many songs recorded by those around at the time. He and Daddy penned "Too Many Women" together, which Daddy recorded on August 11, 1947. While Daddy and Hank put away the booze, Vic was restricted from drinking by a bad heart. Vic and Daddy enjoyed writing songs together and Daddy also co-wrote with Jimmy Selph.

Little Jimmy Dickens

The first time Denny and I saw Little Jimmy Dickens was when he was on a show with Daddy at Roy's Acuff's Dunbar Cave Park in Clarksville, a short drive from Nashville. Dunbar Cave was a popular resort and amusement park with a large lake for swimming, boating, and fishing, and ample space for picnics, if you chose not to eat at the excellent restaurant there. Besides the cave itself, which invited exploration and had guided tours, the cave's mouth had a large, level, flat stone floor on which dances were held. There was an amphitheater on the property as well, with backless wooden benches among the trees facing a big stage. Daddy emceed the Sunday shows and we would all go with him.

Between shows we would hang out at Roy and Mildred's "cabin" just up the path from the amphitheater. Denny had gone backstage one Sunday and was watching what seemed to be a little kid who was getting great response from the audience. Since he appeared to be Denny's age, Denny asked Daddy to invite the little boy to come out and play after he finished his song. And, after he was done with his set, Little Jimmy Dickens did, indeed, come out to "play" with Denny for about an hour outside Roy's house.

One of Little Jimmy Dickens hits, "Take an Old Old Cold Tater and Wait," which gave him his nickname, was originally a 1920s hillbilly song that Dickens learned from Sonny Grubb, a banjo player in Fairmont, West Virginia.

Recitations of poetry were popular on radio broadcasts at that time and drew a lot of fan mail. Hank Williams' "Luke the Drifter" employed recitations as a part of his radio shows. During his early morning radio shows, Daddy recited poems as requested by his listeners. "Old Cold Tater" and "A-Sleepin at the Foot of the Bed" were done as poems by many artists, but it was not until Little Jimmy Dickens came to the Opry that they became popular as novelty songs.

In an interview Micki had with Jimmy Dickens backstage at the Opry he told her, "When I was brand new here in Nashville, one of the first people I met was Milton Estes. Milton was always very good to me, and we became very great friends. Many times he would call me on the phone and say he and the band were doing a show that night in a nearby town for Martha White, and asked if I would like to come along. "

He continued, "Whenever I would be on local radio here, it would usually be on one of Milton's early morning radio shows at WSM. He'd be there, along with Jimmy Selph, Eggy McEwan, Dale Potter, and the rest of them. And whenever I would get to go on the Opry itself, well, it was almost always on Milton's part for Martha White Flour."

Dickens also said it was probably Milton who taught him how to fish. He said Milton would call him late in the evening and ask if he'd like to go fishing with him and some others. The trips would often that them to Kentucky Lake and usually lasted all night long.

"Milton showed me how to fish for bigger fish, and we usually caught plenty," said Dickens.

Their friendship continued offstage and on dry land. Dickens and Daddy once came to a stop at a traffic light on Deadrick Street in downtown Nashville and decided to race to WSM at Seventh and Church for a $500 bet. Dickens had a new Buick convertible and Daddy had a new Rocket Eighty-Eight Oldsmobile. Dickens said he didn't recall who won, but Denny does because he was in the car with Daddy and witnessed the payoff of the wager by Dickens!

Daddy was a practical joker, and this powerful new car of his was a perfect accomplice. Daddy would place a $20 bill on the dashboard and tell an unsuspecting passenger that if he could reach the money from the back seat, it was his to keep. This car had great acceleration so Daddy would hit the accelerator and force the passenger to fall back onto the seat. Whiplash, yes, but money, no.

Dickens recalled that Daddy's greatest talent, to him at least, was that he was always in control.

"He was absolutely the best Master of Ceremonies I have ever known," said Dickens. "And he was the most professional person I ever worked with. He never seemed to be excited or out of control. When he talked about Martha White Flour, it was just like talking about going fishing with an old friend. He was so personable over the airwaves."

Stringbean

One of the best banjo players, along with Grandpa Jones, was David Akeman, otherwise known as Stringbean. As kids, we got a kick out of String's ridiculous costume, and most people never recognized him in street clothes. He had a handsome, albeit craggy, face and was always even tempered. Tall and thin, he took on the name "Stringbean" for his performances.

String did many shows with Daddy, and String's wife, Estelle, was a good friend of Mama's. String did not drive so chauffeuring duties fell to Estelle, except when he was playing a date with Daddy or some other group that could include him as a passenger. Estelle spent many evenings with us, even for sleep overs while String was away, and she was a delightful lady. Since Mama did not drive, Estelle was right at home playing driver for their shopping trips and excursions.

Estelle was a great fisherman and she accompanied anyone who would go with her to wet a line. String went fishing with her and others, but he didn't care much for fishing because it required being on the water in a boat. String couldn't swim so he was uncomfortable if he wasn't on dry land.

Whenever he went fishing with Daddy and his fishing buddies, if the party was more than three then Denny was always paired with String. Denny once asked Daddy why that was and was told that String was part Indian and it was for Denny's safety to be in the boat with a skilled outdoorsman. That was a joke!

Once when he was fishing with Daddy and some others, the boat String and Denny were in capsized. String came up sputtering and floundering in the water, yelling for someone to help him. Denny righted the boat and then went towards String and helped him stand up. When String's feet touched bottom he realized the water was only three feet deep. The rest of the fishing party was hysterically laughing and, once it was over, String laughed along with the rest of them.

The senseless and brutal murder in 1973 of both of them left a wound in Mama's heart since she had been close to Estelle for so long.

Lew Childre

Lew Childre was a vaudeville veteran who found his way onto the Opry stage, using a dobro-style guitar and doing fast paced songs. He had a great rhythm to his numbers, which audiences loved. Daddy liked him, and they shared similar backgrounds but their real connection was fishing. Childre invented many fishing lures throughout his life, and was an avid fisherman just like Daddy.. They often swapped jokes and tall tales backstage at the Ryman.

Jamup and Honey

Jamup and Honey was a comedy team from the old vaudeville and radio days. The act was done in black face, which today is certainly not politically correct, but they were good entertainers and Daddy respected them, especially since they were strictly a comedy act.

Rod Brasfield

Rod Brasfield and his brother, Lawrence or "Boob" were friends from the old tent show days and Daddy spent a lot of time with them bending elbows. Rod was always cordial to all of us, and we socialized with him and his family. He had a big heart and was a sucker for anyone in distress. If he could help relieve stress, he would. One Sunday we were all visiting Rod's home in Hohenwald, Tennessee, where the property had a small pond on it with lots of fish, including bream, the ones with the flashing iridescent colors. Denny and I were given cane poles along with the other guests, and soon everyone had caught at least one bream except me, probably because I couldn't sit still and wait for anything to take the bait. I was nearly in tears over this.

Mama and Daddy comforted me and diverted my attention while Rod went downstream a few feet and tied a fish on my line. At the appropriate time, they all yelled that my bobber was dancing and I should pull in the fish. I landed the "sea monster," and danced with glee at my prowess as a fisherwoman.. Not that I would ever touch the floppy creature after I landed it – it was too slimy and squirmy! This gives some insight into Rod's personality;

he always loved kids, and would tease me and Denny. We loved him, too. It goes without saying that we thought he was the funniest man on earth.

Most of the people Daddy worked with were just plain folks to me and Denny and, as far as their being iconic or rich or special, we thought everybody had a job like Daddy did.

Cowboy Copas

I remember Cowboy Copas as being tall and handsome and a good singer. Since he and Daddy had both been with Pee Wee King they had a lot in common. I remember his daughter, Catha, as being tall and pretty, but not too friendly with me and Denny since she was a little older. I do remember once seeing Catha backstage at the Ryman when she came to borrow a costume from Minnie Pearl for a Halloween party where she was "Minnie Pearl." Minnie helped her, and to me she looked like the real thing.

Gary Copas was my brother's age and they would hang out together at the Opry and in our neighborhood, since they didn't live too far from us. They would not let me pal around with them since I was younger, and a girl as well!

Minnie Pearl

Minnie Pearl had worked with Daddy and Pee Wee King. She was a gracious lady and was friendly with all the Opry members and their families. I recall being present with a crowd of Opry folks at her home when an impromptu party was in full swing. By that time she had married Henry Cannon and they played host to WSM and Opry personnel just like all working families did. Mama remembered how Henry stood at the stove and fried fish for the entire party. Years later I recalled this to Miss Minnie and she remembered the incident. She was always just like "down home" people to us.

Vito Pelletier

Vito Pelletier was chief music librarian for WSM, and Stage Manager for the Opry. He was a distinguished, white haired gentleman and was always polite. We often gave him a ride home after the Opry since he lived near us. I always thought his white hair was amazing.

Owen Bradley

The credentials of Owen Bradley as a musician and record producer are impeccable. He worked with Dinah Shore early on and, as a record producer, produced Patsy Cline, Loretta Lynn, Brenda Lee, Kitty Wells and Ernest Tubb. He first came to WSM as a teenager in 1940, and stayed until 1958, when he became a father of the Music City recording industry. While at WSM, he worked with Daddy on "Noontime Neighbors."

John McDonald was the Farm Director of WSM and had a daily radio show to give farm and livestock reports and, little by little, entertainment was added. By 1946, when Daddy arrived on that scene, it had become a fixture. I interviewed Owen Bradley and during the interview he recalled that for the "Noontime Neighbors" show, Daddy was responsible for the country music guests while

Owen handled the 26 to 30 piece orchestra. It was a variety show and, with Daddy at the helm, it ran smoothly every day.

The show was not scripted except for the farm reports. Owen stated that WSM allowed him to grow and develop the show, just as they allowed the existing shows to grow. He recalled that WSM, in an effort to keep the FCC convinced that WSM's clear channel status remained intact, took "Noontime Neighbors" on the road and did remotes from Memphis, Knoxville, and a host of other cities nearby.

Daddy was part of that endeavor, which made the daily show a lot easier to do because it was fun. Owen said there was no pressure in doing the show, and that Milton was more than a smooth emcee; he seemed to have the knack to move it along smoothly and put those around him at ease. He stated in answer to a direct question that he never saw Milton drunk or drinking at any time he was on the air for WSM. He spoke only in the most glowing terms of his ability as an entertainer and emcee.

Eddy Arnold

I interviewed Eddy Arnold, who stated that he met Daddy when he joined Pee Wee King at WHAS in Louisville, Kentucky.. He spoke in flattering terms about Daddy, and attested that he had been an excellent emcee, a good singer, and that he had a lot of respect for him and liked him and Mama a great deal. Eddy stated that Daddy taught him to sing the harmony parts when he, Daddy, and Curley Rhodes sang as a trio because he was not then, and never was that good at singing harmony. He said Daddy told him which notes he should sing to make the song come out right. He said Daddy was extremely talented, and a wonderful showman and he further stated that Daddy understood showmanship extensively.

After Daddy and Eddy had both moved to Nashville, I recall hearing bits of conversation with Daddy and Mama about Eddy's new manager, Colonel Tom Parker. Daddy more or less withheld any opinion about the venture except to wish Eddy well.

(NOTE: In my biography of Eddy Arnold. I stated that in the summer of 1935, Pee Wee King and J.L. Frank moved to Louisville where King joined Frankie More's Log Cabin Boys on WHAS. The following year, 1936, J.L. Frank organized a group he named The Golden West Cowboys, put Pee Wee King in charge, and found a sponsor, Crazy Water Crystals, a laxative company, for a show on WHAS. In 1937 the Golden West Cowboys consisted of Pee Wee King on accordion, Abner Simms on fiddle, Milton Estes on banjo, Curley Rhodes on bass, Curley's sister Texas Daisy on vocals, and Cowboy Jack Skaggs on guitar. This was the group that auditioned for David Stone, Harry Stone and engineer Percy White for the Opry. The group was hired and on June 4, 1937, made their Opry debut; however, J.L. Frank made Archie Campbell, then going under the name Art Bell, the head of the group when they first joined the Opry. Frank and King insisted that his band members be allowed to join the musicians union. The union at first objected but finally relented and King's Golden West Cowboys were among the first individuals in a country music group to become members of a musicians union, which gave them access to network exposure and, later, country musicians who were union members could record for major labels.)

Joe Zinkan

Joe Zinkan was another Pee Wee King alumnus who worked with Daddy in several different bands and venues through the years. They worked together often, and our families were intertwined through many years. Mama and Lois Zinkan were pregnant during the same time, with me being born in April, 1939, and the Zinkan's' daughter, Sandra, their firstborn, in September of that same year. Even after Joe moved on to Roy Acuff's Smoky Mountain Boys, and Johnny and Jack, to name a few, our families were still close. I have a "souvenir" photograph of the two couples enjoying a rare evening out at The Commodore Club in Nashville.

Joe stayed with the Delmores after Daddy returned to Nashville. Joe was a premier bass player and became a sought-after studio musician when the Nashville Sound was born.

Joe was one of the finest slap bass players anywhere around. I once asked him how he learned his distinctive style, and he told me that a river boat stopped on the river near his home in Indiana and he and his brother sneaked on board to see the show. There was an old black man playing slap bass, and Joe was so fascinated that he came back every night where the boat was docked in order to watch and learn that style.

Red Foley

Red Foley was a popular contemporary of Daddy's on the Opry. We sometimes saw him and his family in the corridors at WSM, but we never socialized with them. For whatever reason, his wife, Eva, chose to keep to herself so her daughters were segregated from the Opry wives and Opry Brats. I know the three girls, Jenny (named for Jenny Lou Carson), Julie, and Shirley recorded a Christmas song with Red. I thought that was just grand, and was a little jealous till I realized I could not sing well enough to do that! I used to hear Daddy and Mama talk in the car on our way home about some of the problems the Foleys were having, and I always felt sorry to hear it. Though not known to the general public at the time it happened, Eva took her own life, and Red was left to finish raising the girls and continue his career.

Hank Snow

I was present at Hank Snow's first Opry appearance and, since not too many folks knew him, I suppose they hesitated to approach him. I recall that he was sitting alone near the back door, near Sergeant Norris, and I kind of felt sorry for him. Little did I know what an important addition he would be to the Opry and country music. Nevertheless, I felt sorry for him and to break the ice in my nine or ten year old brain, I asked for his autograph, which he cheerfully gave. I didn't need or even want an autograph, but thought it might ease his entry into Opry society.

He was always polite as well and probably wasn't in the least feeling "alone" but was probably glad to have the opportunity to sit quietly for a while. He, Pee Wee King, and Daddy were the same size, a fact which I find odd, although I don't know why.

John McDonald

John and Evelyn McDonald were two of Daddy and Mama's closest friends at WSM. John was the farm director at WSM, and worked with all the agricultural agents employed by the State of Tennessee, and gave farm reports daily on WSM. His frequent reports on the many uses of corn cobs drew a lot of fan mail. An imposing figure, he was one of the smartest men in existence, as far as our family was concerned. When not on the air, he and Daddy frequently made stops throughout the State of Tennessee at county fairs, livestock shows, and things agricultural.

John was an amateur photographer and made some excellent family photos for us. John and Evelyn had no children, but holidays were special to them. Every Christmas, John's photographic skills created holiday greeting cards before they were in vogue. They would dress in costume and create a photo vignette for the holiday being celebrated. Evelyn had a degree in home economics and was an authority on all things dealing with the home. When a fan sent Daddy a crate of fresh strawberries, Mama called Evelyn to find out the best way to preserve them. We had jams and jellies and shortcakes running out our ears, but we did not lose a single strawberry to fruit rot. Evelyn could be counted on to offer any assistance Mama needed.

George Morgan

After Daddy was a regular part of WSM, a new young singer arrived on the scene. I remember seeing George Morgan and his wife in the halls at WSM, and once they had their new baby with them. Candy Morgan was named for George's first monster hit "Candy Kisses" and she was a cute baby. Daddy always said that George was one of the best singers he ever heard, and opined that perhaps he was too good!

The Carter Family

Daddy later said the same thing about young Anita Carter after the Carter Family was brought to the Opry at his urging. Anita was his favorite female vocalist, an opinion widely shared by most of the Opry members. She had a glorious voice and, in Daddy's judgment, was totally in control of her vocals.

Sergeant Richard Norris

Sergeant Richard Norris was the "cop on the beat" at the Ryman Auditorium, and was charged with keeping out the riff raff from the stage door and backstage. Affectionately known as "Flatfoot," he was Opry security for a long time. His demeanor was gruff, but underneath that exterior was an absolute marshmallow. The Opry Brats were the only riff raff backstage that I ever knew about, and more than once "Sarge" chased us offstage and away from the RC Cola machine that stood onstage as an advertisement. Denny and Cowboy Copas' son, Gary, were the main offenders who snuck onstage to get a cold drink. Sarge himself was not opposed to instigating their trips to the cooler as long as it included a brew for him. Sarge was always cool about chasing them offstage.

Tootsies

Tootsie's Orchid Lounge is now a Nashville landmark. It fronts on Broadway, but has a back door across from the stage entrance to the Ryman Auditorium. Long before Tootsie Bess' family took over the establishment, it was known as "Mom's" to the Opry entertainers, and in between shows any number of them could be found at Mom's wetting their whistles and biding time. Vito would enlist Sarge's aid in sending a messenger for the next-scheduled act to come back to the stage area.

The Opry Wives Club

Mama was a charter member of the Opry Wives club, which was formed when so many of the wives had to "hold down the fort" while the guys were on the road. No one had heard of a support group back then, but that is exactly what it was. I don't know if a similar group exists today, but these "road widows" meant a lot to each other back then. Some of the wives were Estelle Akeman, Lucille Copas, Sarah Summey (Clell), Mary Claire Rhodes (Curly) and anyone else who wanted to bring a covered dish to the home of the hostess of the month.

There were wives of the musicians and anyone else connected with WSM and the Opry. There were no dues, no rules or bylaws, but plenty of lively conversation and shared experiences, both high and low. Lucille Copas talked about the times when she literally passed the hat on street corners to have money to feed their family while Cope sang to draw the crowd. Once Audrey Williams came but did not stay long because she was afraid Hank had followed her. This was after the incident when he shot at her after they had separated and he learned she had dated someone else. She seemed nervous and apologized for not being more social. She was visibly upset and made her exit early.

The group was not without lots of laughs, though, and Vermell Turner, wife of Zeke Turner, always delivered memorable jokes and was a real cut up. She was well loved by the other ladies. Our home on Baxter Avenue was the scene of a baby shower for Ramona Jones before the birth of her daughter, Eloise.

Vic McAlpin

Before an admission fee to the Opry was set, passes were given away by National Life Insurance agents and staff personnel. One enterprising young man, Vic McAlpin, found a way to "earn" a little money on weekends. He would wangle a handful of passes from whatever source he could tap, and then stand near the entrance to the Opry and sell them as "admission tickets." The unsuspecting fans did not know there was no admission charge.

Vic later became one of Nashville's most successful songwriters. He and Daddy became friends and went fishing together. Vic did not drink because he had a heart problem which prevented him from doing so. Nevertheless, he was always happy to go fishing with Daddy, and also with Hank Williams. He and Daddy collaborated on several songs, and Vic also wrote songs for Hank Williams.

Bill Monroe

Bill Monroe, "The Father of Bluegrass," left his mark on the face of American music, and deservedly so. He was a man who believed in what he was doing. During his climb to the top, the paths of Daddy and Monroe crossed many times during their early careers. The Monroe Brothers, Bill and Charlie, had been at Raleigh around the same time as Daddy, and their brotherly quarrels were legendary. One story I remember that is often repeated in the industry involved one Monroe in Raleigh and the other Monroe in Nashville. The argument became so heated that one said to the other "I'll just come and beat the **%$#*& out of you!" And with that the phone was hung up, the car started and the road trip began, which ended in fisticuffs just as threatened. It's over 500 miles from Nashville to Raleigh.

On one of the days when Daddy was headed downward, he happened to be walking through halls where a recording studio had been set up and where Monroe was recording. Monroe's bass singer had not shown up so he asked Daddy if he would sing bass on some of the numbers, knowing that with his Stamps Baxter training it would be no stretch. Bluegrass is sung in a higher key than normal songs, so even though Daddy was not a true bass, he sang the bass part with ease. Daddy sang on "He Will Set Your Fields On Fire" and Monroe's discography credits Daddy with several sides on his gospel albums.

Another tale I heard repeated by Daddy concerned Monroe's purchase of a farm. After spending many hours searching for just the right place near Nashville, Monroe finally decided on one. The realtor with him suggested they retire back to his office and make out the checks and papers whereupon Monroe walked to the back of his Cadillac, opened the trunk and counted out the purchase price in cash stashed in brown paper bags!

Jimmy Martin

Jimmy Martin was born in Sneedville, Tennessee, just down the road from where Daddy was born. Sneedville is in Claiborne County, as is Arthur, Tennessee. Martin realized a dream by becoming one of Bill Monroe's Bluegrass Boys but after a time his cantankerous and argumentative personality did not stand him in good stead at the Opry or with Monroe. He left Monroe and went out on his own with the Sunny Mountain Boys. He earned his stripes with an audience and was in demand as a performer and enjoyed success in his own right. He employed the Osborn Brothers, who were quite young but extremely talented.

I interviewed Jimmy Martin at a bluegrass festival in Salt, West Virginia, , where he told me that one day in 1954 Jimmy and Bobby Osborne paid a call on RCA record producer Troy Martin, who told Jimmy he had a song he wanted him to hear. The song was written by Daddy and Joe Allison and was first recorded by Gene Autry. Troy Martin played "Twenty Twenty Vision" for Jimmy Martin and the Osbornes. When the song finished, Troy asked "What do you think of that?" Jim Osborne replied, "We can't sing that – it ain't bluegrass" and Jimmy Martin said 'It will be by the time me and the Osborne Brothers get through with it."

"Twenty Twenty Vision" was termed "influential" in an article in *The Tennessean* newspaper following Martin's death in 2006. The song has become a Bluegrass classic, recorded by multiple artists.

Ernest Tubb

Ernest Tubb and Daddy were colleagues and friends at WSM. Denny and I were never in the same age bracket as his kids, but we saw Ernest at WSM and on the Opry. Mama didn't see Elaine Tubb much except when she was backstage or at an Opry function. When Ernest opened his first record shop, it was a huge media event, and was attended by most of the WSM and Opry personnel. In a publicity picture, Ernest is at the microphone with WSM announcer David Cobb, and, over his shoulder are, among others, Johnny Bond and Daddy.

Ernest formed his own publishing company in addition to opening a record shop, and he persuaded Daddy and Vic McAlpin to give him publishing rights to some of their compositions. Hank Thompson, who turned down an invitation to become a regular member of the Opry because of the attendance requirement, which was 26 weekends at that time, told me that he gave publishing rights to "Whoa Sailor" to Ernest, who had Daddy record the song . Even then it was an industry practice to have more than one artist "cover" a song to garner more royalties.

I remember Daddy doing some of the songs on the air that Hank Thompson had big hits with.

Divorce

Daddy did a weekly early Sunday morning show at WSM, and at least once a month Senator Al Gore, Sr., father of former Vice President Al Gore, read his report from Washington in the studio. On occasion he and Daddy would talk, especially after Daddy told Gore that Mama was a Gore from the Livingston area. Gore, of course, knew the family and acknowledged the kinship, albeit distant, and was always cordial even before the kinship was revealed. Years later Senator Gore attended the funeral of Granny Gore in Livingston.

Denny and I began to spend our summer months in Middlesboro with Allie and Lester to allow Mama and Daddy more privacy to attempt to set things right between them. The womanizing and boozing had taken a toll on the Estes marriage, and, try as she might, Mama could no longer endure the situation. Daddy had left home or been asked to leave a number of times, only to return and give it another try. I would like to say that it all worked out for the better but, sadly, it got much worse. The marital tension between them had taken too much out of both of them. Finally, enough was enough, and Mama filed for divorce. Denny and I often talked about the misconception most people have about "staying together for the kids." We both wished divorce had come sooner so as to avoid the constant arguing and turmoil within our home.

The divorce was granted on October 27, 1950. Alimony and child support were granted but Daddy never paid much of it. The court set child support at $100 per week per child, then later reduced, twice, to $50 He was always giving Mama cold checks and she had to chase him down and get the cash. We were in dire straits and yet Daddy seemed to be able to live the life he wanted. Mama worked for the State of Tennessee at a clerical job which didn't pay much.

We lost our home to foreclosure when the second mortgage came due. Daddy had either forged Mama's name or had a girlfriend pose as Mama to get the second mortgage. We were forced to move into a small two bedroom apartment above someone else's living quarters. We didn't have our own entrance and had to go through their living room to the stairway leading to our apartment.

One amusing incident came about because of Mama's "collection efforts." While trying to find Daddy to make good on a cold check he had given to her, she knew he would be at the State Fair doing some of the shows there. She took three buses to her destination and when she arrived at the site, was warmly greeted by all the guys in the band and by WSM personnel who were there doing a remote broadcast. She was told Daddy was in the parking lot, so she left the building. On her way out, she noticed an empty Coca Cola bottle on the steps and, being a good citizen, scooped it up to drop in a nearby trash can.

She spotted his car and walked toward it, unaware she was still holding the empty bottle. Daddy spotted her, bailed out of his car, and shouted to his girlfriend du jour, "Run, Marie, run!" He started circling the car to get away from, Mama, who still held the empty bottle. In a truly Keystone Cops moment, or more like an "I Love Lucy" scene, they chased each other in circles around the car, not really hearing what the other was saying until, finally, Mama sat down on the rear bumper, bottle still in hand, and waited until Daddy arrived at the back of the car. He skidded to a stop, and sat down, too. Then, both panting, Daddy asked her what she was intending to do with the bottle. Realizing she still held her "weapon," they started to laugh together. Once satisfied that Marie was long gone, and that Mama was not going to do physical harm, he gave her cash for the cold check and then drove her home!

Generous visitation rights were given even though Mama was awarded custody of us, but somehow Daddy's preferences seemed to take top billing. Mama would call and arrange for a weekly visit, mostly on school nights so that we could not stay out late because of school. Looking back on those visits, Denny and I both realized Daddy usually got free passes through the radio station or some person he could put the touch on to events he thought we might enjoy. Fact is, he usually only got two passes so he dropped us off, and picked us up after the event. He was usually at a nearby bar until the event was over, so "visitation" was not all that great. However, Denny and I became big wrestling, racing, and baseball fans but after a while we became so disenchanted with not having any time with Daddy that we told Mama not to bother. He never questioned it, nor did he ask why she didn't call and arrange further visitation. Neither did he initiate any visits.

Following the divorce, Daddy was involved with a number of women, one of whom was Frances Walker, widow of the CEO of Haynes Underwear company. The Walkers had previously given me a collie puppy for my birthday in better times. Her husband was still alive at that time, and we went to their farm in nearby Franklin to pick up the dog. Following her husband's death, she began seeing Daddy on a regular basis.

Joe Talbot

Joe Talbot was the steel guitar player for Hank Snow while he was a student at Vanderbilt Law School. He was not Daddy's attorney, but advised him about some of his legal rights during the divorce. Talbot went on to become an attorney and a fixture in the Nashville music industry.

When I interviewed Mr. Talbot at his office about what he remembered of the divorce, he would not allow me to tape record the interview. Talbot revealed that Daddy was involved with the widow Frances Walker, and that her children did not like the situation. Talbot stated that her family felt he was after her money, and went so far as to try to have her committed to keep them apart. Joe Allison later stated that he remembered hearing something about that, but neither of us knew whether it was true. Joe said that Frances was a multimillionaire and Daddy was her big love. Joe didn't think he was after her money but was just trying to find someone to love.

Family Matters

During the summer following the divorce, Denny rebelled at having to take up the slack, as he put it (he had been carrying the male load in our household for a while, like lawn chores, carrying out the trash, etc., but didn't complain until this time) and wanted to go and live with Daddy. Wisely, Mama said OK, and helped him pack his clothes to take up residence in a hotel downtown with Daddy. It only took a week for boredom to set in and Denny decided to come back home, as Mama knew would happen.

Jailed

In December, 1952, Daddy wrote a bad check to a men's clothing store for $59.84. He never made good on the check, and in March 1953 he left the state. Daddy was Missing In Action until September, 1953, when the Davidson County Grand Jury indicated him for feloniously leaving the state, nonpayment of child support and for the bad check. In February, 1954, he received a suspended sentence of 11 months and 29 days and on June 3, 1954, he surrendered after returning to Tennessee and was ordered to serve the sentence. On June 3, 1955 he was released.

Joe Allison

I interviewed Joe Allison on several occasions beginning in November, 1997, because he had been close to Daddy toward the end of his career, and because the two of them were friends and had co-written songs together. These interviews about Daddy gave insight into what happened when everything collapsed. I did not personally know Joe Allison prior to the time I started researching this book. I contacted him and he was extremely affable and willing to meet with me. He was painfully candid and forthcoming with any information about their friendship, so I immediately felt I could trust him and take as truth whatever he revealed about their relationship. He also was very open about his own faults and shortcomings.

Joe knew Daddy when he was going downhill. The booze had gotten Daddy. Joe drank with him and admits he himself was an alcoholic, which is what drew them together. Joe quit drinking but

Daddy never did. Joe saw the wrong end of Daddy's career but also knew him when he was hot.

Daddy's standards were high when staging a show, whether it was the band members or guest stars. On "Noontime Neighbors" it was Daddys's responsibility to get the country guests, and he would not settle for just anybody. He was a great emcee. People believed everything he said – he came across that way. He was responsible for Martha White making a quantum leap into the mainstream.

Daddy first met Joe in 1949 when Joe came through Nashville with Tex Ritter. Joe worked at WMAK when Daddy was on WSM.

Joe remembered Daddy's affection for the vaudevillians in his midst – Lew Childre, Jamup and Honey, and the Duke of Paducah, to name a few. Daddy liked all the old timers. He was from that entertainment school of that time -- the total entertainer--and he felt that most of the old timers could more than hold their own when they performed solo at center stage.

Joe recalled that Daddy sang and played pop music somewhere because he knew all the songs and did shows everywhere. He could work with quartets and sing all four parts in bluegrass and gospel. Joe said that Daddy did a lot of cover songs but never had a big hit on his own. He was a baritone and a really good singer and Joe compared him with Jim Reeves, who had a smooth, mellow voice. After we returned to Middlesboro, the Jim Reeves hit "Four Walls," written by Joe, was released. Mama heard it and thought it was Daddy singing and that he had changed his name to Jim Reeves.

Joe said that Daddy was the best salesman on the Opry and Cohen Williams picked him to promote Martha White and that Daddy absolutely built Martha White, long before Flatt &

Scruggs came on the scene. Daddy built that company into a major enterprise because his long suit was being able to sell over the air. He had a voice that people believed and people would buy anything he told them to.

"I remember he was making $1600 and $1700 a week when most people were making $50 and $75," said Allison. "He was cleaning up. I remember people talking about the amount of money he was making. Today it would be like $40 million a year. He did night shows, morning shows, 'Noontime Neighbors' and remotes from the VA Hospital before the Opry. The VA show was the precursor to the Friday Night Opry because they had so many sponsors they could not get them all on so they [ultimately] went to Friday night from the studio. Milton did those extra shows around and up to the Opry."

"At one time he was almost the guy you had to see to get on the Grand Ole Opry," continued Allison. "If he recommended you, then you got on. It wasn't official but he had that job at one time, back in the days of the Solemn Old Judge. His influence was substantial."

Joe indicated that Daddy recommended the Carters be brought to Nashville from Knoxville in about 1947. After their arrival at the Opry, Joe also had them on his shows in 1949. (NOTE: The Carters came to the Grand Ole Opry in 1950 from Springfield, Missouri.)

"Musicians who came through his band became the super sidemen when the Nashville Sound was born," said Allison. "Jimmy Selph was on every record in the very first days. Tommy Jackson was the fiddle player of choice and if you wanted a hot fiddle player, you called Dale Potter."

Joe was well acquainted with Daddy's passion for fishing and went with Daddy a few times before the really bad days came along. He said once at Kentucky Lake, where they stayed in a cabin with a tin roof, Daddy told him how to catch bass. When they got out on the lake, Daddy kept patrolling around and around and up and down the water. He scanned the horizon and kept looking on either side of the shore as if searching for a landmark. Joe asked him what he was looking for. Daddy said he would let him know when he found it. After a while, Daddy slowed the boat and said "This is it."

Daddy told Joe that the previous day he had anchored a Prince Albert can at a prime fishing spot so he would know where to return next time. Joe said they fished in that one spot the rest of the day, pulling in fish after fish until the boat was literally filled. Joe said he initially doubted the story, but within 30 minutes they were fishing multiple poles and pulling fish out of the water as fast as they could get them in the boat. They caught more than their limit, and were praying not to see a Game Warden. .At the dock they gave most of the catch away, but went home satisfied that it had been a good day. Joe said he never saw anyone catch fish like Daddy could.

Daddy and Hank Williams used to fish some together at the same dock where the Prince Albert incident played out. Daddy also fished with Vic McAlpin, Edwin Craig, and anyone who would wet a line with him.

Milton got fired from WSM a lot but Edwin Craig, president of the National Life and Accident Insurance Company, which owned WSM and the Grand Ole Opry, was a good friend. Milton often took him fishing. Finally the no-shows became more frequent and

Jack Stapp and Harry Stone went to Mr. Craig and told him not to re-hire Milton. The dismissal finally "took."

Joe said that someone called him and said they fired Milton and I told them, so what? He'll be back on Monday; but the firing was not rescinded. Joe was hired not to replace him, but to take up some of the slack caused by his absence. Joe's show did not go on the air right away.

Daddy did Martha White stuff and used the Carter Family and Chet Atkins, but Joe got tired of waiting and went to California and Flatt &Scruggs came on the scene. Eddie Hill came to WSM after Joe, then Ralph Emery. Daddy followed Joe to California to try his luck there. He brought Vicki, his latest girlfriend, with him and they stayed with Joe and Audrey until they returned to Nashville. Incidentally, I have been told by others, not Joe, that Audrey did not like Daddy, making her one of the few who did not like him.

Milton did not leave WSM the same way he went in. It wasn't politically sound to be his friend when he left but it was not like that when he was riding high and everybody wanted to know him because he had influence.

At that time, Daddy needed help, but Joe said he, himself, needed help as well. Daddy had nowhere to go, was earning no money; but you'd never know that because he never discussed his personal life, changed his expression or complained about it. Daddy had the same outlook all the time. He would not share anything private.

"People criticized me for [helping him] but it was not any of their business," said Joe.

On their drinking habits, both in Nashville and in California, Joe said, :"I never saw him try to quit drinking. He would say 'I'm gonna quit one of these days' but he never thought he was doing anything wrong. He would just get real drunk and was real quiet. He did not tear up things but he would drink constantly for two or three days until he passed out."

While staying with Joe on Pennington Bend they wrote some songs that got recorded. Words and melodies came from both of them. They would collaborate on all of it, according to Joe. "20-20 Vision" was recorded by Gene Autry first, and then by Jimmy Martin. Later, in California, came the "Singing All Day and Dinner on the Ground" song that Steve Stone produced for Brush Arbor; that was never released. However, Country Gazette later had a hit version. Their collaborations brought forth a few more songs but none were as well known as those two. Jimmy Dickens recorded a novelty of theirs called "Hey, Worm."

Family Matters

When the Estes' returned to Nashville, in 1959 and 1960, Daddy's girlfriend, Vicki, worked at an upscale clothing store, Gus Mayer, where Mama had purchased her clothing when she was married to Daddy. Mama had a strong sense of style, which dictated that she get the best buy for her money. She was never a "clothes horse" but definitely had a strong fashion sense, which was displayed whether from Gus Mayer or Woolworth. Daddy always had good taste in his clothing, and he chose women with similar tastes. I was told by those who knew Vicki that she resembled Mama physically, but Mama never met Vicki.

All Daddy's legal troubles happened after Mama, Denny and I had moved back to Middlesboro.

When Daddy was released from the Nashville Workhouse on June 2, 1955, he and Vicki were together and lived at various residences in Nashville for brief periods. By late summer of 1955, Daddy had moved to Chattanooga to work at radio station WAGC as a disc jockey. Vicki made the move with him and worked as a waitress. On September 4, 1955, Joe and Audrey drove from Nashville to Chattanooga to accompany Daddy and Vicki to be married. Joe says he was so drunk at the time that he did not remember where they went, but a three year search unearthed a marriage certificate that documents they were married in Rossville, Georgia, just across the state line from Chattanooga. Daddy and Vicki stayed in Chattanooga for a time, then returned to Nashville where Daddy took any job he could find whether in the music industry or not. He began driving a cab. Their last place of residence in Nashville was on North 15th Street.

Vicki developed breast cancer and things went downhill again. Daddy took Vicki to Nashville General Hospital, admitted her and then left town. She died there on September 6, 1961, and her parents had to claim the body and arrange the burial.

Joe said Vicki was a wonderful girl, loyal to Daddy even though at that time he was drinking heavily. She did her best to make the marriage work.

I have thought about his reasons for leaving his wife in the hospital and disappearing. Could it be that all the women in his life who meant anything to him (his mom, my mom, and his last wife) had been cursed by cancer? He just could not face having a third brush with this dreaded disease. Or was Vicki the real heroine here who may have sent him away so that he would not witness her ultimate death?

Joe says that after Vicki died, Daddy went back with Francis Walker again. That was when her kids broke them up.

After Vicki's death in 1961, Daddy began drifting throughout the country. He showed up in Monroe, Michigan at his aunt Bertha's home. While there he went to Detroit where he worked briefly at the Greystone Ballroom in downtown Detroit.

He visited his sister, Allie, in Middlesboro, showing up unannounced, which was an awkward situation because Mama, Denny and I were staying with her pending our getting on our feet. His demeanor was the same as always; affable, jolly, and very entertaining. Allie had an upright piano, which he played and sang and entertained us in fine style. He left the next day, with all his worldly belongings in a shirt box. Allie gave him some money and he just drifted away. That was the last time I saw him.

Family Life

My friendship with Dottie Swan was very close since we both attended Jere Baxter School in Inglewood. Dottie was pretty and talented, and was a part of her parents' act. She began performing with Radio Dot and Smokey when she was barely three years old. When we were reunited at school, we began putting on little talent shows where she was the vocalist and I was emcee and comic relief.

She could yodel and I could mimic novelty songs like Little Jimmy Dickens and Lonzo and Oscar.

We were the hit of the eighth grade circuit. As a result of those efforts, and because of my high grade point average and affinity for performing, I was chosen to emcee the eighth grade graduation/honors banquet. I did not know exactly what was supposed to happen, and simply made my own agenda according to the list of honorees I was given by the teachers and principal.

Index cards are a real boon to any fledgling performer, so I was armed with a sheaf of them, numbered in the order they came up on the program. I also got to eat the rubber chicken at the head table. The entertainment for the evening was a young singer in Nashville who was just launching his career. He also happened to be dating Shirley Foley (I didn't know about this and it wasn't a factor in his performance). I introduced Pat Boone, complete with his white bucks, who really stole the show. I have been a fan ever since.

Mama and Denny were in the audience in that gymnasium/banquet hall that night, and Mama said that her jaw did not come off the floor all evening. She realized that a chip off the block had landed squarely on my shoulders! I just behaved the way I had seen Daddy conduct a show. The gene came out. It did with Denny, too, but several years later.

After I graduated from the eighth grade, Denny and I went to Middlesboro to Allie's so that Mama could get a toehold on how we were to live. I started freshman year of high school and Denny enrolled as a Junior. Mom stayed with Eileen and her husband, Mitchell, for a time, and then Mama went to Oak Ridge to her brother Carson's. She managed to save enough money to come to

Middlesboro and we all stayed at Allie's while Mama found work as a split shift desk clerk at the only hotel in town and eventually landed a job at JC Penney.

In Middlesboro in 1953, Mama received two separate phone calls from Nashville newspapers at the time Daddy was indicted and sentenced by the Grand Jury. I don't know how they found us, but they did. Of course, she knew nothing about Daddy's current problems and so she could not comment. We knew nothing about his February, 1954, suspended sentence, nor of his actually having to serve the sentence for failure to comply with court orders

When Denny graduated high school in 1955, we were destitute of funds, and Allie and Les didn't have any money either, so his Senior Trip to Washington, DC, looked like a no-go for him. Then one day a check arrived from the Davidson County Jury Commission for Mama's witness fee from the time of the divorce! She didn't know she would be paid for testifying at her own divorce trial, but the Lord provides, and He came through this time with just enough money to cover Denny's trip.

Denny joined the Air Force the day after his high school graduation in 1955, and with financial help from his service allotment, Mama and I were able to move from Allie's home into a tiny apartment in a building which had been a funeral home. Our quarters had been the embalming room and had an enormous kitchen (the sinks were really BIG) After about a year, Mama and I managed to leave the embalming room and took a garage apartment just four blocks from downtown Middlesboro so she could walk to work and I could walk to school.

Years later, after Denny returned home from military service, he was between jobs and decided to see if he could be hired as a disc jockey at a local station near Middlesboro. He went to WNTT in New Tazewell, Tennessee, just three miles from the Kentucky-Tennessee border, and was immediately pressed into service, thus beginning a radio career. His talent in radio and gab extended to being able to do play-by-play sports announcing, especially basketball. He became the popular "Voice of the Railsplitters" from Lincoln Memorial University in Harrogate, Tennessee. Sponsors flocked to buy time for his broadcasts. He even went to the basketball TSSAA tournament in St. Louis, where he broadcast the game for the Mutual Radio Network. (Unfortunately, Lincoln Memorial University did not win that game.)

After my high school graduation, I went to work in nearby Pineville, Kentucky, where Allie was Chief Clerk at Selective Service System Local Board No. 4. Allie had drafted Uncle Lester into World War II, and his "Greetings" letter is the only one on file which is signed "Love, Allie." She was distraught that her sworn duty had come to this, but he made it through the conflict and returned home safely.

Since I was now on my own and employed as a secretary, Mama decided to move to Wyandotte, Michigan, with her sister Lois after arranging for a transfer to a local JC Penney store there. Mama said she had raised us to the best of her ability and, since we were adults, we could now go out on our own while she picked up the remnants of her life and moved on.

The Search For Milton

My great-aunt Bessie (sister of Grandma Artie) died in January, 1963, and Allie was charged with settling her estate because she had not left a will and had no children. Bessie owned a small piece of property in Middlesboro and, without a will, this had to be disposed of and the proceeds disbursed to her heirs, Allie and Daddy, who were Artie's children. The biggest snag was in getting a deed signed by all the heirs so that it could be sold. Guess who was the only one who could not sign? Yep – Daddy.

Since he had not been seen or heard from in so long, we all started a search to track him down. There was no internet then, and all of us constantly hit brick walls. At one point I went to Nashville and made inquiries on my own.

In Nashville, Mary Claire Rhodes was immensely helpful in sharing every bit of information and rumor she had heard, and all bases were covered as far as we could go. Mary Claire had been Jim Denney's right hand at the artist bureau at WSM prior to his establishing Cedarwood Publishing Company. Mary Claire made the move with him and practically ran Cedarwood, just as she had the artists bureau, and she had a lot of Nashville music business connections, as did Curley. Mary Claire touched every base she had and went to extraordinary lengths to help us find Daddy. Not all were viable leads, but I came back home and reported to Allie all that I had. Mary Claire continued the search and tracked down various hints and rumors on into the summer of 1963.

Allie continued trying to track him with the leads from Mary Claire and, without telling me, one of Mary Clair's leads actually paid off when Allie tracked him to Oklahoma City and a Salvation Army store. By this time, I really didn't expect him to be found, so I went on about my life.

Southeastern Kentucky was economically depressed, and since there were more economic opportunities in Michigan, I moved there in late April, 1963, to seek work there. I moved in with Mama until I could get established.

In June, 1963, Allie found Daddy in Oklahoma City and corresponded with him. Here is an excerpt from a letter dated June 12, 1963 that I found among Allie's papers after her death. I had not known of this correspondence until that time.

"Dear Sis: Rec'd your letter and was glad and also surprised to hear from you. Sorry to hear of Aunt Bess' death. Send whatever papers you want me to sign and I will have them notarized and mail them back. Also tell me all the news you mentioned. There is no news for me to report except that I am well and hope everyone there the same. Hoping to hear from you soon, Love, Milt."

In an undated letter from him after Allie's initial contact, he wrote "My being connected with the Salvation Army may not be what you think. ... If you haven't mailed the deed yet and are sending it registered, it would be better to send it to me at the store as I am there six days per week from nine until 4:30.

Apparently all the business was transacted satisfactorily and the estate was finally settled. Denny and I each received about $18 as our share of the estate.

The important fact here is that, for whatever reason, Allie kept secret the fact that she had been in contact with him since June. I would have welcomed a chance to at least say hello, regardless of the fact I felt he had abandoned Denny and me.

On August 23, 1963, Milton Estes was found dead in the Hudson Hotel in Oklahoma City. He was 49 years old.

He had apparently checked into the hotel and gone on one huge bender, during which his heart stopped. His death was ruled due to "natural causes." He had died at least a week before his body was discovered. The Oklahoma authorities set about trying to find a relative from the few meager belongings he had with him. Had it not been for Local 257 of the American Federation of Musicians Union in Nashville, Daddy would have been buried in Potters Field. The authorities found an old Union membership card among his effects, and a phone call to the Nashville Local Union reached the one person there who knew we were looking for him.

The Union secretary/receptionist remembered that we were searching for him and made a note to that effect in Daddy's file. She called Allie, and so the job of getting Daddy home for burial began. Allie handled all the details of getting him back to Middlesboro.

At the funeral an open casket was not possible because he had been dead for more than a week before he was found, but the funeral director in Middlesboro, William Shumate, was a boyhood friend of Daddy's, and assured us that indeed it was his body that arrived by rail to be laid to rest at home. The only thing Shumate would reveal to me and Denny was that Daddy's hair was snow white.

Daddy's funeral was held in Middlesboro on Aug 28, 1963. Roy Acuff was always the first on the spot with bail money, and in the end, Acuff was the only Opry member or member of the Nashville music community besides our friend the Zinkans who sent flowers to his funeral. He was buried in Myers Grove Tennessee, near his mother, Artie.

The circumstances of Daddy's death are doubly sad because he did not reach out to anyone, even though the link had been reconnected, at least with his sister.

Following his death, a letter was received from Major Carl Ferrell in the Personnel Department of the Salvation Army in Oklahoma City. He wrote "Very little is known about the men who occasionally seek the services of this Center. ...During his stay here Milton ran two of the Center's stores quite competently. He was friendly but not overly communicative about anything. However, he seemed, generally, to be in good spirits and usually had a joke to tell on checking in from the store each evening.

"As you know, Milton was not living here at the time of his demise. The word that we received was that he had moved to the Hudson Hotel in this city from the Southland Hotel this city about two days before. He apparently went from here to the Southland Hotel.

....Perhaps, in the course of his lifetime something did happen that changed Milton's way of thinking. However, he did attempt to stay on his own and if it had been necessary he could always find employment here. The important fact in my way of thinking is that he maintained himself and was not a burden to his loved ones."

Summary

To have any kind of career in the country music business has been the dream of countless very talented people through the years.

Just attaining that goal has often taken more than some of them ever had to give and, in some cases, once they had given what it took to arrive at their goal, some then had little, if anything left. I have seen several who, once they finally had that dream in their grasp, just let it get away from them. Such a case may be made in this story, since it now appears that once Milton actually grabbed that brass ring, he just gradually loosened his grip on it and then just let it go altogether.

Milton Estes worked as hard, maybe even harder, than most other aspiring young entertainers to get to the top. He learned his singing in small churches and at local school socials. He honed his act in vaudeville and worked as a strolling troubadour in illegal speakeasies during Prohibition. I am not sure to this day if Opry membership had ever been his ultimate goal, but he settled there and, for a while, it seemed he was happy with this choice.

There were several more years of working his way to the top at radio stations and in bands in Birmingham, Alabama, and Raleigh, North Carolina, and Dallas, and Wichita Falls, Texas. Then came the offer from Cohen Williams and Martha White Flour.

Milton Estes had set out from the beginning, it would seem, on a course of pure self indulgence as a self-centered hedonist, apparently on a course of pure self destruction. At first, it was not openly apparent that he could care less about all of the success and acclaim he achieved.

He quickly fit into his duties at WSM. He was very energetic as the primary spokesperson for Martha White Flour and on The Grand Ole Opry. He gladly did all he that was asked to do, and even a little bit more. At that point, he appeared to be headed nowhere but up.

Was all his success too hard to handle? Had it all come with too high a price? He had ample talent and his energy level was astounding at the time he was riding high. There had to be something else going on in his mind during his career.

Connie (Williams) King Brothers summed up the relationship between her father, Cohen Williams, and Daddy, and her remembrances. She remembered that "When things started going downhill for Milton, my Daddy began looking around for someone else but, you know, my Daddy never said a word about Milton drinking.

"I feel like people with real talent that comes out so naturally … and Milton's did. . .and he knew what he wanted from the band……..My Daddy thought that was so great…. I feel like it's hard when an artist has this talent and this great feeling, it sometimes causes them to not have a normalcy in life. I think that's what happens so often to these artists. All their emotions you can see because they feel it. I've seen it so much. ….[T]hey are truly God's richest people, but managing their life is difficult. It puts them in a position where after they do really well they either feel they have to be on their Ps & Qs or have to be someplace relaxing. They will allow themselves to be pushed too far and I feel so often they don't take care of themselves. …They've got to compact it; get it all in. [Milton] had that great charm and ability to not only sell himself but sell you on whatever it was he was selling. Daddy saw that in Milton and realized – he was inclusive with his audience. He brought them into it ….He could milk a crowd better than anybody [my daddy] had ever seen until [later] when Ernie Ford came along. He said Milton and Tennessee Ernie Ford were two of the greatest at milking an audience. That was not the case with Lester and Earl …. They came along at the right time."

Milton Estes grave in Myers Grove overlooks that of his mother, Artie, and is beneath a lone pine tree that hums a lonesome tune when the breeze stirs,

The Legacy

Of all the songs written and or recorded by Milton Estes, very few royalties have been forthcoming from any source. Perhaps his habit of, like Willy Nelson, using songs as a commodity, caused any monies to fall by the wayside. Most of the songs he co-wrote are now in public domain. (NOTE: This is not true. There are 27 songs co-written by Milton Estes registered to BMI. They do not earn money because none are being played on the radio or have not been on recordings that are sold.)

I was contacted by J. Berg, a "fan" from Virginia, who tracked me down and ultimately found me from information given to him by Eddie Stubbs of WSM. Berg stated that he had been pressing for a CD to be put together in Europe of Daddy's recordings. At his urging, Anita Binge of Cattle Records in Europe indeed released a CD made not from the masters but from fairly pristine recordings from another fan in Great Britain. This bootleg endeavor resulted in what I consider highly unethical use of Daddy's music where no one but Cattle made any money. The original record companies still own the masters and therefore do not receive income from this release. The cover picture on the CD is from the Golden West Cowboy years and not even at the time he made the recordings. It would prove far too costly to bring a lawsuit against this bootleg purveyor than to just let it slide. I was not even favored with a courtesy copy of the CD. The CD was listed on the internet for a while at a price of $39 or so, depending on the vendor.

(NOTE: In England the copyright for recordings lasted 50 years after the recording's "publication" or release. That means that all of Milton Estes professional recordings were legally Public Domain.)

I have put together a list of all of Milton Estes professional songs and recordings that I could find.

Milton Estes recordings

1946: Bullet Records
"That's Why I Worry" (Jimmy Selph lead vocal)
"Say You'll Be Mine" (Jimmy Selph lead vocal)

August 11, 1947: Castle Recording Studio: Decca Records
"Swing Wide Your Gate of Love"
"When the Fire Comes Down"
"Whoa Sailor"
"Too Many Women"

December 19, 1947: Castle Recording Studio: Decca Records
"New Wabash Cannonball"
"New Filipino Baby"
"Answer to Drivin' Nails in My Coffin"
"Happy Birthday Polka"
"The Almighty Dollar"
"The Waltz I Waltzed With You"
"Seems Like Yesterday"
"Out in Pioneer Town"

December 30, 1949: Decca
Thirty Pieces of Silver
House of Gold

January 14, 1954: Decca (sang on a Bill Monroe session)
Happy On My Way
I'm Working on a Building
A Voice From On High
He Will Set Your Fields on Fire

April 21, 1949: King Records (Cincinatti)
Red Rosey Cheeks
Hush, Somebody's Calling My Name
I'm on the Battlefield For My Lord

December 30, 1949: Coral
Seems Like Yesterday
The Waltz I Waltzed With You
Thirty Pieces of Silver
House of Gold

January 19, 1950: MGM
E-A-S-T-E-R
Wealth Won't Save Your Soul

Song Written by Milton Estes and registered with BMI
NOTE: All of the songs were co-written.

Are You Sorry You Said Goodbye (with Alton Watson)
Calypso Rock and Roll (with Joe Allison)
Don't You Come Crying To Me (with Jimmy Selph)
End of My Roundup Days (with J.L. Frank and Pee Wee King)

Hear Him Calling (with J.L. Frank and Pee Wee King)

Hey Worm (with Joe Allison)

I'll Call on You in My Dreams (with J.L. Frank and Pee Wee King)

I'm a Wrangler From Old Cheyenne (with J.L. Frank and Pee Wee King and Curley Rhodes

I'm Headin' For Dat Heb N Train (with J.L. Frank and Pee Wee King)

I'm Writing My Daddy a Letter (with Alton Watson)

Just Before Dawn (with J.L. Frank, Pee Wee King and George Dooley)

Keep Step With Jesus (with J.L. Frank, Pee Wee King and George Dooley)

Key to That Beautiful Home (with J.L. Frank, Pee Wee King and George Dooley)

Let Me Wander Again on Smoky Mountain (with J.L. Frank and Pee Wee King)

Little Pony (with J.L. Frank and Pee Wee King and Texas Daisy

My Heart's Broke Baby (with Bill Carrigan)

My Pony and My Guitar (with J.L. Frank and Pee Wee King, and Abner Simms

Old Dusty Saddle (with J.L. Frank and Pee Wee King)

Old Kentucky Hills (with J.L. Frank and Pee Wee King)

Singing All Day and Dinner on the Ground (with Joe Allison and Jimmie Davis

That Old Fashioned Mother of Mine (with J.L. Frank and Pee Wee King)

Too Many Women (with Vic McAlpin)

Twenty-Twenty Vision (with Joe Allison)

We Still Love Our Boy Down in Prison (with J.L. Frank and Pee Wee King)

When the Fire Comes Down (with Wally Fowler, Tommy Harrell and Paul Kinsey)

You Must Have that Pure Religion (with Wally Fowler)

You're a Flower of the Plain (with J.L. Frank and Pee Wee King)

U.K. Album release
Milton Estes and his Musical Millers
Cattle Compact Mono CCD 293

Answer to Drivin' Nails in My Coffin (Jerry Irby) Decca 12/19/47 re 1948

Calling You (Hank Williams) MGM 1/19/50 rel 50

E-A-S-T-E-R (Cliff Rodgers) MGM 1/19/50 rel 50

Happy Birthday Polka (Dewey Bergman and Jack Segal) Decca 12/19/47 rel 48

House of Gold (Hank Williams) Coral 12/30/48 rel 50

Hush, Somebody's Calling My Name (arr: Rosaline Gore) King 4/21/40 rel ca 49

I'm On the Battlefield For My Lord (arr: Rosaline Gore) King 4/21/49 rel ca 49

Keep A-Talkin' Baby (Rudy C. Sooter) King 4/21/49 rel ca 49

New Fillipino Baby (Clark Van Ness ad Billy Cox) Decca 12/19/47 rel 48

New Wabash Cannon Ball (A.P. Carter and Johnny Bond) Decca 12/19/47 rel 48

Out in Pioneer Town (Tim Spencer) Decca 12/19/47 rel 48 or 49

Red Rosy Cheks and Big Brown Eyes (Jimmy Selph)(King 4/21/49 rel ca 49

Say You'll Be Mine (Jimmy Selph) Bullet rec ca 46 rel ca 46

Seems Like Yesterday (M. Estes and J.C. Tex Sumney) Coral 12/19/47 rel 49 or 50

Swing Wide Your Gate of Love (Hank Thompson and Sidney Nathan) Decca 8/11/47 rel 47 or 48

That Why I Worry (Jimmy Selph) Bullet rec & rel ca 46

The Almighty Dollar (Fred Kirby) Decca 12/19/47 rel 48 or 49

The Man At the Table Asleep (Odell McLeod) MGM 1/19/50 rel 50

The Waltz I waltzed With You (M. Estes and J. Selph) Coral 12/19/47 rel 49 or 50

Thirty Pieces of Silver (Odell McLeod) Coral 12/30/49 re: 49 or 50

Too Many Women (Milton Estes and Vernice Johnson McAlpin) Decca 8/11/47 re

Wealth Won't Save Your Soul (Hank Williams) MGM 1/19/50 rel 50

When the Fire Comes Down (Milton Estes, John W. Fowler, Tommy Harrell, Paul M. Kinsey Decca 8/11/47 rel 47 or 48

Whoa Sailor (Hank Thompson) Decca) 8/47/11 rel 47 or 48

Milton sings solo on all tracks except Traces #2, 4, 11, 17 and 23 they are Milton Estes and Musical Miller s

The Musical Millers Quartet on tracks # 6 & 7

Castle Studios Tracks 2, 3 18 and 22

Tracks #6, 7, 8, 9 and 12 in Cincinnati, Ohio

Bibliography

Cusic, Don. Eddy Arnold: His Life and Times. Nashville: Brackish Publisher, 2016.

Estes, Micki. Milton Estes: Phantom of the Opry. Unpublished manuscript.

Hawkins, Martin. A Shot in the Dark: Making Records in Nashville, 1945-1955. Nashville: Vanderbilt University Press & Country Music Foundation Press, 2006.

Pugh, Ronnie. Ernest Tubb: The Texas Troubadour. Durham, N.C.: Duke University Press, 1996.

Ruppli, Michel, compiler. The Decca Labels: A Discography: Volume 5: Country Recordings, Classical Recordings & Reissues. Westport, CT: Greenwood Press, 1996.

Whitburn, Joel. Top Country Singles: 1944-2017.Menomonee Falls, Wisconsin: Record Research, INc. 2017.

www.ingramcontent.com/pod-product-compliance
Lightning Source LLC
Chambersburg PA
CBHW071236300426
44116CB00008B/1061